Praise for
CREATING INCLUSIVE
CAMPUS ENVIRONMENTS

"No challenge is more important than creating the conditions whereby ALL college students can acquire the skills and competencies that will enable them to survive and thrive in the 21st century. As Harper and his colleagues make plain, student affairs educators are key players in helping students convert the rich harvest of out-of-class learning opportunities into developmentally powerful outcomes."

— **GEORGE D. KUH**, Chancellor's Professor and director,
Center for Postsecondary Research, Indiana University

"Although many campuses claim to value the importance of diverse perspectives for students' personal and professional growth, few have an understanding of the 'why' and 'how' of integrating best practices. Harper's book fills a huge void in understanding the 'why' of the imperative for inclusive campus environments for learning and student engagement and also addressing 'how' campuses can begin to develop promising practices. Moreover, the range of institution types examined in this book mandates it as essential reading for all of higher education."

— **KASSIE FREEMAN**, vice president for academic and student affairs
and professor of education, Southern University and A&M College System

"Student learning will be enriched as more colleges and universities purposefully transform into the inclusive, cross-cultural environments envisioned in this inspiring book. Community and two-year college student affairs professionals and others will find this NASPA publication challenging and insightful, yet practical in its approach to theory, good practice models, and ideologies about how to create multicultural spaces, learning, and engagement inside and outside our classrooms."

— **MAGDALENA H. DE LA TEJA**,
dean of student services,
South Austin Campus, Austin Community College

"Harper and colleagues have done a wonderful job of addressing critical issues related to developing environments that lead to student learning in our institutions of higher education. I have learned from them, and trust other readers will as well."

– JOHN H. SCHUH,
Distinguished Professor of Educational Leadership and Policy Studies,
Iowa State University

"Finally, a book for practitioners that speaks to the complexity of U.S. higher education in the 'here and now.' With contemporary data, Harper and his colleagues have put together a text that will help colleges and universities work with enrollments that reflect the changing demographic realities of the United States. From residential liberal arts colleges to state universities and faith-based institutions of higher learning, *Creating Inclusive Campus Environments* should be required reading for all higher education professionals."

– XAVIER E. ROMANO, vice president for student development
and dean of students, Knox College

CREATING INCLUSIVE
CAMPUS ENVIRONMENTS

·····

FOR CROSS-CULTURAL LEARNING
AND STUDENT ENGAGEMENT

NASPA.
Student Affairs Administrators
in Higher Education

SHAUN R. HARPER, EDITOR
Foreword by Sylvia Hurtado

CREATING INCLUSIVE CAMPUS ENVIRONMENTS

○○○○○

FOR CROSS-CULTURAL LEARNING AND STUDENT ENGAGEMENT

NASPA
Student Affairs Administrators
in Higher Education

Creating Inclusive Campus Environments for Cross-Cultural Learning and Student Engagement

Additional copies may be purchased by contacting the NASPA publications department at 301-638-1749 or visiting http://bookstore.naspa.org.

ISBN 978-0-931654-53-4

TABLE OF CONTENTS

TABLE OF CONTENTS (CONTINUED)

Acknowledgments

I salute the courageous few who not only embrace social justice ideologies, but also speak and act against oppression on college and university campuses. Obviously, an edited volume cannot exist without chapters; thus, I am forever grateful to the 22 colleagues and 6 undergraduate students who not only contributed, but also care authentically about what they have written. Also deserving of recognition is Kimberly A. Truong, my doctoral research assistant, who located missing references and microscopic editorial oversights. In addition, I wish to thank the following important people for their support at various stages in the development of this book: Margaret Cyrus, Marybeth Gasman, Ryan J. Davis, Brian L. McGowan, Walter M. Kimbrough, Etta R. Hollins, Beverly Lindsay, Frank Harris III, Estela Mara Bensimon, Amanuel Gebru, Corliss P. Bennett-McBride, and Ontario S. Wooden. Finally, my sincere appreciation is expressed to Melissa Dahne, NASPA director of publications, for her enthusiasm and hard work on this significant contribution to higher education and student affairs literature.

Shaun R. Harper
Higher Education Management Program
University of Pennsylvania
December 2007

FOREWORD

We have much to learn about how to create diverse learning environments in higher education, though advances in research and reflections on practice have helped us along the way. Since the 1970s, the focus has been on increasing the numbers of underrepresented students on campus. Institutions responded by devising programs, creating new roles and positions for student support, and developing initiatives to accommodate diverse student groups. Researchers who studied these changes, however, largely categorized them as reactive rather than proactive; more important, many diversity initiatives were "added on" to existing institutional structures that showed little change despite increasing diversity in the student body.

By the 1980s, the realities of the difficulty in creating diverse learning environments became more apparent. Researchers documented the issues students of color face in higher education, increasing intergroup conflict spawned research on campus climates, and institutions modified their practices to conform with the *Regents of the University of California v. Bakke* 1978 ruling. Though *Bakke* placed constraints on practices focused specifically on race, it also affirmed the importance of racial/ethnic diversity to the environment of speculation, experimentation, and creativity on campus. This later became known as the *diversity rationale* for the practice of building and sustaining multicultural environments. Even though many educators hold general notions that diversity enriches the college environment, many campuses leave student engagement and multicultural learning to chance encounters and student motivation or occasional workshops to help bridge social divides, rather than incorporating diversity into all aspects of learning inside and outside the classroom. With the varying awareness about diversity issues and how to best address them among campus units, student affairs professionals are often left to deal with a wide range of diversity issues that affect students.

Of course, there are exceptions in practice, and those institutions that became recognized for their "inclusive excellence" in the 1990s had an important combination of factors: leadership support; new initiatives and structures that attempted to address intergroup relations and curriculum on diverse populations; innovations that bridged student and academic affairs; and engagement at the level of culture change that began to change daily practice. Just as campuses were making progress, however, additional resistance to racial "inclusiveness" emerged in attacks on affirmative action. The most recent defense of diversity, taken on by the University of Michigan at the Supreme Court in 2003, became a focal point for scholars studying the educational benefits of diversity. The diversity rationale, supported in philosophy, now has a rich empirical base of research on students. It was on the basis of this literature that we finally acknowledged that while representation is essential, interaction across cultural and racial groups is a key component of enacting diverse learning environments on a campus.

What does this mean for student affairs? While we will continue to work at increasing diversity on campus, the next important phase of our work will be movement toward a deeper understanding of issues that divide and separate, and development of initiatives that engage and include. We expect to see advances in practice that involve proactive attempts to educate students for a diverse society. We also expect a broader share of the responsibility for facilitating engagement with diversity on campus—across individuals and units—because it is central to educating students wherever they learn.

I write with optimism because many more of us are engaged in institutional transformation. This volume contains the work of seasoned researchers on diversity issues as well as many emerging scholars concerned about improving diverse learning environments and student affairs practices. This is a hopeful sign for higher education as a field of study and the profession of student affairs. As new issues emerge in fostering intentional practices for cross-cultural learning and engagement, a cadre of individuals who share a common vision will give insight into potential difficulties. It is possible for individuals to transform institutions to achieve diverse learning environments on campus and this, in turn, is critical to advancing progress in the larger society. The individual and collective efforts of this work inspire us to make a difference in the lives of diverse students on college campuses.

Sylvia Hurtado
Higher Education Research Institute
University of California, Los Angeles
December 2007

CHAPTER ONE

○○○○○

Not By Accident: Intentionality in Diversity, Learning, and Engagement

SHAUN R. HARPER AND anthony lising antonio

○○○○○

D erek Bok's (2006) book, *Our Underachieving Colleges: A Candid Look at How Much Students Learn and Why They Should Be Learning More*, offers a balanced critique of American higher education. It describes how satisfied students are with their undergraduate experiences, while arguing that too few leave college having learned to think critically and demonstrate mastery in a diverse democracy. Regarding the ability to comfortably interact with others who are different, Bok suggested: "Success in life often requires it. Employers increasingly demand it. The nation needs it if America is to maintain a cohesive society and an effective democracy with a population splintered by racial, religious, and ideological differences . . . [it's] simply too important to be ignored during such a formative time in students' lives" (p. 222). Unfortunately, this is an area in which college graduates are continually inexperienced and ill-prepared.

Bok is not alone in his appraisal of the negligence with which student learning is approached. For instance, The National Center for Public Policy and Higher Education awarded 50 "Incomplete" grades in *Measuring Up*, its 2000 and 2002 state-by-state report cards. Across all 50 states, the center deemed evidence of student learning both insufficient and inconclusive. Similarly, in its 2006 report, the commission, appointed by U.S. Department of Education Secretary Margaret Spellings to explore necessary areas of improvement in higher education, noted that students do not learn enough in college and employers complain that graduates lack the skills needed for workplace effectiveness. And in the acclaimed documentary *Declining by Degrees: Higher Education at Risk* (PBS, 2005), college students admitted on camera that they learned very little and navigated college with limited educational challenge. In the video, Indiana University Professor George D. Kuh referred to this as "higher education's dirty little secret." Amid all the national discourse about student learning, two things are missing: 1) Critical considerations of the negligence with which student learning through cross-cultural engagement is approached on many campuses; and 2) conversations regarding the role of student affairs educators in creating rich diversity-related learning opportunities.

Quaye and Harper (2007) argued that the onus is typically on students to seek out educational experiences and resources related to race, marginalized identities, and colored histories. Though their focus was on faculty and classroom diversity, the same can be said for student engagement in educationally purposeful out-of-class activities pertaining to difference. Whereas some colleges and universities have a one- or two-course "diversity requirement" in the academic curriculum, it is entirely possible for a student to persist through baccalaureate degree attainment without having meaningfully interacted outside of class with a gay or lesbian peer or someone from a different racial, religious, or socioeconomic background. Although many live together in residence halls, eat in the same dining facilities, and hang out in student unions, there is no guarantee they will learn from the differences they bring to those settings. Yet there is a longstanding erroneous assumption that they will—UCLA Professor Mitchell J. Chang and his colleagues (2005) referred to this as "Magical Thinking." Putting the onus on students ultimately renders many insufficiently prepared for participation in an increasingly diverse workforce and society. Educators, including those in student affairs, must be held more accountable for ensuring students are afforded deep, rich, and challenging learning experiences related to diversity.

Bok (2006) gave virtually no attention to student affairs educators in his book and none were shown throughout the entire two hours of *Declining by Degrees*—not a single dean of students, residence hall director, student activities advisor, or multicultural affairs professional. Could it possibly be that student affairs professionals are not perceived as valuable and serious contributors to learning? The remainder of this chapter is devoted to exploring this question, with an emphasis on cross-cultural learning and engagement. We acknowledge that there are other dimensions of learning for which these professionals should also assume responsibility; however, our focus is specific here given the scope and aims of this book. In the next section, we call for a shift in the way student affairs educators view themselves and their roles on college and university campuses. Following is an overview of the educational benefits associated with diversity and a discussion of the enactment of espoused institutional values. Emphasis is then placed on intentionality in educational practice related to diversity and learning, and the chapter concludes with guidelines for how this should be done.

A Reputation Shift From Icebreakers to Educational Impact

In 1994, the American College Personnel Association (ACPA) released *The Student Learning Imperative*, a document intended to ignite discussion about the role of student affairs professionals in creating conditions and experiences to enhance student learning. Among the assumptions upon which the document was based are: Learning should occur both inside and outside the classroom, but cannot in the absence of purposeful planning, educator expertise, and assessment; the compartmentalization of academic affairs and student affairs hinders the collaboration required to foster rich learning environments; and student affairs professionals are *educators* who share with faculty and others a responsibility for student learning (ACPA, 1994). Characteristics of learning-oriented student affairs divisions were also described. Despite the widespread dissemination and popularity of this document, its ambitious goals remain largely unrealized, as evidenced in three recent situations:

> **Student Affairs = The Human Knot.** An announcement was made in a faculty meeting about an upcoming event that would be attended by several chief student affairs administrators from across the country. Professors were invited to brainstorm possible ways graduate students could benefit from engagement with these vice presidents and deans during their visit to campus. One person asked, "Are they

going to do the human knot?" He laughingly explained, "Whenever I hear 'student affairs,' I think of the human knot and other assorted icebreakers." Faculty colleagues seated around the table also found this humorous—no one offered a different characterization of student affairs professionals.

I Am Effective, I Just Know. A new professional in residence life experienced difficulty in attempting to write an article for publication. She wanted to provide a perspective on a pressing problem of practice, but thinking conceptually about the integration of theory and research into the paper proved to be a challenge. By her own admission, this task was frustrating because the ways she had previously approached the practical dilemma being written about were based on intuition—not much else. "I do not have time in my busy workday to be reflective, read literature, or write out plans," she confessed. The new professional also noted, "I am effective in my practice, I just know it . . . I am there for my students when they need me." Despite these claims, she struggled to find a clear way to convey her supposed educational impact in writing and describe the science upon which her work was based.

Learning Confined to the Academic Side. Seated at the dinner table were a faculty member and mid-level administrators from academic, student, and governmental affairs at five different colleges and universities. The conversation was about recent suicides on their campuses and trends in student mental health. An associate vice president for student affairs (AVPSA) mentioned that institutions are increasingly searching for vice presidents for student affairs with backgrounds in psychological services. The professor asked, "Doesn't being a chief student affairs officer entail other responsibilities beyond mental health, such as student learning?" With a surprised look on his face, the AVPSA exclaimed: "STUDENT LEARNING . . . that is what the academic side of the university is for!"

These examples—all actual, not fictitious—make clear that some student affairs professionals are not thought of (by themselves or others) as educators. In 2001,

University of Pennsylvania Professor Matthew Hartley posed an important question: "Student Learning as a Framework for Student Affairs—Rhetoric or Reality?" In his interviews with senior student affairs officers, Hartley found that institutions were beginning to embrace the concept of student learning, but their approaches and the programming they offered were largely the same as they had always been.

Additional documents calling for a focus on learning have followed *The Student Learning Imperative*. For example, ACPA and the National Association of Student Personnel Administrators (NASPA) convened a group to craft a set of principles for good practice in student affairs (see Blimling, Whitt, & Associates, 1999). Of the seven principles developed, four are particularly relevant to our discussion here: engaging students in active learning; setting and communicating high expectations for learning; forging educational partnerships that advance student learning; and building supportive and inclusive communities. Consistently emphasized across the seven principles is the notion of student affairs professionals as educators and cofacilitators of learning with faculty and students.

Apparently, a paradigmatic shift toward learning has been slow, as student affairs professionals were urged twice more to think of themselves as educators in *Learning Reconsidered* (Keeling, 2004) and *Learning Reconsidered 2* (Keeling, 2006). These reports and the work of the task forces that produced them are useful, yet the concept of "student affairs educators" awaits widespread adoption. Good educators plan, reflect, and identify desired outcomes in advance; thoughtfully select strategies to actualize learning goals; and frame their lessons around published literature and research. We argue here that those who work in student affairs ought to approach learning in general, and learning about diversity specifically, in such ways. Deep learning about power, privilege, and social injustice are unlikely to occur through fun exercises with short-lived opportunities for processing and trivial reflection. Instead of depending disproportionately on intuition, student affairs educators must take into account the available research and theories to identify outcomes and explain complex phenomena related to cross-cultural engagement.

EDUCATIONAL BENEFITS OF DIVERSITY: RELYING ON EVIDENCE

Supreme Court Justice Lewis Franklin Powell's opinion in the 1978 *Regents of the University of California v. Bakke* case established racial diversity in the student body as a compelling interest of the state, essentially arguing that diversity plays an important role in the achievement of educational outcomes. Ten years ago, a group of college presidents came to the defense of affirmative action and publicly acknowledged the educational value of diversity for students:

> We speak first and foremost as educators. We believe that our students benefit significantly from education that takes place within a diverse setting. In the course of their university education, our students encounter and learn from others who have backgrounds and characteristics very different from their own. (Association of American Universities, 1997, p. A27)

Diversity, as a central element of a college education, matters for students. Although it arose out of a legal interpretation of admissions policy, many of us in higher education strongly hold this belief. Given the research produced over the past decade, we have good reason to hold this maxim not only as a belief, but also as a campus priority.

Reviews of the many empirical studies of the educational relevance of diversity are fairly unequivocal (Milem & Hakuta, 2000; Hurtado, Dey, Gurin, & Gurin, 2003; Milem, 2003). Research points to four forms of diversity that can potentially have an impact on students: structural diversity (the extent to which a student population is racially and ethnically diverse); interactional diversity (experiences with others of different races, ethnicities, sexual orientations, and cultures); cocurricular diversity (programming such as cultural awareness workshops and intergroup dialogues); and curricular diversity (academic programs, courses, and course content focusing on diversity) (Hurtado, Milem, Clayton-Pedersen, & Allen, 1999). Below we summarize the empirical research on the first three forms, followed by a discussion of their implications for student affairs. Near the end of this chapter, we introduce an expanded notion of curricular diversity that is directly relevant to student affairs work.

Studies of structural diversity have estimated direct and indirect effects on numerous student outcomes. In terms of direct effects, higher proportions of students of color on campus are associated with more frequent interaction with others from different backgrounds; engagement in discussions concerning difference; and encounters and serious conversations with peers holding different beliefs, opinions, and values. Structural diversity appears to indirectly enhance intellectual and social self-concept, satisfaction with college, retention, racial understanding, and perceptions of the campus climate (Astin, 1993; Chang, 2001; Chang, Astin, & Kim, 2004; Cole, 2007; Engberg, 2007; Gurin, 1999; Pike, Kuh, & Gonyea, 2007).

The majority of research on diversity highlights links between interaction and educational outcomes. Interactional diversity—socializing across racial/ethnic lines, discussing issues of race and cultural difference, and maintaining interracial friendships—has been linked to structural diversity; it has been shown to have strong effects on a vast array of cognitive outcomes, including critical thinking and reasoning; perspective-taking; openness to cognitive dissimilarity and challenge; retention in school; and grade point average. Affective outcomes positively affected by diversity are even more expansive; they include self-concept (intellectual and social); cultural awareness and appreciation; racial understanding; leadership skills; engagement in citizenship activities; pluralistic abilities; satisfaction with college; commitment to racial understanding; motivation; and high postbaccalaureate degree aspirations (antonio, Chang, Hakuta, Kenny, Levin, & Milem, 2004; Chang, Denson, Sáenz, & Misa, 2006; Chang, Astin, & Kim, 2004; Cole, 2007; Engberg, 2007; Pike, Kuh, & Gonyea, 2007; Umbach & Kuh, 2006).

Harvard University Professor Richard Light's (2001) study confirms these findings regarding interactional diversity. Participants in his study reflected on the value that meaningful in-class and out-of-class engagement with peers from diverse backgrounds added to their overall college experiences. All but 9 of the 120 students Light interviewed were able to quickly recall specific examples of ways their learning had been significantly enhanced by interactional diversity. Although diversity-related learning outcomes were cited across all racial/ethnic groups in the sample, White students were clearly affected most positively by engagement with their racially different peers; many elaborated on ideas they would not have learned or even pondered.

As Sylvia Hurtado mentions in the foreword of this book, institutions have been organizing out-of-class diversity activities since the 1980s. These programs typically involve group settings wherein participants engage in dialogue and learning experiences about racism, sexism, homophobia, cultural differences, discrimination, and intergroup conflict (McCauley, Wright, & Harris, 2000). The research here has been conclusive, illustrating positive effects on cultural awareness, racial attitudes, commitment to racial understanding, attitudes toward campus diversity, perspective-taking, and comfort with dialogue across difference (Engberg, 2004). These types of activities are part of the *Enriching Educational Experiences* benchmark of the National Survey of Student Engagement (NSSE, 2007). Such engagement is considered educationally purposeful; when facilitated meaningfully, it could lead to learning and the production of enduring and measurable gains and outcomes for students (Kuh, Kinzie, Schuh, Whitt, & Associates, 2005).

Though the preponderance of research findings reflects the positive effects of diversity, a closer examination reveals complexity worth noting in the data. First, the positive effects of structural and interactional diversity are remarkably consistent and far-reaching for White students, but are less consistent for others. Many fewer direct effects of structural diversity have been found for students of color, and in some studies, negative effects are evident. In Gurin's (1999) extensive analyses, socializing with someone of another race and discussing racial issues (two common measures of interactional diversity) had many fewer statistically significant relationships with student outcomes for the African American and Latino samples. Gurin also found both positive and negative effects of same-race affiliation for these two samples. Also, antonio (2004) examined the effects of racial diversity of student friendship groups; in a study of intellectual self-concept and degree aspirations, he found nearly opposite effects of diversity on White students and students of color. And finally, Hu and Kuh (2003) and Umbach and Kuh (2006) found structural diversity was negatively related to satisfaction and perceived interpersonal support. These findings complicate our diversity mantra, insofar as they disrupt a simple, uniform, and unconditional understanding of racial and ethnic diversity as an educational panacea.

The data also show contradictions of perception and behaviors. Early studies of campus climate indicated an interesting paradox: on diverse campuses, students reported relatively high levels of interracial contact (discussions, socializing, and friendship) alongside campus segregation and racial tension (Astin, Treviño, & Wingard, 1991). Similarly, antonio (2001) found that while a significant majority of students' best-friend networks were racially diverse, a near unanimity viewed the campus as marked by self-segregation. Understanding these complexities is important for student affairs educators who endeavor to increase cross-cultural interaction among students and make good on institutional promises for diversity.

ENACTING ESPOUSED INSTITUTIONAL VALUES

The striking discrepancy between perceptions of self-segregation and a poor interpersonal environment and the prevalence of diverse interaction and friendship suggest the work of achieving the educational benefits of diversity is much harder than it seems. The complexity of effects that diversity appears to have within and between racial groups underscores this difficulty. Several scholars discuss this complexity and offer important insights for institutions. For example, Claremont Graduate University Professor Daryl G. Smith and her colleagues (1997) noted the key to achieving these outcomes was coordination of diversity-related efforts and a focus on inclusion. The comprehensive approach described by Hurtado et al. (1999) identifies the campus climate for diversity as the organizing construct around which to evaluate and build our diversity efforts. And Chang (2002) argued that an overall discourse of learning should compel our embrace and practice of diversity-related policies. It is clear that *diversity for education*, as Chang calls it, must be thoughtful, intentional, proactive, coordinated, and comprehensive. Simply enrolling a diverse student body is not enough. Scattering the campus with assorted diversity programs is also insufficient. Inattention to the entire campus effort is likely to yield, at best, mixed results.

Diversity for education requires serious institutional attention; when commitment is weak, students seem keenly aware of it. For example, the following were student reactions to the topic of diversity at UCLA (antonio, 1998):

> "Bullshit! Yeah, it's great, it's diverse. It's just a shame that these people tend to hang out with who they're related to, or not related to, but with who they have some sort of connection with, just because they have the same ethnic group." (p. 161)

> "If you have the kind of diversity that UCLA has, which is diversity in name but not in practice, it's worthless." (p. 196)

These statements are telling because the quoted students were strong supporters of diversity and both consciously sought out a diverse network of best friends and contacts on campus. Yet, like many of their peers, they could easily identify the geographic locations on campus that are regarded as racial enclaves. And while some students may view ethnic clustering as an individual preference, it is often interpreted as an institutional characteristic, a behavioral manifestation of a poor campus racial climate (Hurtado et al., 1999). Another student astutely remarked, "The problem that I've had with UCLA since I came here from day one, is that UCLA as an academic environment does not promote the kind of dialogue and discussion that it should. And until the University starts doing that, society as a whole will be paralyzed by the polarization that you see taking place every day" (antonio, 1998, p. 197).

Similarly, White and racial/ethnic minority participants alike in Harper and Hurtado's (2007) multi-institutional study of campus racial climates perceived disconnection between espoused and enacted values concerning diversity. Specifically, they believed most talk about diversity was rhetorical and merely for institutional publicity. Many students wanted to interact with peers from different backgrounds, but did not know how to do so. Reportedly, educators on their campuses offered little or no assistance, which put the onus on students to learn from each other. Those who were inexperienced in this regard (e.g., White undergraduates who grew up in racially homogeneous rural towns or Black students from urban areas) found it especially challenging to initiate these types of learning experiences on their own. Harper and Hurtado concluded that such educational negligence contributed to racial segregation and toxic racial climates on the campuses they studied. Perceptions of the climate, therefore, are important to consider, as negative perceptions may discourage interracial socialization and friendship and severely impede the educational promise of diversity (antonio, 2001; Harper & Hurtado, 2007; Hurtado et al., 1999; Hurtado, Dey, & Treviño, 1994; Loo & Rolison, 1986).

The relationship between institutional commitment to diversity, the campus climate, and realizing the benefits of interactional contact is clearly conceptualized in Gordon W. Allport's (1954) Contact Theory of Prejudice Reduction. According to Allport, interracial contact has the greatest potential to foster positive intergroup relations when four conditions are met: individuals are of equal status, individuals share common goals, there is an absence of intergroup competition, and contact is sanctioned by a common authority. These conditions suggest that educators can substantially affect the reach and effectiveness of diversity by attending to how these conditions are fostered on their campuses—but such efforts must be intentional.

On Intentionality in Educational Practice

One possible response to Beverly Daniel Tatum's (1997) question, *Why Are All the Black Kids Sitting Together in the Cafeteria?*, is that educators have not strategically considered imaginative ways to transform dining halls (and other campus spaces) into venues for cross-cultural learning and engagement. Intentionality entails recognizing that segregated space exists and partnering with student groups and colleagues to develop programs that disrupt (if only temporarily) narrow interactional norms. Moreover, an intentional educator would devote an occasional lunch hour to walking around the dining hall asking groups of students what compelled their seat selections, ascertaining their perspectives on the apparent racial separation, and soliciting their ideas for future lunchtime activities that will increase their personal likelihood of interacting with peers who are different. In contrast, a negligent (and dare we say, typical) educator would walk through the same dining hall day after day, notice the constant segregation, perhaps mention it to a colleague, but then ultimately do nothing in response.

Intentionality requires courage, consciousness, assessment, and planning. Courageous educators recognize the presence of various -isms (racism, sexism, heterosexism, ableism, etc.) and oppressive conditions in campus environments, call them to the attention of several others, and respond with deliberation. Those who willingly seek out trends that contradict espoused institutional values are likely to become more conscious of hidden and commonly overlooked realities. In this way, teachers must be willing to become learners and use their discoveries to craft deliberate programmatic and policy interventions. Harper and Hurtado (2007) found that institutions were negligent in assessing the qualitative realities of campus climates and cross-racial interaction. In fact, participants in every focus group indicated it was the first time any institutional effort was made to inquire about the qualitative realities of their college experiences with diversity. Sensible intentionality in practice is virtually impossible in the absence of data that illuminate current trends and areas of necessary improvement.

Effective professors who want students to learn and master a certain concept plan classroom activities designed to yield desired outcomes; student affairs educators who seek to be intentional must treat such work like curricular planning. Interestingly, the term *extracurricular* was replaced with *cocurricular* in the student affairs literature at some point in the 1990s. Yet the curriculum that supposedly exists outside the classroom is rarely written in any formal way and campus activities typically are not strategically tied to predetermined outcomes. Those who are serious and intentional about learning, wherever it occurs, have thoughtfully written plans that guide their educational efforts.

At some point, the sociology faculty at a college got together to determine what students in the major should know. A sequence of courses and possibly other enriching educational experiences were considered as the curriculum was developed. Some professors (the good ones) aligned their individual courses with the agreed-upon goals for student learning embedded in the sociology department curriculum. Consequently, much of what aspiring sociologists learn about their discipline is not by accident. This same systematic approach within student affairs divisions and among individual student affairs educators would reflect intentionality. If college students are to accrue the full range of gains and outcomes associated with diversity and cross-cultural engagement, an actual out-of-class curriculum—complete with learning outcomes, activities and experiences to actualize those goals, and assessment plans—should be intentionally developed, and there must be some personal and institutional accountability for its implementation. Alternatively, using the same unsystematic approaches year after year reflects educational negligence. Knowing that students and society could ultimately benefit from new approaches to cross-cultural learning, but failing to take the necessary steps to intentionally create enabling conditions outside the classroom is downright irresponsible.

CONCLUSION: FIXING THE FAILURE OF STUDENT AFFAIRS

In many ways, this chapter was written in the same spirit as Nevitt Sanford's (1967) book *Where Colleges Fail*. Our position is that many student affairs educators fail to prepare students for participation in a diverse democracy, and neglect to capitalize on the diversity of their campuses in educationally meaningful ways. Simply dumping 1,500 students into a residence hall and concluding they will "magically" learn from each others' differences represents both naïveté and educational negligence in student affairs practice. Likewise, failing marks are deserved when out-of-class activities are not tied to desired outcomes for cross-cultural learning, segregated space goes unnoticed or undisrupted, and students graduate with unchallenged racist and homophobic assumptions about others.

Sanford (1967) made clear the importance of balancing challenge and support in work with college students, and found it necessary for development. We have argued for an expanded conceptualization of challenge and support throughout this chapter. Supporting student development entails being deliberate about creating the conditions that allow students to accrue competencies required for effective citizenship in a diverse democracy. If graduates are sent into the workforce and broader society insufficiently prepared, our view is that educators actually failed to support their development—no matter how enjoyable the students' college experiences were. Though fun icebreakers have a place in the range of things student affairs educators do, the well-planned learning experiences that challenge students to think critically and engage in well-facilitated conversations that develop cultural competencies are more educationally beneficial. The gains and outcomes are too robust and essential to leave to chance—student learning about and through diversity must not occur by accident.

REFERENCES

Association of American Universities. (1997, April 27). "On the Importance of Diversity." *The New York Times*, A27.

Allport, G. W. (1954). *The nature of prejudice*. Reading, MA: Addison-Wesley.

antonio, a. l. (1998). *The impact of friendship groups in a multicultural university*. Unpublished doctoral dissertation, University of California, Los Angeles.

antonio, a. l. (2001). Diversity and the influence of friendship groups in college. *Review of Higher Education, 25*(1), 63–89.

antonio, a. l. (2004). The influence of friendship groups on intellectual self-confidence and educational aspirations in college. *Journal of Higher Education, 75*(4), 446–471.

antonio, a. l., Chang, M. J., Hakuta, K., Kenny, D. A., Levin, S., & Milem, J. F. (2004). Effects of racial diversity on complex thinking in college students. *Psychological Science, 15*(8), 507–510.

Astin, A. W. (1993). *What matters in college? Four critical years revisited*. San Francisco: Jossey-Bass.

Astin, A. W., Treviño, J. G., & Wingard, T. L. (1991). *The UCLA campus climate for diversity*. Los Angeles: Higher Education Research Institute.

Blimling, G. S., Whitt, E. J., & Associates. (1999). *Good practice in student affairs: Principles to foster student learning*. San Francisco: Jossey-Bass.

Bok, D. (2006). *Our underachieving colleges: A candid look at how much students learn and why they should be learning more*. Princeton, NJ: Princeton University Press.

Chang, M. J. (2001). Is it more than about getting along? The broader educational implications of reducing students' racial biases. *Journal of College Student Development, 42*(2), 93–105.

Chang, M. J. (2002). Preservation or transformation: Where's the real educational discourse on diversity? *The Review of Higher Education, 25*(2), 125–140.

Chang, M. J., Astin, A. W., & Kim, D. (2004). Cross-racial interaction among undergraduates: Some causes and consequences. *Research in Higher Education, 45*(5), 529–553.

Chang, M. J., Chang, J. C., & Ledesma, M. C. (2005). Beyond magical thinking: Doing the real work of diversifying our institutions. *About Campus, 9*(2), 9–16.

Chang, M. J., Denson, N., Sáenz, V., & Misa, K. (2006). The educational benefits of sustaining cross racial interaction among undergraduates. *Journal of Higher Education, 77*(3), 430–455.

Cole, D. (2007). Do interracial interactions matter? An examination of student-faculty contact and intellectual self-concept. *Journal of Higher Education, 78*(3), 249–281.

Engberg, M. E. (2004). Improving intergroup relations in higher education: A critical examination of the influence of educational interventions on racial bias. *Review of Educational Research, 74*, 473–524.

Engberg, M. E. (2007). Educating the workforce for the 21st century: A cross-disciplinary analysis of the impact of the undergraduate experience on students' development of a pluralistic orientation. *Research in Higher Education, 48*(3), 283–317.

Gurin, P. (1999). *Expert report of Patricia Gurin, in the compelling need for diversity in higher education.* Gratz et al. v. Bollinger et al., No. 97-75321 (E.D. Mich.) Grutter et al. v. Bollinger et al., No. 97-75928 (E.D. Mich.). Ann Arbor: University of Michigan.

Hartley, M. (2001). Student learning as a framework for student affairs—rhetoric or reality? *NASPA Journal, 38*(2), 224–237.

Harper, S. R., & Hurtado, S. (2007). Nine themes in campus racial climates and implications for institutional transformation. In S. R. Harper & L.

D. Patton (Eds.), *Responding to the realities of race on campus: New Directions for Student Services, No. 120*. San Francisco: Jossey-Bass.

Hu, S., & Kuh, G. D. (2003). Diversity experiences and college student learning and personal development. *Journal of College Student Development, 44*(3), 320–334.

Hurtado, S., Dey, E. L., Gurin, P., & Gurin, G. (2003). The college environment, diversity, and student learning. In J. Smart (Ed.), *Higher education: Handbook of theory and research* (Vol. 18, pp. 145–189). Amsterdam: Kluwer Academic Press.

Hurtado, S., Dey, E. L., & Treviño, J. G. (1994, April). *Exclusion or self-segregation? Interaction across racial/ethnic groups on college campuses.* Paper presented at the annual meeting of the American Educational Research Association, New Orleans.

Hurtado, S., Milem, J. F., Clayton-Pedersen, A. R., & Allen, W. R. (1999). *Enacting diverse learning environments: Improving the climate for racial/ethnic diversity in higher education institutions.* ASHE-ERIC Higher Education Report, No. 26. Washington, DC: George Washington University, Graduate School of Education and Human Development.

Keeling, R. P. (Ed.). (2004). *Learning reconsidered: A campus-wide focus on the student experience.* Washington, DC: National Association of Student Personnel Administrators and American College Personnel Association.

Keeling, R. P. (Ed.). (2006). *Learning reconsidered 2: Implementing a campus-wide focus on the student experience.* Washington, DC: American College Personnel Association, Association of College and University Housing Officers–International, Association of College Unions International, National Academic Advising Association, National Association for Campus Activities, National Association of Student Personnel Administrators, and National Intramural-Recreational Sports Association.

Kuh, G. D., Kinzie, J., Schuh, J. H., Whitt, E. J., & Associates (2005). *Student success in college: Creating conditions that matter.* San Francisco: Jossey-Bass.

Light, R. J. (2001). *Making the most of college: Students speak their minds.* Cambridge, MA: Harvard University Press.

Loo, C. M., & Rolison, G. (1986). Alienation of ethnic minority students at a predominantly White university. *Journal of Higher Education, 57*(1), 58–77.

McCauley, C., Wright, M., & Harris, M. E. (2000). Diversity workshops on campus: A survey of current practice at U.S. colleges and universities. *College Student Journal, 34,* 100–114.

Milem, J. F., & Hakuta, K. (2000). The benefits of racial and ethnic diversity in higher education. In D. J. Wilds (Ed.), *Minorities in higher education, 1999–2000* (pp. 39–67). Washington, DC: American Council on Education.

Milem, J. F. (2003). The educational benefits of diversity: Evidence from multiple sectors. In M. J. Chang, D. Witt, J. Jones, & K. Hakuta (Eds.), *Compelling interest: Examining the evidence on racial dynamics in higher education* (pp. 126–169). Palo Alto, CA: Stanford University Press.

National Center for Public Policy and Higher Education. (2000). *Measuring up 2000: The state-by-state report card for higher education.* San Jose, CA: Author.

National Center for Public Policy and Higher Education. (2002). *Measuring up 2002: The state-by-state report card for higher education.* San Jose, CA: Author.

National Survey of Student Engagement (NSSE). (2007). *Experiences that matter: Enhancing student learning and success, annual report 2007.* Bloomington, IN: Indiana University Center for Postsecondary Research.

Pike, G. R., Kuh, G. D., & Gonyea, R. M. (2007). Evaluating the rationale for affirmative action in college admissions: Direct and indirect relationships between campus diversity and gains in understanding diverse groups. *Journal of College Student Development, 48*(2), 166–182.

Public Broadcasting Service. (2005). *Declining by degrees: Higher education at risk* [Televised documentary]. (Available from PBS, 2100 Crystal Drive, Arlington, VA 22202).

Quaye, S. J., & Harper, S. R. (2007). Faculty accountability for culturally-inclusive pedagogy and curricula. *Liberal Education, 93*(3), 32–39.

Sanford, N. (1967). *Where colleges fail.* San Francisco: Jossey-Bass.

Smith, D. G., Gerbick, G. L., Figueroa, M. A., Watkins, G. H., Levitan, T., Leeshawn, C. M., et al. (1997). *Diversity works: The emerging picture of how students benefit.* Washington, DC: Association of American Colleges and Universities.

Tatum, B. D. (1997). *Why are all the Black kids sitting together in the cafeteria? And other conversations about race.* New York: Basic Books.

Umbach, P. D., & Kuh, G. D. (2006). Student experiences with diversity at liberal arts colleges: Another claim for distinctiveness. *Journal of Higher Education, 77,* 169–192.

U.S. Department of Education. (2006). *A test of leadership, charting the future of U.S. higher* education: A report of the commission appointed by Secretary of Education Margaret Spellings. Washington, DC: Author.

CHAPTER TWO

○○○○○

Student Voice and Sensemaking of Multiculturalism on Campus

STEPHEN JOHN QUAYE

WITH DONNA K. LIN, CULLEN R. BUIE, MELISSA ABAD,
ADAM LABONTE, JOANNA GREENBERG, AND JESSE W. HALL

○○○○○

Multiculturalism is one of the most commonly used words in colleges and universities. As the U.S. population becomes increasingly diverse, many administrators have recognized the need to recruit and retain students from various cultural backgrounds. Even so, few students have sustained opportunities to articulate their perspectives on and experiences with diversity. Many institutions merely espouse an appreciation of cross-cultural learning, providing minimal concrete suggestions for enacting this supposed campuswide commitment to multiculturalism and inclusiveness. When educators create the expectation that students appreciate those different from themselves, without student input, students often become resentful. If student affairs educators and faculty are to foster inclusive environments leading to cross-cultural learning and engagement, they must develop ample opportunities for students' voices to be shared and heard—promoting healthy exchanges across social and cultural differences.

This chapter responds to the need to listen to student perspectives about multiculturalism in their institutions. First-person narratives from six undergraduate students are presented here. The authors represent different cultural backgrounds:

an Asian American woman, an African American man, a Latina, a White man, a lesbian, and a gay man. The students describe their experiences with multiculturalism and critique[1] how their institutions constructively and marginally deal with issues of difference. Each writer offers relevant examples that help readers understand the importance of student voice and sensemaking around multiculturalism. The chapter concludes with an integration and synthesis of the themes identified in the six narratives, and a reemphasis of the merit of capitalizing on student insights to create inclusive campus environments that are respecting of differences.

DONNA, ASIAN AMERICAN WOMAN, THE UNIVERSITY OF TEXAS AT AUSTIN

I cannot say that I am perfectly multicultural because I hold prejudices, whether conscious or unconscious, and I perpetuate stereotypes. As a student leader on a campus of nearly 50,000, I am a second-year resident assistant, an honors student, a member of a national multicultural sorority, have a part-time job, and am actively involved in other student organizations. I have greatly enjoyed my experience at The University of Texas at Austin (UT Austin) and feel that my undergraduate experience has been of great value. However, as a student and person of color, I have grown to view issues of diversity honestly and frankly. I recognize both the strengths and weaknesses of the environment around me. It is not my goal to damage the reputation of the institution of which I have been fortunate to be a part; but it is important to express how I have felt as a student of color at a predominantly White university.

As a student and person of color, I can vividly recall situations that made me feel unwelcome at my own university. Because I am a young woman of Asian descent, most people assume that my socialization experience has been similar to that of a White person's, and I find this unfair. My concern about racial/ethnic minority issues and my sincere effort to educate myself on the topic often surprises and impresses others. If a Black student feels the same about systems of oppression and hegemony as I do, this does not come as a surprise to others. Yet, it is impressive to my peers that I, an Asian woman, feel oppressed and strive to resist systems that are already in place. I often find I have to work harder to gain others' respect and almost prove that I have the knowledge it takes to be credible.

I have since found myself in leadership roles with increasing responsibilities on campus, and have undergone "diversity training" and "multicultural awareness" sessions designed to expand my horizons and test my personal cultural limits. Through these experiences, I have come to feel the term *diversity* is an overused and empty buzzword. It often seems as if the word is used to establish a person as "accepting" of people of color. In a world where it is politically and socially taboo to express prejudice or bias toward people from nonmainstream (meaning non-White) culture, the word diversity has become bland and meaningless. What does being diverse really entail? I have found that in my personal interactions with others, people who typically describe themselves as "diverse people" are those who engage in tokenism (e.g., "I have a Black friend," or "I know an Asian person"). Tokenism, and the ability to note how many friends from particular cultures one has, does not reflect true multiculturalism, in my opinion.

I have seen too many peers sit in the same room espousing their beliefs that we must truly make an attempt to understand one another to live in a diverse world, but make comments in private that are both ignorant and prejudiced. These peers, who are friends, classmates, and coworkers whom I respect and admire, have expressed continually how they think diversity-related awareness training is useless. Yet, some of these people are the first to say behind closed doors that racism is no longer a problem of the present; it was a problem 40 years ago that no longer applies. It is not that I dislike the ideals of what I think of as "perfect multiculturalism," which is what I think people mean when they use the word diversity. The possibility of living in harmony with others, who differ from me in a multitude of ways, while trying to understand what makes them different and embracing those differences, obviously appeals to me. But the term diversity is used and overused so often that society has lost sight of what the word is supposed to mean. Diversity sometimes strikes me as simply a keyword that communicates to others: "I (person, institution, corporation, or other entity) am accepting of people of color." Unfortunately, up to this point I have been unable to judge the sincerity of such statements.

UT Austin is a proud Southern school with a strong Southern identity and unique Texan pride embodied in the physical layout, the design of buildings, demographics of the student body and alumni, and even the physical landmarks on campus. In my college search, I chose UT Austin out of six other large predominantly White universities based on its quality of education and low tuition. I could not afford to visit the UT Austin campus before committing and enrolled without ever seeing the school. I came to Austin in the fall of 2002, pleasantly surprised to see a large, centrally located campus with a thriving college life. One day early in the semester, I took a walking tour across campus. I found myself on the South Mall, otherwise known as the Main Mall, an open lawn flanked by three buildings on each side and lined with statues of historically important Southern men. Stopping to learn just who these men were, I found a statue of Jefferson Davis, the president of the Confederacy during the American Civil War. To my surprise, I also discovered a statue of Robert E. Lee less than 50 feet away. One can only imagine my chagrin when I realized that all the statues on the Main Mall were testaments to the wealthy, White, Southern men of the Confederacy and its legacy of disenfranchisement, oppression, and racism.

As I began taking courses about diversity and became more involved in multicultural events on campus, I learned the statues were only part of a larger set of hidden meanings. The campus has an East Mall, a West Mall, and a South Mall, but no North Mall. The statues all face the Capitol building, and all point to the south. The statues turn their backs to the north, as if it does not even exist. The lone statue of a person of color is Dr. Martin Luther King Jr., who is cast in bronze and tucked away in a grassy knoll of the East Mall, farther away from UT Austin's Main Building than the statues of the Confederate heroes. Ironically, most of the underprivileged, disadvantaged, and Latino and Black population of Austin resides in East Austin. I have not undertaken the research, but am willing to make the assertion that most of the buildings on campus are named after wealthy White donors. UT Austin has streets bordering campus named after well-known racists, people who supported the creation of "separate but equal" facilities that removed the threat of people of color attending UT Austin.

My assessment of the student body is by no means objective; I consciously surround myself with people who see eye-to-eye with me on many diversity-related issues. Most of my closest friends and acquaintances hold values similar to my own, and many of my activities outside of the classroom focus on these beliefs. However, I do not see students around me passionately committing themselves to issues of diversity. The courses I take in minority studies and social equality are normally populated with two types of students: (a) those, like me, who are interested in equipping themselves with the knowledge necessary to make a difference (although whether or not they choose to take action in the future remains to be seen); and (b) students who take the class to fulfill a requirement. I have found the latter type sometimes learns a great deal and becomes the first type of student, but the majority sit passively through the class, earning decent grades, rarely contributing to class discussions and squirming with discomfort in times of heated conversation.

I cannot say with certainty that administrators overestimate student engagement in cross-cultural interaction. I assert that every student engages in some sort of cross-cultural interaction daily, inevitable at such a large school with a relatively multicultural student body. What is certain is that not all students come away with a new perspective or a changed mindset, or even recognize the value of cross-cultural learning. The number of cross-cultural interactions a student engages in all depends on the person's tendency to reach out to others and to test his or her own boundaries. I have noticed that interracial dating is relatively uncommon on campus; though friendships can be wide and varied across cultures and races, romantic relationships are normally limited to the same ethnic background.

For UT Austin to fulfill the promises it makes to prospective and current students, it needs to take a sincere, active role in promoting cross-cultural interaction. As an incoming student of color from another state, I sensed that the university expected students to be immersed into a large, heterogeneous mix of students and automatically interact with others. While there is some level of reality in this expectation, the reality is that students will automatically seek out what is familiar to them. To promote multiculturalism on campus, UT Austin has proposed a requirement that all students take one cross-cultural or diversity-related course. The administration has also hired a vice president of diversity and community engagement. These initiatives are positive steps, especially because addressing diversity awareness at a large university has no perfect solution.

If these steps toward improvement become reality, then the university is making a sincere effort to address not only the needs of students of color, but all students at UT Austin. Furthermore, the university must actively recruit faculty and staff of all cultural backgrounds to effectively reach students. I do not know the makeup of UT Austin's faculty, but I see a clear lack of faculty of color in my field of study. I am often at a loss at how to pursue a career in higher education and would like to turn to a role model who may understand my needs. I understand the Asian American population in this country is young, primarily made up of first-generation children who are encouraged to pursue certain careers and fields of study, so it is often difficult to find faculty of color in other disciplines. However, there must be other ways to address the academic needs of students of color to ensure their success.

The unfortunate side of these steps toward improvement is that they were borne out of a series of disturbing events. On Martin Luther King Jr. Day in 2003, cowards who disrespected university property and the values, morals, and ethics of Martin Luther King Jr. threw eggs at the statue. UT Austin police said surveillance cameras installed around the statue and the East Mall were broken. On the same day, a wreath of lilies was draped around the neck of the Robert E. Lee statue on the Main Mall. These incidents occurred after several fraternities at UT Austin wore racially offensive shirts and painted their bodies in black paint, wearing "blackface" at themed parties. In August 2004, Dr. King's head and torso were spray-painted silver by two men who were caught on camera, but never identified. Former UT Austin President Larry Faulkner then formed the Task Force on Racial Respect and Fairness, and out of that came proposals for students to take 6 hours of multicultural studies and the appointment of a full-time administrator specializing in diversity. It is unfortunate that it took such blatant acts of ignorance and racism to illustrate the dire need for the university to promote multiculturalism among students.

As an out-of-state, first-year student, educators expected me to interact with other students from across Texas and the world automatically, finding my niche at UT Austin with ease. As a student of color coming to a large university alone, I lacked guidance, role models, and advisors. Even as a junior, I find my residents and the younger students I advise often experience difficulty figuring out "where they really belong" at UT Austin. In particular, students of color often find themselves as token representatives of their races, making it extremely difficult for them to decipher and shape their own identities, while deciding what they want to gain from their undergraduate experiences.

I can say with confidence that I will graduate from The University of Texas at Austin having actively sought out new experiences, knowledge, and information. I have tested my comfort levels and encouraged myself to go beyond what I already know. Many students will leave this institution and hundreds of other institutions ill-equipped for reality, having never taken a course addressing cross-cultural interaction or racial/ethnic minority issues, having grown up in a town where people of color were a small population, or having never attempted to understand how the cultural experience of a person of color differs from a White person's experience. Most of these students are not prejudiced or racist, nor do they believe they are better than people of color. Furthermore, not all these students are White. These students have not formulated an understanding of power, privilege, prejudice, oppression, and resistance as they apply to society. Although they are bright, educated, and well-prepared in other domains to fulfill the responsibilities of entry-level and lower-level management positions, the most successful high-level management and administrative positions will ultimately be held by people who are well educated on issues of multiculturalism.

Cullen, African American Man, The Ohio State University

In my transition from high school, I had an idealized view of diversity programs and multicultural initiatives. I grew up in a middle-class neighborhood that was about half Black and half White. At the time, I viewed diversity programs as mechanisms to aid all cultures and ethnicities in understanding one another. Upon entering a major institution of higher education, I gained a very different, more realistic view of such programming. To my shock and dismay, diversity initiatives were often contrary to my needs and those of other ethnic minority groups.

As a Black student at a predominantly White university, I took special interest in any programs that were labeled with the term diversity. In my opinion, Black people (more specifically, Black students) are one of the biggest reasons why diversity has become what it is today. Throughout most of the history of American higher education, White males were virtually the only group offered admission to the major academic institutions in this country. There was no need to develop committees and hire personnel to cater to the needs of a diverse student population because other groups were virtually invisible; colleges and universities inherently satisfied the needs of White males. The first group to raise a major protest to this unfair system was African Americans; their successful protests opened the door for similar movements by other students previously excluded from higher education. Students quickly learned, though, that admission into the university was not enough; they would also have to fight to receive the same treatment as their White male counterparts once inside. To address the needs of the various groups, colleges and universities began forming administrative support networks for the many different populations. After a few years, many institutions began to go back to their old ways, but in a far subtler manner.

After years of having unique organizations to support the needs of various student populations such as women, Black, Latino, and Native American students, and students with disabilities, many institutions began to view the needs of these groups as similar. Though the needs of these groups have some overlap, each group needs its own attention because in many cases their needs are different. Unable to recognize this, many institutions have consolidated their support offices for these specific student populations into a single office that is supposed to satisfy every student's needs. Often, this office is labeled with the terms diversity or multicultural, which I find troublesome.

While Blacks, Latinos, and other groups have made progress against discrimination, White women have outpaced us all. For example, most law schools in the 1960s were comprised almost solely of White men. Today, White women often make up the majority of law students while other groups struggle to maintain numbers that are often lower than their percentage of the general population. Around 2004, five of the 11 Big Ten university presidents were White women. Will racial/ethnic minority people ever achieve this kind of representation at a university's highest level? Since women have, the cultures of colleges and universities have moved from catering solely to White men to catering to White students. White women have been able to succeed where most other groups have failed. They have altered the everyday workings of colleges and universities where their needs are considered in almost every arena. Until the cultures of colleges and universities can accept the presence of all students, focused attention will be needed to satisfy the desires of the various student populations.

An institution that is welcoming to only one portion of the student body seems to meet only the majority's needs rather than the needs of the entire student population through diversity programs. When a college or university takes various underserved or underrepresented groups and gives them all one outlet for their unique needs, the result is one organization that does much work but does not adequately satisfy any of its constituents. For instance, Black students at Ohio State had been fighting for various rights and privileges for decades. As a result of their picketing, protesting, and (in some cases) other activities detrimental to their academics, Black students established a Black Cultural Center, a Minority Affairs

Program, and a Black Studies Department. Recognizing that the overwhelming number of White students inherently suppressed Black culture, the Black students started an African American Heritage Festival, a weeklong event to celebrate African American culture. Most might think the university would applaud Black students for our passion and willingness to go beyond what is required in the classroom. Yet every year, Black students fight to keep the programs that our predecessors helped establish. Often, the attacks on programs for Black students have come under the name of diversity.

About five years ago, the university started a Multicultural Center to promote the celebration of various ethnic groups. In doing so, though, they took power away from each of the existing student services offices to create this one center. Instead of reporting to the vice president for student affairs, the ethnic student services offices began reporting to the director of the Multicultural Center. Ideally, each group would have kept the same autonomy it had before, but this simply was not the case. When budgets were cut, the funding of ethnic organizations was the first to go; each group began fighting for funds from a smaller source. Because Black students had been enjoying many so-called privileges, other groups believed it was time that Black students shared our programs with others.

Many sought to turn the Black Cultural Center into the Multicultural Center, and others wanted to turn the Black Heritage Festival into a celebration of all ethnic groups. Why should Black students suffer for the sake of multiculturalism? After all the years spent as slaves, fighting, and working, Black people still do not live a life free of racial discrimination. As long as students need Black History Month to denote historical facts that teachers should have taught them in elementary school, services for Black students on predominantly White campuses will be needed. Instead of benefiting each of the different ethnic groups, the Multicultural Center placed the groups in opposition for resources. In the end, White students get to go to one place if they want to experience various cultures, but students of diverse backgrounds only see their programs diminish for the sake of diversity.

Unlike White women, Black students and other ethnic groups have not been able to alter the fabric of society into something more sensitive to their needs. In this country, White people can still live and work in places where they do not have to interact on an intimate level with anyone not of their race. White women have made strides far and above almost any other group because White men cannot escape socializing with White women, though they can avoid Blacks, Latinos, and Native Americans. White men have mothers, daughters, sisters, wives, and partners who can help them see that discrimination based on sex is wrong. How many other disadvantaged groups are so close to the power source? This closeness has given White women the opportunity to step into areas of power formerly held by White men, and once in place, they could begin forming institutional cultures that cater to their needs as well. Unfortunately, racial/ethnic minority students still do not receive similar treatment and advantages as White students. It seems that diversity programs in their present form are temporary solutions to a more permanent problem.

Let's face it: our society is not ready for multiculturalism. White students at The Ohio State University complained about a weeklong Black Heritage Festival without realizing that every other week of the year is White Heritage Festival by default. Look at the way diversity programs and multicultural initiatives are justified by the administration: underlying the administration's argument is that diverse environments enhance the education of White students. Celebrating diversity because it is the right thing to do is not enough; there has to be some benefit for White students before it can be accepted. As a result, institutions are left with diversity programs that do not meet the needs of any of its constituents, but instead allow White students to get a small, bland taste of other cultures.

MELISSA, LATINA, NORTHWESTERN UNIVERSITY

The Latino family I have at Northwestern University has been an important part of my time in college. My experience at Northwestern started with the Summer Academic Workshop (SAW), an academic program meant to ease the transition of a group of incoming Latino and African American students. The classes would not count for credit at Northwestern, but I thought it would be a good opportunity to meet other first-year students. Though the program cut a month out of my summer, I also thought it would be a good opportunity to wake up my brain before fall classes started.

I do not remember much about the chemistry and math classes I had every morning or the writing classes that met each afternoon. The best part of the program was in Jones, our summer residence hall. There were about 40 first-year students and 7 upperclass student counselors in a residence hall suited for more than 200 people, so we had a lot of room to move around. The warm weather and undemanding classes allowed us to spend almost every night staying up dancing, talking, or playing games around campus. The campus became ours those three weeks, and we became really close in a short period of time. Student affairs educators ran the program, and we interacted most with the coordinators of Latino and African American Student Affairs.

Lisa, the coordinator of Latino/Hispanic Student Affairs, recruited me instantly to participate in New Student Week. She wanted the SAW participants to attend a Latino luncheon sponsored by her office; there, I met other Latino students. She also wanted me to meet Latino leaders on campus to acquaint me with the Latino student organizations. "The Latino Experience," held the same night as the luncheon, was sponsored by the Latino student organizations; there, I met other Latinos and more upperclass students. I was excited to see so many others like me. Deerfield Academy, my former high school, was a small East Coast boarding school, and I was one of 18 Latino students. At Northwestern, I was one of a few hundred; coming from a large Hispanic family, I was glad to have a new one.

My first year, I became heavily involved in Alianza, the Latino Student Cultural Organization. I helped build our homecoming float and danced down Sheridan Road the night of the homecoming parade. I also went to events the organization sponsored for Latino Heritage Month. My work–study job was in the Office of Undergraduate Admissions. I worked with the Latino recruitment division and helped pair prospective students with enrolled students; I also hosted a few prospective students on my own.

My relationship with Lisa also enabled me to attend events planned by her office. Her big event was LatiNU, which brought a band, food, and performers to kick off the celebration of Latino Heritage Month. I remember arriving early and staying until the event ended. A group of SAW students who had built a strong relationship with Lisa were there that night. We danced to the Afro-Caribbean music and enjoyed the Puerto Rican food. Another event her office sponsored was Friday afternoon tertulias. They encouraged Latinos to practice Spanish, but they also helped us catch up on news and events within the Latino community. Lisa kept the family together at Northwestern through events she planned and her availability to students, no matter how involved they were on campus.

I spent time in her office not only talking about issues relating to the Hispanic community and the events she planned and facilitated, but also asking for advice about classes and other organizations in which I was involved. She encouraged me to apply for the executive board of Northwestern's Diversity Conference, and I became cochair. Because I knew I wanted to spend my junior year abroad, I wanted to take a Spanish course each quarter. To make sure I fulfilled my personal goals, she suggested I minor in Spanish, and I enrolled in Spanish and Latin American Literature courses in my first and second years. Taking these courses helped me maintain my writing skills and also served as useful background for my courses in Spain.

My other first-year activities included the Undergraduate Leadership Program and Carib Nation, the Caribbean Student Cultural Organization. I became one of the founding members of the Carib Nation Dancers, a group of Northwestern students who choreographed dances and performed at events for prospective students. We also performed at Carib Fest, the annual Memorial Day festival to celebrate Caribbean culture. Like LatiNU and Alianza salsa parties, this event drew students not only from the Black and Hispanic communities. White students also attended these events, and many White students looked forward to the quarterly salsa parties.

As a first-year student, I was glad to have both the African American and Latino communities. Through SAW and the student organizations, I met many students who were interested in social change and cultural celebration/exploration. We were highly involved in cultural organizations, but were also connected to different parts of the larger Northwestern community. The organizations and the physical spaces that the university allocated us brought us together; they became places where we could share our frustrations with other members about the problems we faced in classes. We often found ourselves overcommitted and holding leadership positions not just in cultural organizations, but in mainstream organizations as well. The resources we found through peer networks and strong mentor relationships with the coordinators in the Multicultural Affairs Office helped us with time management and encouraged the projects we took on as students and as community activists. It was important to us to disperse ourselves because we wanted to reach out to the communities and educate both our White and our ethnic minority peers. We viewed ourselves as bridging different parts of the larger Northwestern community, and the Multicultural Affairs Office helped us do so. Educators understood the types of responsibilities we faced as students and as children in our home families. They also understood the social pressures

that came with being high-achieving students of color and the conflicting expectations from our families, peers, and professors.

As a student of color on a predominantly White campus, I was aware of the
complexity of the choices my African American and Latino peers had to make.
When I was a first-year student, Lisa and my upperclass peers nominated me
to participate in the Freshman Emerging Leadership Program. Two other SAW
Latino alumni were in my group. Of the 10 others, one was Asian American.
Everyone else in the group, including the faculty moderator, was White. We met
every Monday during winter quarter to discuss issues of campus life and leadership education. One week we got into a discussion on affirmative action and the
notion of a diverse campus. I remember explaining to the group the important
relationships students of color have with each other. There are those who use their
ethnicity to further their academic and professional careers and breed doubt and
insecurity among those who do not. We have two choices when we come to college.
Some of us, a Latino person in the group admitted, got involved in high school
cultural organizations to gain leadership positions that made us better candidates
for college admission, and chose not to get involved in college. They chose to disas-
sociate because they wanted to assimilate and ignore the debate on affirmative
action. Others (e.g., me) need the community of students in cultural organizations
and the resources of a multicultural affairs division in student affairs.

The Multicultural Affairs Office and the organizations are important
because they give us the space to celebrate ourselves and our accomplishments.
In addition, they offer students a space "to be." I have participated in leadership
programs like this and have had to explain myself and my student involvement
choices to White students over and over again. In high school, I was frustrated
by my peers' ignorance, but participation in cultural organizations has taught me
the language to defend myself and to educate my peers. Visits with Lisa and the
conversations I have had with peers at Northwestern allowed me to learn how
to explain the importance of ethnic organizations without being defensive. Most
White peers and faculty cannot relate to the positions we adopt as students of
color on predominantly White campuses. I have found that at Northwestern, the
most intelligent and capable students of color burn themselves out because we
spread ourselves across the board. We need the community and the Multicultural
Affairs Office to ease the burden of socially educating our campuses. While I
recognize Northwestern has many steps to take before it offers students of color

adequate facilities, what we have has positively affected my experiences here; prepared me to be a more ambitious student; and trained me for the challenges that I overcame as a college student.

One of the most telling memories of New Student Week my first year occurred in a small group of racially mixed peers. We were walking to the student center and talking about the Black Family Reunion, the African American Student Organization event for first-year students. There was a White student with us that night, and as we discussed the events, he asked where the White support group was on campus. I responded that it was Northwestern University. He fell silent and my Black friends smiled and agreed with me. No one would doubt his eligibility or his intelligence. They would not question his choice of organizations to join or what career path he chose to follow. We needed our peers of color who served as a network of support because they were the few who understood our individual and collective experiences.

As a senior who has gotten involved in a variety of organizations on campus, traveled abroad, and worked with professors on different projects, I realize I am an asset to my communities of color. Though I spent a year abroad, I continued to build relationships with younger students to inform them of the opportunities available to them and to support their decisions. We need each other because we remind ourselves why we attended schools like Northwestern in the first place.

ADAM, WHITE MAN, UNIVERSITY OF TAMPA

If you can, imagine going from a small town with one stoplight, where the people all think the same and pretty much look alike, to a city and college campus where the people come from different backgrounds, beliefs, and heritages. This is what it was like when I left my home and entered college. The first advice I would offer new students is to get involved. I would tell them to go out and meet people who may or may not be like them. It is not likely that a person can get along with everyone, but by taking a chance with meeting new people, one can get to know others better and easily form great friendships that may last beyond college.

Getting involved on campus is the best idea I had when I arrived. I became involved in several organizations, including Student Government, the Residence Hall Association, and a leadership group offered through our Student Activities Office. As I got to know people and made new friends, I came to see that the state of diversity programming at the University of Tampa was much better than at my high school, but still not at a level I deemed acceptable or satisfactory. Coming from a small Massachusetts town, my experience with and exposure to diversity was very limited. I graduated in a class of about 120 students, 99% White. Even in high school, I knew my town was not representative of larger society. I was not really involved in any organizations in high school, instead choosing to work.

We had several diversity-related events in my first year of college: diversity was the theme of our Leadership Retreats; a diversity walk brought together students of different backgrounds and celebrated our differences; and a new student organization was created to promote diversity. Toward the end of the year, the university hosted a one-day conference on embracing diversity. Although some of these programs were well attended, I felt diversity was not that well regarded on my campus.

I would like to think of myself as different from everyone else, but I know this is not the case. Reflecting on my experience as a first-year student, the most memorable instance of people working together is one where a common characteristic of the group actually held it back from realizing its goal. At our Spring Leadership Retreat, we had to brainstorm ideas for values to add to the retreat's list of Top 10 Values. About 30 ideas were written down, and a group of about 50 student leaders was to narrow the list to 10. At first, some were easily removed, consolidated with another value, or unanimously dismissed. After more discussion, another five were removed. We were down to about 15, and after an hour of some people refusing to let a value be scratched off the list and complaining about the true "Webster's definition" of some of the words, the facilitators finalized our list of Top 12 Values. This event is memorable for me because although we were all different, we shared a characteristic of exhibiting leadership qualities, and the room full of like-minded people argued over little ideas so much we could not get our goal accomplished. It made me realize that everyone has a personal sense of leadership and values, and these conflicting values can impede progress.

There are many White students at the University of Tampa, and it appears that a larger percentage of these students are apathetic compared to racial or ethnic minority students. While the university tries hard to promote diversity, I do not think cross-cultural interaction and diversity programming are where they should be. The problem does not come from a lack of effort by those like me who wish to promote diversity, but from a lack of interest in anything extracurricular from a large portion of the student body. Another problem I find is that students have a tendency to hang out with people like themselves, often distancing themselves from others. Sorority sisters seem to socialize with their chapter members, the swim team eats meals together, National Pan-Hellenic Council events are attended by mostly African Americans, and so on. Students who may be interested in meeting and becoming friends with someone from a different cultural background may feel they do not fit in a prospective friend's group.

White students are not very involved in diversity programming on campus. Being actively involved in several organizations, I notice that the same small number of students are involved in many organizations, while a large number of students are not involved at all. Unfortunately, many of my White peers are not involved in diversity programs because they perceive diversity as an almost forced integration into their lives and not as an opportunity to learn from and embrace differences. Some of these students may feel they do not belong with others because they fear being seen as arrogant, privileged, or ignorant on issues of diversity, or some may feel the different groups will not accept them. I also think there continues to be a small group of people who do not desire diversity and do not want to associate with different groups.

Personally, I cannot pinpoint any particular reason why I became involved in diversity programming on campus. It could be because I think the best ideas can be created by a group of people who are not all alike. It could also be because I find it interesting that people can be so unlike me, yet we can end up at the same university and in the same group to learn from each other. I enjoy learning about different cultures and how families celebrate them. I am still taken aback when I hear friends of mine dismiss a person they do not even know simply because they do not "like" that person's heritage, or when they label a person because they attribute a particular characteristic of theirs to their entire race. Unfortunately, I have heard this on several occasions; stereotyping is a common problem. I have been involved discussions of how certain actions might seem offensive to others, even though that is not one's intention. Examples included calling a behavior or practice "ghetto" or "retarded." This also helped me think about words I may have been using that could be offensive to different groups.

I have gained much more from my involvement in diversity programs and activities than I have contributed. I have been involved in many discussions about diversity at different colleges and have candidly offered my opinions on what problems exist and what beneficial outcomes can accrue when diversity is embraced at the University of Tampa and elsewhere. White male students are least interested and most underrepresented in diversity programming at the university. I cannot identify any single reason, but I have my theories. First, many people of my race and gender are so wrapped up in themselves or getting good grades or just hanging out with friends that they do not really want to get involved. Also, White students have a greater feeling of independence and feel less need to belong to groups. I offer a different perspective to the group, because students gain so much more when they become involved in activities on campus. Not only do they make great friends and make more connections, but they also have a good time.

Nobody has ever questioned my commitment to diversity. I am an honest person and am committed to my beliefs. I did not get involved to enhance or network myself into a great paying job upon graduation. I got involved because I truly believe that to bring about changes, students must make a difference and show commitment and personal stake in these activities. Diversity programs appealed to me because they were not available in my high school. Surrounding myself with people who are too much like me will just lead to boring conversation and few opportunities for learning.

The word diversity is all-encompassing, and it does not refer exclusively to racial/ethnic minority students. By getting to know students from all walks of life, we gain a greater respect for different cultures and also the opportunity to form friendships that can last a lifetime. These programs should definitely include White students so they can gain an understanding of unfamiliar cultures, and also allow members of racial/ethnic minority groups to get a perspective from a group they may not fully understand. By believing that White students should be excluded from diversity programming, we lose the whole concept of diversity and embracing differences among each other.

JOANNA AND JESSE, QUEER STUDENTS, NEW YORK UNIVERSITY

Attending college in New York City, arguably one of the most diverse places on the planet, you inevitably get a second education in what multiculturalism means and the potential it holds. New York is alive with diversity; walking down the city streets, we could not remember what it was like to live in a place where everyone looked the same. One thing Joanna *can* remember is what it felt like to know that because of her sexual orientation, she was different than everyone else she grew up around in her small suburban Long Island town. When Joanna came out as a lesbian at 15, she was lucky to do so to a supportive network of friends and family. While her experience was generally positive, there were very few other queer people around; she was cognizant of her difference and aware that, to many, she was "that one"—not just *a* lesbian, but *the* lesbian.

Similarly, Jesse's experience was not marred by violence or a notable lack of support, but it still made him different, odd—literally queer. Growing up on the other side of the country, Jesse came out at 14 in a supportive, private Catholic high school in the San Francisco Bay area. His overall experience was also positive, but he, too, was one of a very small minority of queer students in his high school. The problem was isolation, limitation, and a total lack of recognition of his identity through much of his experience.

Coming to New York University (NYU) to start college was quite a change for both of us. We both joined Outspoken, a campus peer education group dedicated to lesbian, gay, bisexual, and transgender (LGBT) student issues, and were instantly thrust into a community of queer people and allies that was incredibly vast in scope. NYU has a large queer community that is as diverse as the city itself, with members of all races, religions, and orientations.

In this narrative, we use LGBT and queer synonymously. We define LGBT as lesbian, gay, bisexual, and transgender—an acronym that encompasses several different identities. Queer, once a derogatory term, has been reclaimed by the LGBT community as an umbrella term that encompasses all minority orientations. We use these interchangeably since both aptly describe the range of identities we discuss. An ally is a person who does not identify with a particular group but still supports its cause and actively participates to work for it; in this case, straight or heterosexual people. NYU's administration is supportive of its queer community, funding our office and many queer-related events every month.

However, it is not the queer community that makes the most influential impact on students' diverse experience in relation to LGBT issues. Rather, it is the degree to which LGBT students are integrated into everyday life at NYU. This integration makes our campus a shining example of multiculturalism in college. We imagine that most students at NYU know at least one queer person. In the course of a four-year education, it would be impossible not to meet or come across peers from the LGBT community. No one seems particularly surprised by or uncomfortable with this. Acceptance and open-mindedness is the norm on campus, not the exception as it may be at other institutions.

This safe environment is partially the result of our peer education work; hundreds of students have undergone "Safe-Zone" training in queer issues and creating a more welcoming campus climate for LGBT students. In the three-hour Safe-Zone training workshop, participants list assumptions and deconstruct them; learn about breaking down the gender binary; and discuss the fluidity of sexual identity, among other activities. One of the most potent activities we lead is one taken from an analogy in the book *Why Are All the Black Kids Sitting Together in the Cafeteria?* (Tatum, 1997). In the *moving sidewalk* analogy, the author notes that just because people are not *actively* participating in racist or other marginalizing activities, they are not accomplishing anything toward its elimination. Imagine a moving sidewalk that moves toward complete marginalization of a group. We all start in the middle of this sidewalk. Some actively walk toward the marginalizing end, with increased speed due to the sidewalk's movement. Some actively walk against it, with increased difficulty against the movement. Finally, some simply stand still, not actively moving in either direction. Rather than staying still, we suggest those people are moving, though not as quickly as those actively moving, in the direction of marginalization. Apathy is not just unproductive—it is antiproductive.

In a more passive way, another large contributing factor is the environment of the city and its inherent diversity. Whatever the cause, it is certain that the overall acceptance and integration of LGBT students within the campus community has greatly enhanced not just our college experience as queer students, but the college experiences of all NYU students regardless of sexual orientation. Students here are exposed to a colorful fabric of humanity, and no one here is "in the norm" in any respect. Our work is to end the types of experiences we had by preventing isolation of individuals, which can occur even in seemingly accepting environments. NYU students learn to respect the many different backgrounds and experiences from which we all come. This makes us all more well-rounded, capable not only of living our lives with the open-mindedness developed here, but also spreading this open-mindedness to others. Multiculturalism must then be fostered to the fullest extent on campuses not only to provide a safe space for students from all cultures, but also to provide a full, enriching, and useful education to college students.

The discussion of multiculturalism begs the question of how exactly this all comes to fruition. It is easy to list endlessly romanticized ideas of how to change the world: Education. Exposure. Asking questions from both sides. Compromise. Commitment. Thinking outside of everyone's box. Constant conversations. Writing letters to your congressional representative. Talking to your parents. Talking to children. Getting involved. Getting into the media. Watching the news. Writing books. Writing movies. Being healthy. Living and loving, and so on. As inspiring as these lists become, they do not really answer the question: How do we make progress happen? How exactly do we advance change to create this welcoming and accepting community? To answer these questions, it is important to examine the focus of one's work. The focus must begin not small, but specific. We are not downsizing goals but seizing the attainable. A focus on college communities is an educated one. As college students, our largest audiences, our biggest strengths, our common experiences all involve the very campuses in which we live and learn.

The best point of reference for us is our own institution. NYU is known for having a progressive attitude and free-spirited population, as well as housing a very large LGBT student population. This, of course, creates a very unique college experience that may be difficult with which to identify, especially for undergraduates at more conventional or conservative institutions. Still, these are important, but certainly not essential, tools to develop a healthy and active community that accepts all identities and works to empower students, to voice concern, and to create progress. An empowering environment is just as important if one's college or university has a population of LGBT students the size of NYU's or if there are only one or two queer students, like in our high schools. The size of the LGBT population is but a tiny aspect of the empowering environment a college or university can create. Though specifics vary across institutions and our experiences can only reference that of a liberal university in the middle of New York City, LGBT students should be able to attend any postsecondary institution for any reason and should not have to consider safety or acceptance as criteria for their decisions. All colleges and universities should be equally safe and accepting. Any campus can and every campus should be actively supportive of and deliberately open to students of all identities, the way that NYU supports multiculturalism. Our examination of NYU's successes as a multicultural campus is one with the intent to set precedent and provide ideas we hope will result in action.

When looking specifically at NYU and the way LGBT issues are handled and supported, there will obviously be practices done well and others in need of improvement. No college, progressive or otherwise, does this perfectly. NYU does well in its recognition of identities, efforts toward education, and desire for progress. A university looking to expand its empowerment of LGBT students should focus first on recognition. It should be universally known across the campus where the LGBT Office is and where people can get information. Constituents of colleges and universities should also know what LGBT means. Recognizing that these identities exist on the campus is vastly important. It is easy to talk about LGBT issues as if they are abstract, but it is important to remember that real people face bad treatment because of their sexual identities every day. LGBT issues should be recognized, celebrated, talked about, and realized. Education is the next step. NYU is constantly retooling and expanding its efforts on the education of identities, coming out issues, being an ally, heterosexism, gender issues, stereotypes, transgender issues, sexual fluidity, HIV/AIDS and sexually transmitted infections awareness, gay rights, and marginalized identities within the LGBT sphere. Education can never be seen as work to be finished, but rather a constant, frustrating, rewarding, growing, ever-in-progress work. A commitment to education becomes a commitment to progress.

Keeping the tone structured and constructive rather than insolent and sophistic, we now examine some areas needing improvement at NYU—not to demean our university, but to suggest change and promote progress. Student engagement is the key to success for any LGBT program. However, student involvement needs to be just that—of the students, by the students, and for the students. Our success with Outspoken has largely been based on its creation as a student-run organization. Outspoken has traditionally encouraged student leadership and innovation where members create and facilitate their own programs and workshops. The creation of such an organization changed the role of LGBT work across our campus. The shift from emphasizing recognition to accenting education marks a progression, the next step. Students are best able to recognize their own needs and understand the best ways to communicate with peers. With initiative, students have a level of challenge and opportunity unachievable with administration-run programming. The emphasis on student engagement, as opposed to a more administrative-oriented involvement, fosters greater interest, maintains commitment, and engenders a sense of ownership among students. It also develops leadership in students, rather than expecting them to participate in prearranged programs. NYU often loses its focus on the student—and invaluable input and breadth of voice—when it tries to establish larger administration-run programming. All college campuses have a vast range of personalities and experiences in their student bodies. We hope colleges continue to capitalize on that amazing opportunity and allow education for social progress to occur with students at the center.

Recognition from the administration is absolutely essential to the promotion of widespread social progress on a college campus, but the administration must act in a support role—it should not create the programs, nor should it censor students from creating their own. Administrators should guide, not control. Otherwise, the school risks student rejection as well as blindness to actual student needs. More important, recognition from the administration should come in the form of active listening. Listen to students with ideas and help realize them. Listen to students with concerns and help address them. Listen to students with problems and help create solutions for them. The administration and the student body absolutely must work together, for students have the passion and the will, and the administration holds the keys to the way.

COMMON THEMES ACROSS STUDENT NARRATIVES

In their book, *Good Practice in Student Affairs*, Blimling and Whitt (1999, p. 160) assert: "An inclusive campus community requires staff and students who are comfortable with people from any culture, and whose attitudes, language, and behavior reflect awareness and sensitivity to other cultures and backgrounds." The authors also note several characteristics of supportive, inclusive communities: the visibility of diversity, the availability of groups where students can find comfort, and the open discussion of controversial issues. The premise is that campus environments that are welcoming to learners value student contributions and actively encourage cross-cultural dialogues. The students' narratives exemplified these qualities of multiculturalism—each identified key experiences related to the influence of student voice in identifying factors that promote inclusiveness. Four themes from the narratives form the foundation for this section: (a) the value of cross-cultural interactions, (b) the need for culturally-centered student organizations, (c) the role of same-culture mentors, and (d) the importance of student ownership in diversity issues. The combination of these four practices can lead to important learning outcomes among students.

CROSS-CULTURAL INTERACTIONS

The narrative authors' collegiate experiences illuminate the meanings students make from multiculturalism when educators develop intentional mechanisms to facilitate cross-cultural engagement. The authors noted that students are rarely afforded opportunities to interact meaningfully with their peers across social differences. Donna encountered stereotypes and assumptions and described racism on her campus during a remembrance of Martin Luther King Jr. With ample opportunity to explore assumptions and engage differences, students might have confronted their stereotypes of Asian American students and understood the implications of their racist actions. Blimling and Whitt (1999) observe that students often associate with those who are like them, so it is not surprising that they are hesitant to leave their comfort zones to explore differences. Adam's experience as a White male student underscores this point, as he communicated the lack of interracial interactions among his White peers.

CULTURALLY-CENTERED STUDENT ORGANIZATIONS

Joanna and Jesse in their essay referred to Tatum's book *Why Are All the Black Kids Sitting Together in the Cafeteria?* (1997). Tatum's work prompts readers to explore continued segregation on today's campuses despite laws prohibiting separate but equal status. The racially/ethnically homogenous campuses that four of the six authors attended resembled White racialized spaces that denoted the presence of students of color as abnormalities. In response, Melissa became actively involved in the Latino student organizations on campus, which helped develop her Latina ethnic identity. Cullen's story illuminates what happens when institutions treat racial/ethnic minority students as a monolithic group and collapse specific cultural organizations into a comprehensive Multicultural Center. Though these centers provide important assistance to students of color and their White peers, they are often underfunded and yet expected to rid the campus of discrimination and serve as havens for racial/ethnic minority students. As Cullen mentioned, students in each cultural group have unique needs that are often overlooked without racially/ethnically-focused organizations. Institutions should examine the importance of specific organizations devoted to the unique needs of culturally diverse learners to give students places to share their frustrations, develop their voices, and partner with their peers to navigate the campus context.

CULTURALLY-SIMILAR MENTORS

The six writers referred to the relative ease with which White students can identify mentors at predominantly White colleges and universities. By contrast, the underrepresentation of racial/ethnic minority and LGBT educators makes it more difficult for these students to find mentors to help them navigate the campus environment and meet their personal and professional goals. Few students are fortunate enough to attend institutions like New York University with its awareness and acceptance of LGBT and racial/ethnic minority students. Higher education administrators must actively recruit and hire faculty and student affairs educators who represent their multicultural campus populations. Students need to be actively exposed to differences in order to learn from them. The Latino family Melissa found at Northwestern University largely escaped Cullen's experience. While most of Adam's contacts are White, he still needs White mentors who understand the complexities of inclusiveness and multiculturalism for Adam and his White peers to engage differences.

STUDENT OWNERSHIP IN DIVERSITY ISSUES

This final theme is the crux of the chapter. Top-down multiculturalism makes it difficult for students to make sense of differences and see their roles in diversity on campus. Joanna and Jesse noted their participation in Outspoken, a *student-run* organization. I emphasize student-run because it demonstrates how learners construct their understandings of diversity and actively appreciate those who hold different values, views, and backgrounds when such opportunities are provided by educators. If open discussion of controversial topics is to occur, issues important to students must serve as the foundation for discussion (Blimling & Whitt, 1999). Both Donna and Melissa took leadership roles in several campus organizations and experienced learning outcomes because of their involvement.

By choosing these opportunities, they made meaning of their experiences and considered what multiculturalism meant from their respective vantage points. Similarly, Adam used his contrasting small-town and college experiences as the context for his learning, while Cullen's African American background enabled him to contemplate the role of multicultural centers on campus. Each author is of a different gender, sexual orientation, and racial/ethnic identity. Their collective experiences give insights into the importance of student voice in cross-cultural learning and demonstrate the learning outcomes when students take initiative and respond to the realities of multiculturalism on their campuses.

CONCLUSION: LISTENING TO AND LEARNING FROM STUDENTS

The student narratives illustrate the gains accrued when educators invite students to communicate their perspectives in classroom and cocurricular learning venues. Educators rarely ask learners to discuss their perspectives in meaningful ways; the norm is the authority figure posing the questions and directing the topics that students should deem important. This chapter proposes a shift from educators as repositories and dispensers of knowledge to active facilitators of learning through dialogue and participation with students. A prerequisite to multiculturalism and inclusiveness is openness to the unique contributions of students in their own words. The stories from Donna, Cullen, Melissa, Adam, Joanna, and Jesse illustrate how students make sense of multiculturalism and the complexities they face in cross-cultural discussions. The advice from Jesse and Joanna is worth repeating and serves as a useful reminder for those who work with college students: "Listen to students with ideas and help them realize them. Listen to students with concerns and help address them. Listen to students with problems and help create solutions for them." Listening to and learning from students enables them to develop their voices and recognize their roles in contributing to inclusive campuses that are welcoming of diverse learners.

REFERENCES

Blimling, G. S., & Whitt, E. J. (1999). *Good practice in student affairs: Principles to foster student learning*. San Francisco: Jossey-Bass.

Tatum, B. D. (1997). *Why are all the Black kids sitting together in the cafeteria?: And other conversations about race*. New York: Basic Books.

NOTES

[1]Each student's narrative is written in present tense, as all were undergraduates when they wrote for this book. Most have now graduated.

Chapter Three

○○○○○

Research on Race and Ethnic Relations among Community College Students

William Maxwell and Diane Shammas[1]

○○○○○

D espite dramatic demographic, political, and cultural changes in North American society, there is a remarkable absence of scholarly research on student race relations and campus climates in community colleges. Political forces have struggled over immigration and affirmative action policies, including the landmark court case University of California v. Bakke (1978) and the more recent Grutter v. Bollinger (2003). Demographic trends show that the proportion of racial and ethnic minority students doubled in the colleges from 15.7% to 30.3% between 1976 and 1996 and will continue to increase in the next 25 years (Kee, 1999). Yet a recent review of the burgeoning scholarship on this issue refers almost entirely to 4-year university settings (Hurtado, Dey, Gurin, & Gurin, 2003). Given this significant gap in the literature, this review addresses two central questions:

> *Research Question 1:* How have scholars previously examined relations among community college students from diverse racial and ethnic groups?

Research Question 2: What are promising future theoretical topics and research methods for studying relations among community college students from diverse racial and ethnic groups?

For the purposes of this review, the students of interest are those who attend community colleges with considerable structural diversity (i.e., those who attend 2-year colleges other than tribal colleges, historically Black colleges, overwhelmingly White colleges, and others populated almost entirely by one cultural group). This chapter begins with a brief description of several theories of race relations among diverse racial and ethnic students. These theories are borrowed mainly from the social sciences and 4-year college literature. The remainder of the review examines empirical studies of diversity and campus climate in community colleges. We do not conclude this review with a list of findings or future research suggestions because few well-established conclusions can be drawn from the literature. Rather, we focus the discussion in each section on future research opportunities instead of deferring them to the conclusion.

In addition to student race and ethnic relations, which is the subject of this review, community college scholarship has also considered race and ethnicity as discrete categories. These studies are outside the scope of this review but have included, for example, analyses of success rates among student groups, instructional and programmatic efforts designed for diverse students, and relations between diverse students, faculty, and staff (see, e.g., Cejda & Rhodes, 2004; Nora, 2004; Rendon, Hope, & Associates, 1996; Townsend, 2000).

THEORIES ABOUT STUDENT RACE RELATIONS

The preeminent theories of student race relations rarely comment on community colleges. As such, the theories discussed in this section depend heavily on the 4-year college literature. Note that although the most cited theories emphasize the psychological features of diversity efforts, this analysis will also address the social factors of diversity and, where the limited literature permits, the cultural dimensions of diversity.

FUNCTIONAL THEORIES

The prevailing perspective on campus diversity is drawn from Allport's (1954) contact theory. This theory proposes that intergroup interaction can reduce prejudice among college students, given four conditions: (a) equal status of the groups in the college setting, (b) common goals, (c) inter-group cooperation, and (d) support of authorities, law, or custom. Contact theory has successfully reached across scholarly disciplines to address psychological, social, and cultural features of race relations and has received wide acceptance among behavioral and social scientists and higher education researchers (e.g., Brown & Hewstone, 2005; Pettigrew, 1998). The contact hypothesis has been used to imply that equality within the college, communication, and common values readily occur within American colleges to foster prejudice reduction. Scholars have applied this theory frequently in research on 4-year campuses but not often to community colleges.

Gurin, Dey, Hurtado, and Gurin (2002) have advanced a similar theory, which they posited the potential benefits of diversity efforts in 4-year colleges. A central thesis of this perspective is that efforts to increase diversity on American campuses have led to democracy outcomes, which include knowledge and awareness about other cultures, civic cooperation, and integration in settings such as classrooms, voluntary organizations, and the workforce. Like contact theory, this functional perspective also assumes open communication and relatively equal status among students in American colleges. This line of analysis has rarely been applied to research on community college students.

ACCULTURATION AND ASSIMILATION THEORIES

The preceding psychological approaches are paralleled by long-standing functional perspectives in sociology in theories of immigration, ethnic stratification, and inevitable assimilation. These lenses are quite relevant to community colleges because these institutions are on the front lines in the education of recent immigrants. Gordon (1964) defined structural assimilation as consisting of several kinds of social relations subsumed under two categories: secondary relationships in colleges and workplaces and primary relationships such as friendships and cliques. The emphasis on communication and assimilation in these sociological perspectives is very similar to the emphasis on cultural and social involvement in higher education theories of integration and engagement (Pike & Kuh, 2005;

Tinto, 1997). In general, these theories focus on communication and cooperation instead of power differentials and the social exclusion and competition experienced by some students at culturally diverse colleges. Although they do not emphasize campus conflict, Bean and Metzner (1985) have adapted a functional approach to pay special attention to the cultural groups off campus from which students may draw social support (see, e.g., Person & Rosenbaum, 2006).

CONFLICT THEORIES

Various conflict theories focus on the tension and struggle among racial and ethnic groups. A central implication from conflict perspectives is that campus intergroup processes are closely linked to structures of domination and reproduction in the societal context of the college (Omi & Winant, 1994). These theories implicitly suggest that disadvantaged students tend to respond to discrimination with resistance or alienation. However, these theories tend to underemphasize how students from marginal cultures willfully cooperate with and accept the practices and beliefs of the dominant culture.

A few recent innovations in conflict theory have attempted to refine the conceptions of intergroup struggle and to incorporate the insights of assimilation perspectives. Integrated threat theory (Stephan & Stephan, 2000) and social, dominance theory (Sidanius & Pratto, 1993) both suggest that conflicts emerge between those who are trying to acquire material resources and those who are trying to retain them. Assimilation processes have been acknowledged by recent conflict theories in new conceptions of dissonant, consonant, and selective acculturation that tend to discount the notion of full assimilation (Portes & Rumbaut, 2001).

A very different theoretical approach concerns such conflicts as the subtle racial insults experienced by African American students at primarily White universities. These conflicts have been analyzed through the lens of critical race theory (Solórzano, Ceja, & Yosso, 2000). Critical race theory advocates a method for developing personal insight and understanding the organizational structure that leads to covert discrimination in U.S. institutional settings. This is a potentially useful method in community colleges, where racism is less overt and where an ideology of a welcoming and open door is prevalent. For a time, particularly in the 1980s, scholars frequently reported overt racial conflicts on 4-year campuses but they did not often monitor these struggles in the community colleges (Farrell & Jones, 1988).

Glaring racial and cultural divides found in the de facto ethnic and racial tracking of students into remedial and college-level courses have attracted little research from a conflict perspective. Although the classroom is the only place on campus where many community college students are engaged, enrollments by race and ethnicity vary extremely among classrooms (Maxwell et al., 2003). Conflict theories could explore whether there are processes by which minority racial and ethnic groups are marginalized from more rigorous college courses. Although theories about race relations on 2-year college campuses are few, there have been empirical studies of intergroup race relations at community colleges. We discuss these studies in the following section.

EMPIRICAL STUDIES OF STUDENT RACE AND ETHNIC RELATIONS IN COMMUNITY COLLEGES

In the paragraphs that follow, we examine ethnically diverse student relations along a few dimensions of assimilation—acculturation, and secondary and primary structural assimilation—as well as two student conflict variables: discrimination and prejudice. Most of the available research comes not from academic and scholarly periodicals but from the practical and action-oriented publications of college institutional research offices, government administrative centers, and education associations. Most of the studies available in national databases were conducted in the blue (democratic) states, particularly on the West Coast, some in the Midwest and northeastern region, and very few in other regions.

STUDIES OF CAMPUS RACIAL CLIMATE

Several researchers have examined racial climates at community colleges. There are several dimensions of campus climate, including social relations among diverse groups of students, friendliness, comfort, belonging, college support of diversity, safety, and equitable treatment by staff, faculty, and students. Despite the fair number of campus climate studies conducted within individual community colleges, there has been only one national study. In 1997, the American Association of Community Colleges (AACC) surveyed 1,450 community college presidents and administrators, of whom 360 replied (Kee, 1999). The central measure on the questionnaire asked administrators and presidents to rate campus climate on a 5-point scale: contentious to harmonious. None rated their colleges with a score of 1 at the contentious pole of the scale; 21% of participants rated their colleges as harmonious with a score of 5; and 39% rated their colleges as 4, somewhat harmonious. Almost one third, 31%, selected the midpoint score of 3, a mix of conflict and harmony. Seven percent indicated the score of 2, for somewhat contentious campus climates.

Given the low response rate, the limited theoretical depth of the analysis, and the reliance on only one unvalidated measure of racial climate, these national data must be used with caution. However, the study does suggest that a majority of community college presidents perceive their campus climates as harmonious and that a substantial proportion of the nation's colleges are also perceived as less than harmonious.

RESEARCH AT INDIVIDUAL COMMUNITY COLLEGES

With the exception of the AACC study, the majority of data on individual community college campus climate is found in 17 studies in the 1990s of one or more community colleges. The samples have typically not been randomly selected and have only modest indications of being representative. However, many of these samples do not appear to be unrepresentative and many are large, with more than 600 students. For example, one of the studies surveyed approximately 13,000 students at 25 different college campuses (Washington State Board, 1997).

However, without any theoretical uniformity or solid conceptual base for these studies, the particular measures used varied considerably in content. For example, London (1978) and Weis (1985) conducted ethnographies, Person and Rosenbaum (2006) both conducted interviews and surveyed respondents, and three studies explored a few student focus groups (Clements, 1997; Weissman, Bulakowski, & Jumisko, 1998; Willett, 2002). This lack of uniformity dilutes the comparability of the studies and likely accounts for much of the variation in findings.

In broad terms, the research findings from individual colleges portray many campuses—particularly those on the West Coast—as welcoming and supportive social zones. Questionnaire surveys were administered at 39 campuses: 32 colleges were described as positive by 85% or more of the students, although it must be cautioned that the estimates for the 25 Washington colleges were statewide averages that may obscure group differences at individual campuses (Arnold, 1995; Hart, Lufkemeier, & Gustafson, 2002; Milwaukee Area Technical

College, 1988; San Diego Community College District, 1994; Washington State Board, 1997; Willett, 2002). Four of the college climates were rated by 70% to 84% of the students as positive (Clements, 1997; Howard Community College, 1998; Mattice, 1994), and three campuses were rated as positive by 48% to 58% of the students (Boughan, 1992; Lee, 1994; Luan, 1995).

To some extent, positive campus climate ratings can be attributed to the predominance of White students who typically rate the racial and ethnic climate as higher than do non-White students. For example, in a focus group conducted by Weissman et al. (1998) at a 75% White suburban Chicago campus, a White student ironically remarked, "It is so diverse here. I think it's great" (p. 33).

Minority students do not always rate campus diversity climates lower than do White students. For example, for the 13,000 students at the 25 colleges surveyed by the Washington State Board (1997), on average, 96% of Asian American, Latino, and White students and 87% of African Americans rated their campus climate as positive.

The positive description of campus racial climates at many individual colleges is largely consistent with the AACC study cited earlier. Furthermore, these positive studies do not show the strident kinds of White racism reported in two ethnographies conducted in northeastern states in the 1970s and 1980s: verbal intimidations, physical threats, antagonistic group depictions of other groups, covert hostility, and an absence of informal contact outside the campus (London, 1978; Weis, 1985). Perhaps this is evidence that the racism perceived by many as prevalent on community college campuses in decades past has dissipated or changed forms. We might also attribute differences in findings to variations in geographic region or methods of research.

These individual campus climate studies have established important foundations for the future study of racial and ethnic climates in community colleges. The samples are large, and although they are not random, they are not easily discounted. In general, many of the studies used technically proficient measures often borrowed from a common item pool such as those provided in the California Postsecondary Education Commission (1992) publications.

The most basic limitation of these studies has already been mentioned: the absence of explicit and consistent theoretical foundations, although Person and Rosenbaum (2006) is an important exception. For example, theoretical development is needed to expand the concept of climate to include prejudice, tension, exclusion, struggle, and discrimination.

Various methodological advances are warranted as well. Very few studies have relied on interviews, focus groups, or observation. These methods of exploration could be used to develop initial conceptual frameworks for understanding current campus race relations. Several specific technical questionnaire issues may also be raised: response-set bias from stating almost all the survey items in a positive tone and halo effect bias from grouping all of the ethnicity items together. Standard survey procedures for randomly varying item valence and mixing various topics in the sequence of items would resolve these problems in future research. Most studies have not attempted to reconcile item divergences or develop an overall measure of the climate. Thus, for example, in a very diverse San Francisco East Bay suburban college (Arnold, 1995), where 84% of the students agreed with the single item "there is respect for differences in race/ethnicity" and 90% agreed with the item "I feel welcome," 32% also agreed that "tension between different cultural groups that leads to verbal abuse or physical violence is a problem" and 31% reported that they did not feel "physically safe and secure on campus." Finally, none of the studies described above reported efforts to ascertain the reliability or validity estimates for the survey items. Future research must thus address the development of multi-item scales and ascertain the reliability and validity of the meaning of the measures.

Another uncertain feature of the research methods is the unusually large percentage of students who selected the neutral response category or did not respond to questionnaire items concerning race relations on campus. The number of neutral responses and nonresponses comprises as much as two thirds of otherwise large samples. Although some reports discard all neutral and missing responses, these data are in fact related to important student perceptions including uncertainty, fears, and tensions (Howard Community College, 1998; San Diego Community College District, 1994). Future research can deal with these issues by incorporating neutral and missing responses as an important form of response, by developing other measures that elicit a more direct form of negative or positive response, and by directly examining the nature of related fears and uncertainties.

DISCRIMINATION AND RACISM AT COMMUNITY COLLEGES

Conflict theories posit that intergroup racial competition, struggle, and discrimination are likely present at diverse colleges. However, only about one third of the studies examined discrimination on campus. On most of the campuses where racism was studied, less than one fifth of the students reported that they were the targets of discrimination. For example, in the San Diego Community College District (1994), where Whites comprise slightly more than half of the student population, 13% of students indicated that they had frequently or occasionally "been discriminated against because of my race/ethnicity," and a clear majority of each ethnic category indicated that they had "never" been discriminated against. Similarly, at a suburban Chicago campus where three quarters of the students are classified as White, a Latino student in Weissman et al.'s (1998) focus group commented,

> I felt better when I came to CLC because I don't look at people as a color. When you are in the outside world, people look at you and judge you. Here at CLC, it doesn't matter if you are young, old, what color, and that is what the great part about it is. (p. 34)

To a substantial extent, these findings parallel earlier evidence of relatively harmonious campus climates. Yet in the Chicago focus group, a Latina recounted, "When I first started in class when I was walking in, they said, 'All those Hispanics are stupid and all are in gangs. All they do is drink.' Automatically, they all thought bad of me" (p. 34). Racism and discrimination are not far away from many classrooms and campus networks. Although the resilient Latina quoted above went on to say, "By the end of the class I had my good points. . . . They finally respected me" (p. 34), the threat of rejection and inequity lurks for many under the amiable surface of academe. It may be the uncertainty of the threat that leads so many of the students to be reluctant to answer some survey questions about race relations and that leads many other respondents to select the neutral or unsure response categories.

Although in these studies some students from each ethnic background reported that they had encountered discrimination, people of color were about 10% more likely to report discrimination than were White people. For example, at the four colleges studied in San Diego, only 10% of Whites indicated that they had experienced discrimination, compared to 18% of African Americans, 22% of Asian Americans, and 12% of Latinos (San Diego Community College District, 1994). Black and White students at Milwaukee Area Technical College (1988) reported corresponding discrimination levels.

Future research needs to explore the nature and the frequency of prejudice, racism, and discrimination on community college campuses. The limitations of the past decade's survey research methods—the high rates of neutral responses and nonresponses and conceptually vague measures that underestimate discrimination rates—indicate that future research must investigate whether the rates of subtle discrimination, racism, and neglect are considerably more accurate than the relatively optimistic reports in the current literature. For example, in an exception to prevailing questionnaire methods, a Maryland campus survey included a detailed list of 18 different types of racial bias, and 38% of the students indicated that they were the recipients of at least one of the 18 types of discrimination, about twice the discrimination rate usually reported (Boughan, 1992). The implication should be obvious: Researchers need to develop detailed theories of discrimination and corresponding measures so that the targets of racism can fully report their college experiences.

RACIAL RELATIONS IN THE CLASSROOM

Classrooms are the focus of student campus activity and are the most likely spaces of intergroup contact among students, many of whom are part-time students and leave the college immediately after class. Despite the focus of the colleges on classroom learning, there has been almost no research about the interpersonal racial processes occurring in diverse classrooms.

Participation rates in classroom activities may vary among races. In a Washington State Board (1997) study of 25 community colleges, about half of African American students reported that they frequently asked questions in class, which is more than any other ethnic group. Asian American and Latino students participated the least in class discussions; only about one third said that they frequently asked questions.

Some minority students expressed uncomfortable classroom experiences of loneliness or tokenism. Weissman et al. (1998) reported that these students wished for more minority students in their classes and that many did not want the teacher to ask them to explain the attitudes or behavior of their ethnic group. Mattice

(1994) cited students who wrote, "Of all the classes I have taken at COC [College of the Canyons], I have been the only African American enrolled. Sometimes I ask myself what I am doing at COC. This has nothing to do with me sensing any prejudice or discrimination at all" (p. 38).

Future research could address the extent and nature of these tensions in classrooms, including loneliness and racial and ethnic tokenism. In addition, studies could examine whether the loneliness of isolated minority community college students as compared to residential students in 4-year colleges is partially alleviated by the opportunity community college students have to return daily to their homes and familiar social networks. Researchers might also examine whether the threat of unalleviated racial isolation at a residential college leads many to enroll at a local 2-year or 4-year commuter campus.

College teaching could also benefit from research on race relations in the classroom. For example, contact theory could be explored for the development of strategies for building equal classroom status positions among racially and ethnically diverse students. Research using theories of structural diversity may consider its application to intergroup relations and cross-group and same-group formations; dominance theories can help inform the emergence of competition for scarce resources and rewards; and critical race theory can be applied to identify practices of unconscious group privilege and discrimination in the classroom.

STUDIES OF RACE RELATIONS IN STUDENTS' SOCIAL LIVES

Previous research suggests that few community college students are socially integrated in extracurricular campus networks (Dougherty, 1992). Similarly, the Washington State Board (1997) study found that 70% to 80% of students spent fewer than 7 hours outside class on campus per week. Correspondingly low levels of social interaction were reported at colleges in rural California (Willett, 2002), in Maryland (Boughan, 1992), and in New York's Westchester County (Lee, 1994). In Weis' (1985) study of social interaction, one East Coast urban college instructor reported, "While there is no overt hostility between black and white students in classes, at the end of classes, they don't see each other at all" (p. 57).

Despite the skepticism of many observers over whether there is social life at community colleges, several studies indicate that some students feel they have friends at the colleges. Of the students at the four relatively diverse colleges in the San Diego Community College District (1994), 61% agreed with the statement

"I have many friends at this campus." Similarly, Person and Rosenbaum (2006) reported findings on same-group versus cross-group friendships in Latino campus enclaves. However, few other community college scholars have paid attention to the current debate about the benefits of same-group versus cross-group friendships in research on schools, 4-year colleges, and other institutions (antonio, 2004). Although previous studies of community college student relations have shown some student interest in contact across cultural divides, there has been little examination of cross-group friendships. In several different California colleges, approximately 70% to 90% of the students reported that "students of similar racial/ethnic backgrounds tend to 'hang out' on campus together" (San Diego Community College District, 1994) or "stick with their own clique" (Arnold, 1995). A student at a Los Angeles suburban college said,

> I think that the different ethnic groups do everything they can to separate themselves. In the cafeteria the blacks, the whites, the brown, and the what have you, seem to have their own tables. But then again, I only see it sometimes because I am a part-time student. I do know that in the classroom every ethnic group gets along and helps each other out when it comes to study groups. (Mattice, 1994, p. 54)

A basic premise of functional theories is that large groups such as community colleges are founded on communication. Questionnaire survey responses about intergroup relations have produced various findings. When asked about communication among students on campus, students of all racial and ethnic categories generally report that "diverse groups communicate well," and substantial numbers from all races report a desire to interact with other students outside their cultural group (Mattice, 1994). Similarly, about 70% to 90% of the students at three different colleges in California agreed with various survey items such as "I value making friends with students of other cultural and ethnic backgrounds" (Arnold, 1995; Mattice, 1994; Willett, 2002). When survey questionnaire items are framed differently, however, a shift in results appears. Fewer Whites, as compared to other ethnic groups, expressed a desire for more intergroup communication (Mattice, 1994; Washington State Board, 1997). In a northern California suburban college, 55% of students surveyed agreed that "there is a lack of communication among students of different ethnic/cultural groups at [this college]" (Arnold, 1995). Future research on functional theories of community colleges needs to examine additional evidence and interpret this tension with the theories' basic assumptions about communication.

Some of the studies mentioned previously also explored questions about cultural dominance on college campuses and struggles for resources across racial and ethnic groups. At the few colleges where these matters have been researched, the majority of community college students are not concerned about or familiar with such issues. For example, Arnold (1995) reported that fewer than half of the students at a diverse San Francisco East Bay college responded to the item "Some ethnic groups here dominate or have an unfair influence on the decision-making process in student clubs, organizations, and government." Of those who did respond, 54% agreed that some ethnic groups dominated or held an unfair advantage on campus (Arnold, 1995). Similarly, at a southern California campus only 35% of White students agreed with the statement, "There is not enough interaction among different racial/ethnic organizations at [the college]" (Mattice, 1994), considerably less than the 51% of Latinos and 61% of Asians and Pacific Islanders who agreed with the item (Mattice, 1994). Student comments from this latter survey illustrate several different points of view:

> To strengthen diversity, have more clubs for students . . . more social things. While I think the clubs and organizations for separate ethnic backgrounds are helpful in educating those who belong, it also helps to separate and exclude others who may be interested in learning about different cultural backgrounds. The more ethnic clubs [the college] has, the greater the segregation will become among students. (Mattice, 1994, pp. 52–53)

A basic necessity in future research on intergroup relations is the use of both conflict and functional theories, and negative as well as positive measures. In the survey items cited above, approximately 70% of the White students expressed interest in friendships and contact with persons of other racial and ethnic groups. But the limited validity of single survey items, which are positively phrased, must be considered in future research. Our analysis suggests that when surveys include a mix of positive- and negative-worded items, more comprehensive findings can be revealed. For example, when students rated the variable survey item "The amount of interaction . . . between individual students of different racial/ethnic groups" as "too much, about . . . right, [or] not enough," differences in responses were striking (Mattice, 1994). Only 29% of Whites reported not enough interaction, compared with 36% of Native Americans, 45% of Latinos, 50% of Asians and Pacific Islanders, and 69% of African Americans surveyed (Mattice, 1994).

Although many White students are interested in more intergroup contact, future research might inquire whether White students are the most isolated from intergroup activity and, if so, why? Past research has not significantly addressed fears, threats, prejudice, discrimination, and the dynamics of intergroup struggles in the colleges. It is time that these theoretical topics become central elements in our research. Future research can also ask why several studies have demonstrated that African American students have been the most active and interested in expanding their contacts with other races and how these interests can be leveraged in developing more civil attitudes and relationships among all groups.

OUTCOMES AND BENEFITS OF INTERGROUP RELATIONS

There has not been definitive research on the impact of race and ethnic relations, although the limited evidence is consistent with the interpretation that the outcomes are positive. In the Washington State Board (1997) survey, approximately one half of the 13,000 students reported substantial progress in response to a question about how much progress they experienced in "getting along with diverse people," with minority students about 5% to 10% more likely than White students were to report this level of progress. About half of these students reported that they were "clearer about ... their own values" with little variation among ethnic groups on this survey item. Open-ended student survey responses regarding the diversity impact of two Massachusetts colleges included the following:

> I have developed a respect for every human being ... learned to take others into consideration, I have grown mostly in my relations with other ethnic people, and I enjoy it. ... I also have a lot more respect for people of different races ... although I have always been active in anti-racism, I found that I am more sensitive to this and more receptive to people's feelings. (Clements, 1997, pp. 9–10)

A basic shift needed in community college outcomes research methods is a movement away from these one-shot surveys and case studies toward both qualitative and quantitative longitudinal designs. Simply asking people if the college has had an impact on them offers thin research grounds for confidence in the estimates of impact or the assurance that the outcomes are any different from what the student might have experienced if not at the college.

Future research on outcomes has many promising topics. Will opportunities for supportive and equitable participation for minorities provide the opportunities needed for academic success? Although community colleges are lauded as democratic colleges, research is needed on the consequences of community college diversity relationships for intergroup civility in workplaces and neighborhoods and for the responsibilities of citizenship. Threat and fear are likely to accompany periods of demographic change in the colleges. White flight has been a consequence in the past. Research is needed for strategies that allay fears and prejudice and nourish cooperation.

CONCLUSION

This review of student ethnic and race relationships has not generated a list of theoretical findings. Other than depicting some campuses as having a positive diversity climate, the research has been too atheoretical, diffuse, exploratory, and based on weak methodological designs to establish any set of conclusions. Furthermore, relatively few relevant publications can be found in scholarly journals because most of the research has been recorded in institutional reports. The evidence in these latter reports has raised many fascinating questions. Therefore, instead of empirical conclusions, we have included suggestions for future research in each section of this review.

We cannot overemphasize the point that this entire field of study requires a new generation of community college theorists and debate to lay the groundwork for future research. For example, there is some evidence that students perceive racial and ethnic cooperation and tolerance on college campuses. Yet there is no community college race relations model that adequately explains why there is so little overt struggle over resources and status among cultural groups. There are fruitful analyses of the relative absence of class conflict in the colleges (Brint & Karabel, 1989; Dougherty, 1994) but not of the muted racial competition and tensions over intergroup domination. Exploratory ethnographies, such as the groundbreaking work by Weis (1985), are very rare in community college research and would be a useful source of theoretical insights on such a topic.

We call for a new wave of studies in the coming decade of shifting demographics and increased immigration to understand relations among diverse racial and ethnic groups and ethnoreligious groups, including Arab and Muslim Americans. Research and action are needed to counter the recent climate of international terrorism and fear that has permitted hostility toward and even vicious oppression of some minorities and international students. This concerted effort needs to take place across all regions of the United States.

We look forward to the ideas that scholars will develop to understand the kinds of relationships that emerge among students in culturally diverse classrooms and campuses. This research can move beyond the description of campus climates to analyzing the determinants and consequences of various diversity climates. The first step in advancing this line of research is having a fundamental commitment to expanding current theoretical frameworks and to applying more rigorous methods to the studies. Longitudinal studies will be particularly useful. We look forward to a lively debate on these issues.

REFERENCES

Allport, G. (1954). *The nature of prejudice*. Cambridge, MA: Perseus.

antonio, a. l. (2004). The influence of friendship groups on intellectual self confidence and educational aspirations in college. *Journal of Higher Education, 75*, 446–471.

Arnold, C. L. (1995). *Chabot College campus climate survey results: Fall 1994*. Hayward, CA: Chabot College Office of Institutional Research.

Bean, J. P., & Metzner, B. S. (1985). A conceptual model of nontraditional undergraduate student attrition. *Review of Educational Research, 55*, 485–540.

Boughan, K. (1992). *Student perceptions of the racial climate at Prince George's Community College, Spring 1992: A preliminary report*. Largo, MD: Prince George's Community College, Office of Institutional Research. (ERIC Document Reproduction Service No. ED346925)

Brint, S., & Karabel, J. (1989). *The diverted dream: Community colleges and the promise of educational opportunity in America, 1900–1985*. New York: Oxford University Press.

Brown, R., & Hewstone, M. (2005). An integrative theory of intergroup contact: The effects of group membership salience. *Advances in Experimental Social Psychology, 37*, 255–343.

California Postsecondary Education Commission. (1992). *Resource guide for assessing campus climate (Commission reports 92-24)*. Sacramento, CA: Author.

Cejda, B. D., & Rhodes, J. H. (2004). Through the pipeline: The role of faculty in promoting associate degree completion among Hispanic students. *Community College Journal of Research and Practice, 28*, 249–262.

Clements, E. (1997). *Creating a campus climate that truly values diversity*. Bedford, MA: Middlesex Community College.

Dougherty, K. J. (1992). Community colleges and baccalaureate attainment. *Journal of Higher Education, 53*, 188–214.

Dougherty, K. J. (1994). *The contradictory college: The conflicting origins, impacts, and futures of the community college.* Albany: State University of New York Press.

Farrell, W. C., Jr., & Jones, C. K. (1988). Recent racial incidents in higher education: A preliminary perspective. *Urban Review, 29*, 211–233.

Gordon, M. (1964). *Assimilation in American life: The role of race, religion, and national origins.* New York: Oxford University Press.

Grutter v. Bollinger, 539 U.S. 306, 123 S. Ct 2325 (2003).

Gurin, P., Dey, E. L., Hurtado, S., & Gurin, G. (2002). Diversity and higher education: Theory and impact on educational outcomes. *Harvard Educational Review, 72*, 330–366.

Hart, K., Lutkemeier, J., & Gustafson, C. (2002). *Analysis of Shasta College student survey results, Fall 2002.* Redding, CA: Shasta College Planning and Research Office.

Howard Community College. (1998). Student *satisfaction: The 1998 YESS survey results (Report 101).* Columbia, MD: Author.

Hurtado, S., Dey, E., Gurin, P. Y., & Gurin, G. (2003). College environments, diversity, and student learning. *Higher Education Handbook of Theory and Research, 18*, 145–190.

Kee, A. (1999). *Campus climate: Perceptions, policies, and programs in community colleges (Research Brief AACC-RB-992).* Washington, DC: American Association of Community Colleges.

Lee, M. M. (1994). *SUNY student opinion survey, 1994, sections I-IVB: Student characteristics, why students select Westchester Community College, college services & facilities, faculty & classroom, and college climate.* Valhalla, NY: Westchester Community College, Office of Institutional Research.

London, H. B. (1978). *The culture of a community college.* New York: Praeger.

Luan, J. (1995). *Cabrillo students' campus climate survey*. Aptos, CA: Cabrillo College.

Mattice, N. J. (1994). *Campus climate survey*. Santa Clarita, CA: College of the Canyons. (ERIC Document Reproduction Service No. ED374854)

Maxwell, W., Hagedorn, L. S., Cypers, S., Moon, H. S., Brocato, P., Wahl, K., et al. (2003). Community and diversity in urban community colleges: Coursetaking among entering students. *Community College Review, 30*, 21–46.

Milwaukee Area Technical College. (1988). *MATC student opinions regarding discrimination and MATC institutional attitudes toward women and minorities*. Milwaukee, WI: Author. (ERIC Document Reproduction Service No. ED300064)

Nora, A. (2004). The role of habitus and cultural capital in choosing a college, transitioning from high school to higher education, and persisting in college among minority and nonminority students. *Journal of Hispanic Higher Education, 3*, 180–208.

Omi, M., & Winant, H. (1994). Racial formation in the United States. New York: Routledge.

Pettigrew, T. F. (1998). Intergroup contact theory. *Annual Review of Psychology, 49*, 65–85.

Person, A. E., & Rosenbaum, J. E. (2006). Chain enrollment and college enclaves: Benefits and drawbacks of Latino college students' enrollment decisions. In C. L. Horn, S. M. Flores, & G. Orfield (Eds.), *Latino educational opportunity. New directions for community colleges no. 133* (pp. 51–60). San Francisco: Jossey-Bass.

Pike, G., & Kuh, G. (2005). First- and second-generation college students: A comparison of their engagement and intellectual development. *Journal of Higher Education, 76*, 276–300.

Portes, A., & Rumbaut, R. G. (2001). *Legacies: The story of the immigrant second generation*. Berkeley: University of California Press.

Rendon, L. I., Hope, R. O., & Associates. (1996). *Educating a new majority.* San Francisco: Jossey-Bass.

San Diego Community College District. (1994). *Campus climate student survey, spring 1994.* San Diego, CA: Author.

Sidanius, J., & Pratto, F. (1993). The inevitability of oppression and the dynamics of social dominance. In P. M. Sniderman & P. E. Tetlock (Eds.), *Prejudice, politics, and the American dilemma* (pp. 173–211). Palo Alto, CA: Stanford University Press.

Solórzano, D., Ceja, M., & Yosso, T. (2000). Critical race theory, racial microaggressions, and campus racial climate: The experiences of African American college students. *Journal of Negro Education, 69,* 60–73.

Stephan, W. G., & Stephan, C. W. (2000). An integrated threat theory of prejudice. In S. Oskamp (Ed.), *Reducing prejudice and discrimination* (pp. 225–246). Mahwah, NJ: Lawrence Erlbaum.

Tinto, V. (1997). Classrooms as communities: Exploring the educational character of the undergraduate population. *Journal of Higher Education, 68,* 375–391.

Townsend, B. K. (2000). Integrating nonminority instructors into the minority environment. In S. R. Aragon (Ed.), *Beyond access: Methods and models for increasing retention and learning among minority students. New directions for community colleges, no. 112* (pp. 85–93). San Francisco: Jossey-Bass.

University of California v. Bakke, 438 U.S. 265, 98 S. Ct. 2733 (1978).

Washington State Board for Community and Technical Colleges, Education Division. (1997). *The effect of race and ethnic background on students' community and technical college experience (Research Report 97-5).* Olympia, WA: Author.

Weis, L. (1985). *Between two worlds: Black students in an urban community college.* Boston: Routledge & Kegan Paul.

Weissman, J., Bulakowski, C., & Jumisko, M. (1998). A study of White, Black, and Hispanic students' transition to a community college. *Community College Review, 26*(2), 19–42.

Willett, T. (2002). *Gavilan College campus diversity climate survey, 2002.* Sacramento, CA: California Community Colleges, Office of the Chancellor. Retrieved June 1, 2006, from http://www.gavilan.edu/research/reports/cc02.pdf

NOTES

[1] The authors published a previous version of this chapter in the April 2007 issue of *Community College Review* (Volume 34, Number 4). Reprinted with permission.

CHAPTER FOUR

○○○○○

Student Resistance to Cross-Cultural Engagement: Annoying Distraction or Site for Transformative Learning?

SUSAN R. JONES

○○○○○

"I just don't know why we still have to talk about [race]. I just think it makes it worse when we dwell on it. I am sure it is bad and everything, but it isn't going to make it better to keep talking about it. Let's just get over it."

"Well, I am sure that I do have some advantages because I am White, but I sure don't want to call it racism because that just sounds so harsh."

"The classroom was not, in my opinion, educational, it just felt like most of the time it was 'diversity is great and all minorities and people that aren't middle class or upper class are that way because they could not have helped it.' Which is so not true."

"You should not be forced to change your values. I would not recommend this [course] unless all you want to do is talk about poor people."

"The most challenging was trying to answer questions that really didn't interest or pertain to me. It's hard to have opinions or feelings about something you aren't specifically passionate about."

These illustrative quotes are from undergraduate students engaged in a service–learning course with significant cross-cultural engagement. They provide a glimpse into the challenges and complexities of creating inclusive environments and promoting cross-cultural learning for all students. Despite increasing evidence that programming and educational interventions effectively promote cross-cultural learning, little attention is paid to the resistance that inevitably surfaces—primarily among White students—to the challenges encountered in learning environments that emphasize diversity and social justice. Though tempting to locate the impetus for resistance in the students themselves (e.g., they just don't get it), student affairs educators need to understand where resistance comes from and work to turn it into an opportunity for transformative learning (Jones, 2002; Jones, Gilbride-Brown, & Gasiorski, 2005). This chapter explores resistance both theoretically and practically as a "site" for transformative learning through examples of service–learning, residential life, and campus programs that aim to promote cross-cultural learning. Drawing from the critical pedagogy literature, the term *site* is purposefully used to describe what happens in a physical space (e.g., classroom, student organization, intergroup dialogue program, community service project) as well as a social location influenced and mediated by patterns of power, privilege, and social identities. In particular, I explore *what* students are resisting, *why* resistance occurs, and the *contexts* in which resistance emerges and takes shape. In addition, I offer suggestions for working through resistance and turning it into greater willingness to engage with cross-cultural learning opportunities. In this context, resistance can be distracting and even annoying to the well-intentioned facilitator. Understanding where resistance comes from and what it looks like, and then anticipating its presence, can help transform resistance from annoying distraction into cross-cultural learning and engagement.

WHAT IS RESISTANCE?

Students are resisting active engagement in issues related to diversity and social justice education and perceived challenges to prevailing conceptions of self, others, and compelling social issues of the day. The concept of resistance first emerged in the scholarly areas of Black studies and critical theory as a way to explain student resistance to schooling and dominant cultural discourses (Fordham & Ogbu, 1986; Giroux, 2003; McLaren, 2003). Fordham and Ogbu's pioneering research found African American high school students developing what they termed an "oppositional identity" as a strategy to protect themselves against racism and microassaults on their sense of self, and to cultivate an identity in opposition to what was expected of them in a dominant setting (like school). McLaren (2003, p. 91) described resistance as representing "a resolve on the part of students not to be dissimulated in the face of oppression; it is a fight against the erasure of their street-corner identities."

More recently, critical theorists have related the phenomenon of resistance to curricula and educational programs that emphasize social justice, equity, and activism. Because multicultural education and interest in cross-cultural learning grew out of the Civil Rights Movement, anything related to multiculturalism and diversity is frequently perceived (and resisted) as decidedly political (O'Grady, 2000). Early multicultural initiatives in higher education were created to "give voice" to the experiences of students of color and other marginalized groups; they were viewed as "a form of resistance to oppressive social relationships" (Sleeter, 1996, p. 10). The attempt to meet the needs of underrepresented groups and respond to their interests resulted in a plethora of so-called diversity initiatives. This educational context then gave rise to resistance from majority students who failed to see themselves in discussions about diversity and multicultural issues. For these students, diversity education was at best about "those others" and at worst just another agenda pushed by liberal university administrators. Cross-cultural learning and engagement seemed a far-off possibility, despite this stated goal by many student affairs educators.

More specifically, Butin (2005) offered four prevalent conceptualizations of student resistance to social justice education and cross-cultural learning: resistance as failure, resistance as unknowing, resistance as alienation, and resistance as uncaring. He offered an additional one of his own: resistance as identity (re)construction. Briefly described, student resistance as *failure* locates the problem of resistance squarely with the student and results in the oft-stated comment, "This student just doesn't get it." Resistance as *unknowing* suggests that a student is not developmentally ready to grapple with such complex content, nor is at the stage of (racial, cognitive, or cultural) identity development to understand. Resistance as *alienation* is anchored in neo-Marxist critical theorists' analysis of schooling as a normative process and evident in students' efforts to maintain a cultural identity in the face of the hidden curriculum of a school. Resistance as *uncaring* emerges from Whiteness studies, described as "the refusal and avoidance of the realization of [W]hite privilege and how it is embedded within our society's very practices, structures, and thoughts" (Butin, 2005, p. 172). Noting that all four conceptualizations view "student resistance as a fixed response—be it due to cognitive inadequacy, lack of racial identity self-comprehension, or desire to maintain a privileged status" (p. 174)—Butin offered an alternative conceptualization of resistance: resistance as *identity (re)construction*. He suggests that resistance is part of an ongoing and dynamic process of maintaining and reformulating a sense of self. Accordingly, "such resistance can be understood as the performance of an ongoing process of decisions meant to obscure the constant destabilization and reconstruction of a purportedly coherent identity. In other words, my students refuse to see themselves in 'someone else's shoes' because it would reveal the frayed construction of their own sandals" (pp. 175–176).

WHY STUDENTS ARE RESISTING

Theorizing resistance from a critical perspective places privilege and identity at the center of analysis. It suggests that students are resisting challenges to self that come from social justice and cross-cultural learning; instead of meeting the challenges, they are drawn to repetition and resistance (Kumashiro, 2002). The desire for repetition is seen in the way privileged identity categories (as well as educational practices) are repeated over and over without scrutiny or critique such that they become normalized "regimes of truth" (McLaren, 2003, p. 91) and "grand narratives" (Sullivan, 2003). Kumashiro explained, "In fact, people often consider some practices and relations to be part of what schools and society are supposed to be, and fail to recognize how the repetition of such practices and relations—how having to experience them again and again—can help maintain the oppressive status quo of schools and society" (Kumashiro, 2002, p. 68). Student resistance to anti-oppressive education and cross-cultural learning is then understood as a desire for repetition, the persistent inscribing and reinscribing of what is known and taken for granted. Drawing on the work of Deborah Britzman (1998), Kumashiro wrote:

> Students, at least subconsciously, want learning that affirms their identities, experiences, perspectives, and values. However, she [Britzman] also tells us that, to learn in anti-oppressive ways, students need to do much more than learn that which affirms how they already understand themselves and what they already believe. Simultaneously and contradictorily, students also need to interrupt their desire to see their identifications, perspectives, and values repeated. They need to interrupt their resistance to disruptive, disaffirming knowledge. (Kumashiro, 2002, p. 70)

Higginbotham (1996) noted that student resisters are often responding to the challenge of examining their own privileges, in turn questioning the facilitator's expertise and the "facts" presented in discussions of race, class, and gender. Kumashiro (2002, pp. 70–72) identified three situations in which he found his students resisting: resistance to thinking differently about themselves, resistance to thinking differently about "good" teaching, and resistance to thinking differently about what it means to learn. Elsewhere, Kumashiro (2000, p. 43) shed additional theoretical light on why students are resistant to antiracist teaching and cross-cultural learning: "It could be argued that we unconsciously desire to learn only that which affirms our sense that we are good people and that we resist learning anything that reveals our complicity with racism, homophobia, and other forms of oppression."

Finally, in several recent mixed-method studies exploring students' conceptions of themselves and others as privileged or oppressed, Chizhik and Chizhik (2002, 2005) found that students' resistance is related to their overwhelming sense of privilege, downplaying the importance of oppression in society, and unwillingness to commit to social change. They suggested that students' preconceived ideas of privilege and oppression help explain resistance to the discourse of multicultural education and that emotions (such as guilt) play a key role in facilitating student learning and motivation to act in socially responsible ways.

Exploring the *why* of resistance reveals the complicated dynamics at work. Many students come to college and university campuses from very homogenous neighborhoods and schools with little exposure to multicultural settings (Chang,

Denson, Saenz, & Misa, 2006; Hurtado, Milem, Clayton-Pedersen, & Allen, 1999; Tatum, 1997). Resistance to diversity and cross-cultural learning opportunities emerges directly from such background experiences; some students cling tenaciously to the familiar and what they know and understand. With no reason, motivation, or encouragement to examine their own social identities and privileges, they seek (knowingly or not) to maintain their former selves in new environments, including college, and resist any perceived challenges.

CONTEXTS IN WHICH RESISTANCE TAKES SHAPE

Any educational initiative, program, course, or other context with a focus on cross-cultural learning, diversity, multicultural education, social justice, and/or antiracist pedagogy holds the potential (and likelihood) to create both inclusive learning environments and resistance to such learning. As noted by Higginbotham (1996, p. 204), "This innovative teaching may be applauded, even if only with smiles or nods, from students generally ignored or marginalized in the traditional curriculum. Yet these same curricular modifications can represent major changes for the more privileged students in the classroom." Though he was writing specifically about classroom-based learning, Higginbotham's observation holds true for activities and initiatives sponsored by student affairs educators, many of whom hope to integrate cross-cultural learning opportunities into their work.

The site or space where such learning and resistance takes place can be conceptualized as a *borderland*—an educational context where student experiences challenge their dominant ways of knowing and understanding (Hayes & Cuban, 1997). The cognitive dissonance that emerges requires students to resolve their perceived conflict between old ways of knowing and new experiences. In the service–learning context, students are crossing both literal and psychological borders as they move into unfamiliar environments, communities, and social situations, and call into question what they thought they understood about themselves and others. Clark and Young (2005) described the potential for "changing places" through service–learning but also cautioned that, in this movement, students can either become "intercultural collaborators" or merely "commentators on diversity" (Peck, Flower, & Higgins as cited in Clark & Young, p. 73). Hill Collins (2000, p. 458) went further, suggesting that the dialogues across difference promoted by service–learning and other cross-cultural learning opportunities often look like voyeurism as "the privileged become voyeurs, passive onlookers who do not relate to the less powerful, but who are interested in seeing how the 'different' live."

Authentic dialogue in the borderlands and becoming an intercultural collaborator require a willingness to trade spaces, engage in authentic learning, and (re)negotiate one's sense of self and place in the world. In a study on student understanding of diversity in the context of service–learning, Jones and Hill (2001) found the cross-cultural learning environments of the community service settings enabled students to cross boundaries, negotiate the complexities of individuality and commonality (e.g., what we have in common and what is distinctive), and engage in cultural learning that produced new understandings of self and other. This understanding emerged from face-to-face contact with community members whose life situations were very different from their own, finding common ground by working together at the community service sites, and developing empathy and compassion as a result (Jones & Hill). Cross-cultural learning initiatives provide these opportunities and the possibility of resistance to them.

How Does Resistance Look?

Resistance shows up in many educational settings, including residence hall programming, academic classes, student activities, and even resident assistant training. Diverse settings themselves may evoke resistance, though rarely. More often, the perceived message conveyed by cross-cultural learning programs provokes a reaction from some students. Stated differently, the sheer presence of diverse others does not automatically promote cross-cultural learning (nor resistance); the opportunities for cross-cultural learning that such numbers present, and the interactions that result, produce the greatest benefits (Chang et al., 2006). The possibility of resistance is integrally connected to these opportunities and potential benefits, which is why it is vital to understand and engage resistance as it emerges.

Resistance to cross-cultural learning and engagement comes in many forms—from the brutally obvious to the silent, obscure to transparent, and planned to unintended. Resistance can appear as simply not showing up for programs to open hostility to their content and process. In one of the earliest pieces focused on student resistance to multicultural scholarship, Higginbotham (1996) identified resisters as active, silent, and absent, noting that educators often pay the most attention to active resisters. Below are several scenarios illustrative of the resistance that may emerge.

SCENARIO ONE: WHY DO WE HAVE TO TALK ABOUT [RACE]?

In a diversity training session for student organization leaders, a student affairs educator working in the leadership programs office was discussing the influence of race and White privilege in leadership, relationships, and community service contexts. The goal: more student organization leaders would participate in community service and then integrate experiences with social responsibility, civic engagement, and diversity into the mission and activities of their organizations. One third of the students in the session were students of color and there was a balance in gender. Many of the White students reported significant involvement in community service activities in high school and their views of leadership were typically hierarchical. Students of color were quite vocal and positive about the training, saying it was about time that student organizations actually address issues of race, class, and gender.

The students prepared for the training by reading Peggy McIntosh's "White Privilege" essay and an article by Beverly Daniel Tatum on racism. When the facilitator began the discussion about racism and White privilege, the students of color were quite receptive and immediately started to voice their reactions to the readings, drawing on their experiences and opinions as student leaders and on campus generally. Most of the White students were quiet, but after a few minutes, one of the White male students raised his hand and said:

> I just don't know why we still have to talk about this. I just think it makes it worse when we dwell on it. I am sure that it is bad and everything, but it isn't going to make it better to keep talking about it. I am sure that I do have some advantages because I am White, but I don't want to call it racism, because that just sounds so harsh. Let's just get over it.

To which a female student of color responded, "That's the point, it's supposed to sound harsh because it is."

SCENARIO TWO: THE PROVOCATEUR

In a service–learning class (taught by a student affairs educator), some students met their community service requirement by volunteering at a local AIDS service organization very close to campus. The cramped quarters of this organization that provided nutritious meals to people living with AIDS was in the basement of a nearby church. Working alongside longer-term volunteers at the organization, it became very clear to the instructor that the students had very limited, if any, exposure to AIDS and people living with the virus. Students often referred to their very sheltered, hometown environments where they learned, as one student said: "If you're gay and a White male, then you're dirty and that's why you have it. They did something bad and therefore deserve what they got."

Several students in the class came from fundamentalist religious backgrounds, which made their beliefs on the connection between homosexuality, sin, and AIDS all the more firm and unyielding. During one class session, the instructor was trying to disabuse students of the notion that only "dirty gay White guys" contracted HIV and structured discussion around the ideas of privilege and homophobia as it related to working at the AIDS service organization. The instructor tried to make the point that individuals don't choose to be gay by asking the student, "When did you decide you were heterosexual?" The student replied, "When did you decide you were a pedophile?"

SCENARIO THREE: BLAMING THE VICTIM

During the week-long resident assistant (RA) training, a session on appreciating diversity used the well known Privilege Walk activity. About 25 students, a third of whom were students of color, were in the RA group. The facilitator, a White woman and new residence hall director fresh out of graduate school, was eager to use this activity because she found it very illuminating and moving when she participated in it. She believed the exercise was a great way to help students understand the concepts of privilege, racism, and oppression, to point out how the playing field is not level, and to get them talking with one another.

Lining up the RAs on the grass near a campus residence hall, she instructed the group to take a step forward or backward to represent their responses to a series of statements. She began:

> If your ancestors were forced to come to the U.S., take one step back.
> If you ever took vacations out of the country, take one step forward. If
> you were raised in a rented apartment or house, take one step back. If
> you were taken to plays or art galleries by your parents, take one step
> forward. If you were ever called names because of your race, ethnicity,
> or sexual orientation, take one step back.

As she moved through her list, the resident director noticed the African American female RAs, now clustered in the back of the group, appeared not to be paying attention and were chatting about other things. Meanwhile, the White males were competing with one another for "first place."

At the conclusion of the activity, the resident director began processing the Privilege Walk and almost immediately conflict erupted. An African American woman began:

> I don't know why we need yet another activity to remind students
> of color of 'their place' in this world. This activity seems designed to
> reinforce all kinds of stereotypes and assumptions about who I am and
> where I come from. I didn't become an RA for this kind of treatment.

To which a White female RA responded: "Geez, I think you are taking this way too personally. I think it is so good that we are talking about these issues. I had never really considered my privileges before this." And the African American female retorted: "Well, this is easy for you to say. You have the luxury of obliviousness. I do take this personally, because it is personal, it is my life."

These scenarios poignantly depict the complexities of diversity work and the challenges inherent in creating inclusive learning environments. Whether the context is service–learning, residence life, student activities, leadership programs, or most any other area in student affairs, resistance is bound to surface when cross-cultural learning and engagement is an objective (and even when it is not!). Resistance takes shape very differently among White students and students of color and this, too, contributes to the complexity of facilitating cross-cultural learning. White students resist because of deeply ingrained privileges that have escaped scrutiny, lack of exposure to those different from themselves, and the absence of developmental complexity to recognize privilege in the first place (Jones, Gilbride-Brown, & Gasiorski, 2005). White students indicate they are "sick and tired" of hearing about race (Johnson, 2006). Students of color resist because they are sick and tired of hearing about White students being sick and tired. Engaging with White students in these contexts requires too much energy, risk, and vulnerability, with little hope of reciprocal effort.

Resistance emerges across contexts and social identities. For the students working at the AIDS service organization, religious values and perspectives (which cut across race entirely) influenced resistance. Though many campus diversity and cross-cultural learning initiatives focus on cross-racial interactions, resistance is also evident in challenges to students' other social identities and privileges: social class, culture, gender, sexual orientation, and religion, for example. As Johnson (2006) pointed out, "When it comes to the problem of privilege and oppression, privileged groups don't want to hear about it at all because it disturbs the luxury of obliviousness that comes with privilege . . . Privilege similarly encourages people to be self-centered and unaccountable to others" (pp. 121, 123), which is how resistance often looks when it surfaces in educational programs focused on diversity and cross-cultural learning.

A Word About Silence and Not Showing Up

Resistance is easier to deal with when it appears in obvious and visible ways. Much harder to contend with is the resistance reflected in not showing up for diversity-oriented events and activities—another way students avoid cross-cultural learning and engagement. Students who avoid such programs are much harder to reach than those who attend, even those whose presence might be difficult for the facilitator and other participants. Silence, though distinctly different from avoidance, may also be construed as resistance.

Being present but silent and nonparticipatory may be a defense mechanism. Privileged students may not be eager to acknowledge their own advantages or change their thinking about themselves and others, while students of color may need to protect themselves against a potentially hostile environment. Indeed, Higginbotham (1996) made this point: "Members of less privileged groups are often accustomed to silence and avoidance as resistance strategies, unless in a safe setting, for example, when their numbers are greater as in women's studies and racial-ethnic courses" (p. 209).

Finally, the Internet is emerging as a powerful vehicle for the expression of resistance. Chat rooms, Facebook, MySpace, and other online venues are increasingly the *places* where students say exactly what is on their minds. A recent example is the dialogue about race on Facebook by Johns Hopkins University students. As reported by the *Chronicle of Higher Education* (Read, 2006), a campus fraternity used Facebook to advertise a "Halloween in the Hood" party, describing Baltimore as "the HIV pit" and encouraging those attending to dress in "regional clothing from our locale like bling bling ice ice, grills, and hoochie hoops." The Black Student Union responded to the invitation, on Facebook. These postings sparked a lively debate about what constitutes racism and racist behavior on the campus, though very few students attended a forum held on campus. Online communities, often hidden from the educator's gaze, may provide another place where student resistance emerges. Reaching these student resisters—whether absent, silent, or communicating "anonymously" in a virtual community—is vital. Many writers have noted that systems of oppression and privilege are maintained through silence, that silence is often read as support for these systems, and that silence has great costs of for all individuals (e.g., Johnson, 2006; Tatum, 1997; Wise, 2005). Educators may need to reframe how such cross-cultural learning and diversity programs are presented and facilitated.

SUGGESTIONS FOR PRACTICE: WORKING THROUGH RESISTANCE

Student resistance to cross-cultural learning and engagement is impossible to avoid. The very nature of this work, with necessary emphases on inclusion, social justice, power, privilege, and oppression, invites resistance. Educators must anticipate its presence, understand what resistance represents, and work through it with students. In fact, the transformative potential of resistance comes in the opportunity to help students shift from resisting challenges to *their positions* of power and privilege to resisting the very structures that produce systems of oppression and privilege. Johnson (2006) conceptualized this idea in the movement from taking the path of least resistance to learning ways to resist the path. He argued that individuals are socialized to participate in social systems by taking paths of least resistance, or choosing those decisions for which they encounter the least resistance. This is akin to the metaphor of the moving airport walkway that Tatum (1997) used to explain the dynamics of resisting racism. The forward momentum of the walkway will take an individual to a destination (racist behavior), even while standing still on the walkway (the path of least resistance). Only when the individual turns around and moves in the opposite direction, walking faster than the walkway, will active resistance—and the opportunity for active antiracist behavior—occur. Such is the possibility of choosing alternatives to the paths of least resistance and learning to resist the structures that are barriers to cross-cultural learning and engagement. What might this look like?

First, as educators and facilitators of cross-cultural learning, we must examine our own assumptions, biases, and paths of least resistance. We often set up these learning opportunities by asking students to go places that we ourselves either have not been, or worse yet, are unwilling to go. This is a sure-fire recipe for failure, significantly reducing the likelihood of transforming resistance in the direction of inclusion and social justice. Said differently, we hold the potential to serve as powerful role models for students in demonstrating how to get started in cross-cultural learning. Johnson (2006) thoughtfully argued:

> If we choose different paths, we usually won't know if we're affecting other people, but it's safe to assume that we are. When people know that alternatives exist and witness other people choosing them, things become possible that weren't before. When we openly pass up a path of least resistance, we increase resistance for other people around that path, because now they must reconcile their choice with what they've seen us do, something they didn't have to deal with before. . . . This suggests that the simplest way to help others make different choices is to make them myself, and to do it openly. (p. 134)

We also need to let students know that this is a life's work, not a requirement to be met with one class, an activity with a pre and posttest to measure change after one training, or a skill set with a checklist for success. Cross-cultural learning is complicated, complex work that takes commitment over the long haul. Students have very real fears of making mistakes or saying the "wrong" things; sharing our own journeys, and in particular the mistakes we have made along the way, will model for students that learning from our mistakes is probably a necessary component to this learning.

Cultivating relationships with students and creating a community in which students cultivate peer relationships is critically important. With a foundation anchored in respect and trust, dialogues can move participants out of their comfort zones and into places where new learning takes place. Creating this safe space for dialogue is easier said than done; what constitutes safe will differ among individuals. Communities of support must be created where students can seek support from others like them, as well as from those who might challenge their ideas. In my service–learning classes, peers provide both affirmations and challenges and students appreciate both from their classmates. Students are more likely to take risks if they see peers engaging in critical thinking and cross-cultural dialogues (Jones, Gilbride-Brown, & Gasiorski, 2005).

This strategy of cultivating relationships, building community, and encouraging learning from peers is also related to the "power of self-generated knowledge" (Tatum, 1992) and "viewing students as capable participants in the journey" (Baxter Magolda, 2000). This suggests the importance of engaging students where they are developmentally (racial identity, psychosocial and cognitive development), validating what they currently know, and providing experiences that challenge assumptions and promote new learning. Exercises, activities, or other assessments of where students are developmentally and what previous cross-cultural experiences they have had will give a facilitator important clues about where resistance might come from, and how to structure peer learning and cross-cultural facilitation. For example, if students are resisting discussion about privilege in regard to race, the facilitator might consider another social identity (e.g., gender, sexual orientation, religion, culture) with which students might identify (Jones, Gilbride-Brown, & Gasiorski, 2005).

Recognizing students as capable and the power of self-generated knowledge also cultivate student agency in cross-cultural learning environments and commitment to social change. Whether working in small groups or engaging in larger activities around a common interest or cause, the seeds of coalition-building are planted to further cross-cultural learning. A recent example of this occurred when several student organizations at the University of Maryland, College Park came together to protest the "real Christians don't sin" message of three evangelical preachers from Soulwinner Ministries preaching from the school's free speech zone. In response, a coalition of Campus Crusade for Christ, the Pride Alliance, Latino Student Union, and other cultural and religiously-based student groups organized a counterprotest, each going up on stage and confessing sins. The result: a dialogue across groups that typically were not known for their common interests.

The research on student resistance to social justice education (which may be seen as an umbrella for cross-cultural learning) documents resisters' emotional reactions including feelings of anger, despair, and shame (Tatum, 1994). Navigating these emotions in the context of cross-cultural learning programs is difficult but critical to the learning of all students, and to the creation and maintenance of a safe and inclusive environment. Discussions must be facilitated in a way that does not silence the resisters while also not intimidating other participants. Resisters need to know their voices are heard, too; their resistance will be further fueled if they feel shut down. Sometimes follow up with active resisters is more appropriate outside the learning context, rather than in front of everyone (Jones, Gilbride-Brown, & Gasiorski, 2005). Highly structured activities may also help with managing volatile emotions in these settings; students must be clear about learning objectives and desired outcomes, and educators must provide direction and feedback along the way.

Finally, helping students recognize their own "spheres of influence" (Tatum, 1997) breaks down some of the resistance that comes from feeling overwhelmed by the enormity of social justice work and powerless to make a difference. Tatum wrote, "While many people experience themselves as powerless, everyone has some sphere of influence in which they can work for change, even if it is just in their own personal network of family and friends" (p. 204). Similarly, Johnson (2006) implored, "Start where you are and work from there. Make lists of all the things you could actually imagine *doing* . . ." (p. 153). Drawing further from Johnson's work, resistance can be engaged and transformed by helping students recognize how privilege operates. Also important is understanding our own role in the systems that maintain it, and learning to listen carefully (which Johnson notes is very difficult for members of dominant groups). Paying attention and listening then serve as the building blocks for action and determining what is the "something I can do."

Fully engaging the resistance that emerges in cross-cultural learning is challenging work, essential to the learning process itself. Viewed as identity (re)construction, resistance is always in the process of becoming and "un-becoming." As un-becoming as resistance might look to a facilitator of cross-cultural learning initiatives—whether in the residence halls, campus programs, service–learning, or any number of educational contexts—resistance reflects an individual's struggles to negotiate and renegotiate the self in complex learning environments. Here lies the possibility of transforming resistance to cross-cultural learning into resistance against the structures that make cross-cultural learning necessary and important in the first place. This is what bell hooks (2003) called the "pedagogy of hope," stretching the boundaries of educational practice to include "the life-enhancing vibrancy of diverse communities of resistance" (p. xvi).

REFERENCES

Baxter Magolda, M. B. (2000). Teaching to promote holistic learning and development. In M. B. Baxter Magolda (Ed.), *Teaching to promote intellectual and personal maturity: Incorporating students' worldviews and identities into the learning process: New Directions for Teaching and Learning, No. 82* (pp. 88–98). San Francisco: Jossey-Bass.

Butin, D. W. (2005). Identity (re)construction and student resistance. In D. W. Butin (Ed.), *Teaching social foundations of education: Contexts, theories, and issues* (pp. 161–187). Mahwah, NJ: Lawrence Erlbaum Associates.

Chang, M. J., Denson, N., Saenz, V., & Misa, K. (2006). The educational benefits of sustaining cross-racial interaction among undergraduates. *Journal of Higher Education, 77,* 430–455.

Chizhik, E. W., & Chizhik, A. W. (2002). A path to social change: Examining students' responsibility, opportunity, and emotion toward social justice. *Education and Urban Society, 34*(3), 283–297.

Chizhik, E. W., & Chizhik, A. W. (2005). Are you privileged or oppressed? Students' conceptions of themselves and others. *Urban Education, 40*(2), 116–143.

Clark, C., & Young, M. (2005). Changing places: Theorizing space and power dynamics in service–learning. In D. Butin (Ed.), *Critical Issues In Service–learning* (pp. 71–87). New York: Palgrave.

Fordham, S., & Ogbu, J. (1986). Black student's school success: Coping with the burden of "acting White." *Urban Review, 18,* 176–206.

Giroux, H. (2003). Critical theory and educational practice. In A. Darder, M. Baltodano, & R. D. Torres (Eds.), *The critical pedagogy reader* (pp. 27–56). New York: Routledge Falmer.

Hayes, E., & Cuban, S. (1997). Border pedagogy: A critical framework for service learning. *Michigan Journal of Community Service–learning, 4,* 72–80.

Higginbotham, E. (1996). Getting all students to listen: Analyzing and coping with student resistance. *American Behavioral Scientist, 40*(2), 203–211.

Hill Collins, P. (2000). Race, class, and gender as categories of analysis and connection. In M. Adams, W. J. Blumenfeld, R. Castandeda, H. W. Hackman, M. L. Peters, & X. Zuniga (Eds.). *Readings for diversity and social justice: An anthology on racism, anti-Semitism, sexism, heterosexism, ableism, and classism* (pp. 457–462). New York: Routledge.

hooks, b. (2003). *Teaching community: A pedagogy of hope.* New York: Routledge.

Hurtado, S., Milem, J., Clayton-Pedersen, A., & Allen, W. (1999). *Enacting diverse learning environments: Improving the climate for racial-ethnic diversity in higher education.* ASHE-ERIC Higher Education Report Volume 26, No. 8. Washington, DC: George Washington University.

Jones, S. R. (2002, September/October). The "underside" of service–learning. *About Campus, 7*(4), 10–15.

Jones, S. R., Gilbride-Brown, J., & Gasiorski, A. (2005). Getting inside the "underside" of service–learning: Student resistance and possibilities. In D. Butin (Ed.), *Critical Issues in Service–learning* (pp. 3–24). New York: Palgrave.

Jones, S. R., & Hill, K. (2001). Crossing High Street: Understanding diversity through community service–learning. *Journal of College Student Development, 42*, 204–216.

Johnson, A. G. (2006). *Privilege, power, and difference* (2nd ed.). New York: McGraw Hill.

Kumashiro, K. K. (2000). Toward a theory of anti-oppressive education. *Review of Educational Research, 70*, 25–53.

Kumashiro, K. K. (2002). Against repetition: Addressing resistance to anti-oppressive change in the practices of learning, teaching, supervising, and researching. *Harvard Educational Review, 72*, 67–92.

McLaren, P. (2003). Critical pedagogy: A look at the major concepts. In A. Darder, M. Baltodano, & R. D. Torres (Eds.), *The critical pedagogy reader* (pp. 69–96). New York: Routledge Falmer.

O'Grady, C. R. (2000). *Integrating service learning and multicultural education in colleges and universities*. Mahwah, NJ: Erlbaum.

Read, B. (2006, November). Facebook posters spar on race. *Chronicle of Higher Education*. Retrieved November 6, 2007, from http://chronicle.com/wiredcampus/article/1708/facbook-posters-spar-on-race

Sleeter, C. (1996). *Multicultural education as social activism*. New York: SUNY Press.

Sullivan, N. (2003). *A critical introduction to queer theory*. New York: New York University Press.

Tatum, B. D. (1992). Talking about race, learning about racism: The application of racial identity development theory in the classroom. *Harvard Educational Review, 62*(1), 1–24.

Tatum, B. D. (1997). *Why are all the Black kids sitting together in the cafeteria?* New York: Basic Books.

Wise, T. (2005). *White like me: Reflections on race from a privileged son*. New York: Soft Skull Press.

Chapter Five

Student Affairs and Cultural Practice: A Framework for Implementing Culture Outside the Classroom

Toby S. Jenkins and Clayton L. Walton

An office with bookshelves holding texts about the importance of diversity, with posters and wall art that advertise poetic multicultural mantras, and a desk scattered with pictures of students from various racial and ethnic backgrounds, cultures, ages, and orientations.

A conference room occupied by dedicated student affairs educators and a diverse group of student leaders meeting to discuss and assess the progress of campus climate improvement efforts.

An orientation session in the student union packed with fresh and excited minds ready to take on the challenge of higher learning, and an equally excited facilitator who convincingly explains how cross-cultural learning and social justice will permeate all aspects of their educational experience.

A CULTURAL LEARNING IMPERATIVE FOR PROFESSIONAL EDUCATORS

P lanning cultural programs is a longer, deeper, and more involved process than probably imagined, while valuing multiculturalism too often takes the shape of an abstract concept—a broad professional ethic. The challenge is to put values into action by making our value for multiculturalism an actionable priority. Many student affairs professionals are committed to the *ideals* of multiculturalism and inclusion. But those who are truly serious about making real and strong change recognize that a major component of growth involves building the knowledge, skills, and comfort needed to effectively approach issues of multiculturalism (Hurtado, 1996). It is essential to enhance educators' abilities to create culture—not just to believe in it.

Many Web-based resources, research clearinghouses, and campus initiatives developed for educators overwhelmingly focus on faculty issues, transforming the curriculum, creating inclusive classrooms, and sharing effective pedagogical strategies (Garcia & Smith, 1996; Quaye & Harper, 2007). Failure to include student affairs educators into the work of multicultural education—particularly with regard to transformative practice—may give the impression that diversity outside the classroom does not require the same deep, intentional, and studied thought as classroom curricula.

Learning, as a broad ethic, should be embraced throughout the campus environment. Strong multicultural learning environments emphasize and place priority on change both inside and outside the classroom. This chapter considers the role of student affairs educators in such work. We describe attributes and behaviors of cultural practitioners; discuss cultural practice and actionable space on college campuses; and make clear what constitutes educationally meaningful cultural practice. We conclude the chapter by introducing our Tri-Sector Model of Cultural Practice, along with programming examples based on the model.

WHAT IS A CULTURAL PRACTITIONER?

Multicultural education, as a field of practice, is primarily concerned with advancing the cause of social justice. The field is centered on illuminating and eradicating inequities in educational practices, structures, and resources to make educational environments more inclusive. Multicultural spaces of learning— whether in a classroom, cultural center, or student activities office—are transformative and activist spaces of resistance to educational oppression. Creating this transformation is the work of many cultural practitioners on college campuses. Some coordinate equal access programs, facilitate mentoring experiences, develop institutional transformation plans, and critically examine environments, policies, and materials to ensure they are inclusive. Others are charged with implementing programs and initiatives after the institution identifies a need to enhance learning and cross-cultural engagement.

Cultural practitioners put culture into practice and transform it from a value or professional ethic into an action-oriented set of behaviors and activities on campus. They are more than advisors who perform the narrowly conceived role of student organization support; they do the work of creating and implementing education-ally meaningful cultural programs. They understand the need for student-created cultural programs as well as institutionally planned cultural events, recognizing that all students (even the most actively engaged student leaders) benefit from periodi-cally being participants and learners. Cultural practitioners also accept institutional responsibility to support and provide cultural experiences that enhance learning, development, and feelings of inclusion among diverse student populations. They acknowledge that students cannot continue to be the primary initiators of cultural programs on college campuses. Programs and events planned by student affairs educators must be relevant, imaginative, and intentional. Cultural practitioners have dual roles as educators and programmers. They do more than educate audiences on culture—they critically understand the architecture of various cultures and replicate, enact, and engage these experiences on the campus.

CULTURAL PRACTICE AND ACTIONABLE SPACE

Creating educationally meaningful cultural experiences on campus involves two layers of learning: (a) the acquisition of practitioner knowledge and ability to facilitate such experiences, and (b) the enhancement of student learning through engagement in the experiences, programs, and initiatives educators create. The construct of actionable space can be used to understand the process of cultural growth for educators as well as students. It examines personal agency in four types of spaces: embodied, reflective, dialogue, and actionable (Sharma-Brymer, 2005). These spaces can be physical environments, experiences in classrooms, out-of-class activities, or participation in exercises with time for reflection, dialogue, or acting on issues of culture. *Embodied space* and *reflective space* include inward reflective behaviors in which identity, values, history and culture influence an individual's present orientation and thought processes.

Gorski (2000) offered three strands of transformation that drive the work of multicultural educators: (a) self transformation, (b) school/institutional transformation, and (c) the transformation of society. The transformation of the professional engaged in multicultural practice includes reflecting deeply on personal values, thoughts, experiences, and prior learning on critical issues of difference. More than that, it includes relearning and transforming the way we think and interact with others, particularly our students. In his personal reflection on the topic, Gorski (2000) wrote:

> As an educator, I have a dual responsibility to engage in a critical and continual process to examine how my prejudices, biases, and assumptions inform my teaching [practice] and thus affect the educational experiences of my students . . . Only when I have a sense for how my own perceptions are developed in relation to my life experiences can I truly understand the world around me and effectively navigate my relationships with colleagues. I also have a responsibility to my students to work toward eliminating my prejudices, examining who is (and is not) being reached by my teaching style, and relearning how my own identity affects their learning experiences. To be an effective multicultural educator, and indeed an effective educator, I must be in a constant process of self-examination and transformation. (p. 2)

To make meaningful inroads toward creating inclusive multicultural environments, student affairs educators must engage in this deep sense of reflection on both their personal multicultural orientations and the broader meaning of the work they do.

Giving voice to their reflections and to the critical evaluation of the world then constructs the *dialogue space*. Through meaningful dialogues with colleagues and mentors, educators talk about their personal cultural orientations, abilities, and professional shortcomings. Along this cultural growth continuum, professionals typically begin to discuss critical issues and questions that frame their professional philosophies: What is multicultural education or why is a multicultural environment important to me? What does it mean to be a professional who engages in cultural practice? Such reflection and dialogue should result in an asserted stance, action, or personal agency (Sharma-Brymer, 2005). For student affairs professionals, the agency involves orienting themselves as cultural practitioners and the action is creating educationally meaningful cultural programs for and with students.

EDUCATIONALLY MEANINGFUL CULTURAL PRACTICE

We have mentioned several times that cultural practitioners do not merely plan campus events; they create *educationally meaningful* cultural programs. So, what exactly do we mean by this? Below are five standards by which program concepts and ideas can initially be measured:

1. **Educationally meaningful cultural programs are comprehensive.** They provide full, deep, and rich learning experiences for students. They may have multiple dimensions and include diverse components tied to a set of measurable outcomes; learning is offered in a variety of textures and styles.

2. **Educationally meaningful cultural programs are intentional.** They take into account the various identity stages of students and consider the potential impact of programming on student growth and development.

3. **Educationally meaningful cultural programs model the way for students in their content and concept.** These programs are more complex than what students themselves may be able to create. They reflect the professional abilities of the cultural practitioners who create them.

4. **Educationally meaningful cultural programs are logistically excellent.** They involve stakeholders in planning to ensure all bases are covered, from content to marketing. They begin with conceptualized goals and learning outcomes. They are developed by mapping out a well-timed, detailed and exhaustive logistical plan that considers every detail of the program, culturally transforms environments, uses culturally authentic catering, and anticipates (and plans for) potential problems.

5. **Educationally meaningful programs are generationally relevant, understanding contemporary students' needs, interests, and potential program opportunities.** Educators must recognize that

the life experiences and popular culture of any generation tell much about where that generation is culturally located. To move and to grow students to where we would like them to be, we must first meet them where they are (Howe & Strauss, 2000).

THE TRI-SECTOR MODEL OF CULTURAL PRACTICE

If the *actionable space* of a cultural practitioner is the creation of educationally meaningful cultural programs, where does one begin? Programming is not a series of isolated events or disconnected ideas; it must be approached as a comprehensive portfolio of cultural programs that provide holistic growth opportunities for students. An exhaustive cultural program portfolio should allow students to experience the same embodied, reflective, dialogue, and actionable spaces that were critical for the practitioners.

The Tri-Sector Cultural Practitioners Model is a practical framework for any professional whose primary charge is to serve multicultural communities in a cocurricular capacity—particularly in student activities and leadership, multicultural affairs, or cultural centers. The model organizes cultural interaction around three critical spheres: *Cultural Education, Cultural Engagement,* and *Cultural Development*. It also offers a level of intentionality that is critical—it conceptually creates a form of practice in stark contrast to a one-size-fits-all approach to diversity programming. This cannot be executed effectively through a single program that includes a little bit of everything (social, academic, and personal development). Nor can program offerings be focused solely on one dimension (i.e., a single diversity lecture). Instead, the model suggests that we need to create program portfolios—collections of quality cultural programs that serve very different purposes. Just as we need programs that are solely educational, we also need programs that are completely social or fully dedicated to the personal development of students. All these types of programs can be developed through a cultural lens. This overall portfolio should intentionally consider how students are provided spaces to understand themselves (embodied space), reflect on ideas and issues (reflective space), discuss critical issues (dialogue space), and engage in action (actionable space). This action could be demonstrated by developing an asserted stance, a change in ideology, an increase in participation, a motivation to become a leader, or a desire to serve as an agent for the advancement of social justice.

The collective outcomes of such programs should contribute toward predetermined actions such as learning, appreciating, understanding, or engaging culture. To do cultural education well, we need to fully develop programs that separately consider each of these dimensions and offer students multiple venues through which they can engage issues of culture. Below, we share the practical implementation of this model by providing detailed descriptions of a few of the programs we developed using this framework. Only one program example is listed under each sphere of the model; in practice, we offer numerous cultural engagement experiences for students. Typically, we host three or four programs under each area during an academic school year.

Figure 5.1. The Tri-Sector Model of Cultural Practice.

CULTURAL EDUCATION PROGRAMS

Cultural education programs allow students to interact with the critical knowledge needed to fully understand and focus on the history, practices, and infrastructure of various cultures. Lectures, panels, and brown bag discussions have been typical offerings. Creativity and innovation in cultural education programs has been slow to develop on most campuses. To engage students outside of the classroom, we have to provide meaningful and bold experiences not found in the classroom. Here is a programmatic example:

The LENS: Popular Culture Education Series is a multilayered program series that gives students opportunities to critically explore the content and influence of popular culture. Popular culture is and will continue to be a driving influence domestically and internationally. In this program, popular culture includes all mass-produced and popular forms of expressing and experiencing culture: music, cinema, print media, television media, travel, and tourism. These educational opportunities let students critically examine the impact of this powerful cultural mechanism on the world and improve their understanding of critical consumerism. The LENS includes a Pop Culture Workshop with Experiential Tour, A Pop Culture Forum, and a Pop Culture Symposium.

FIRST PROGRAM COMPONENT:

Pop Culture & History Workshop with Experiential Tour by The Institute of Karmic Guidance: This two-part session first engaged students in an interactive workshop that explored how popular media have influenced social understanding of Black history and culture—particularly their influence on participants' personal perceptions of the culture. The workshop was followed by a trip to Washington, D.C., to participate in the city tour, African Influences on the District of Columbia. By challenging the typical lack of critical tourist evaluation, the experiential tour helped students understand that even simple forms of popular culture (such as travel and tourism) can offer opportunities for deeper learning through critical questioning about the shared history of communities, cities, and nations.

Learning Outcomes:

- To encourage the exploration of alternative forms of education and to illustrate how critical learners challenge the process, content, and intent of education.

- To provide a concrete complement to the theoretical ideas shared in the lecture by allowing students to visit and see the historical concepts through experiential learning.

- To promote student cultural learning through exposure to new cultural information and experiences.

SECOND PROGRAM COMPONENT:

Pop Culture Forum: Lyrical Legacies: Art in the Spoken Word featured a conversation and poetry readings by poetic elders Sonia Sanchez and Amiri Baraka, and the young poetic artists/lyricists Ursula Rucker and Black Thought from The Roots, a hip-hop band. The conversation provided an intimate look into the life challenges, growth outcomes, and the continued insight shared by these extraordinary artists expressing their life experiences through their written art. In a "fireside discussion," the artists shared selected pieces and talked about racism, politics, womanism, sexism, poverty, love, history, family, and other facets of life. This program sought to expose students and the local community to the idea that experiencing life is less a matter of finding the answers than asking the right questions—and that art, whether performed or painted, is a canvas to express a community voice.

Learning Outcomes:

- To expand student exposure to and understanding of how art, as an expression of culture, can be used to critique, reflect, and evaluate society.

- To expose students to diverse social perspectives across several generations of artists.

- To begin developing critical thought about popular culture among students and to grow understanding of the linkages between classical poetry and more popular forms of literary art including spoken word and hip-hop lyrics.

THIRD PROGRAM COMPONENT:

Pop Culture Symposium: Past, Present, & Future of Hip-Hop Culture: The Pop Culture Symposium is a one-day event structured to examine one topic in popular culture from an academic, social, political, and artistic perspective, and through diverse styles of learning. Hip-hop culture has become a dominant force in the last 20 years, carrying influence in musical, fashion, cinematic, and political arenas. To create educational spaces relevant to the experiences of our students, it is almost obligatory for institutions to offer students opportunities to better understand the influences and effects of this culture.

This event was constructed to inform participants and to challenge them to broaden their intellectual perspective of hip-hop. The forum leveraged the social and educational expectation of art to be reflective, meaningful, and relevant to the communities that consume it (Karenga, 1996). The collection of programs brought together scholars, performers, political activists, and vocal and visual artists. Students could critically examine this complex topic through day-long panel discussions, art exhibitions, interactive workshops, and off-campus programming.

Learning Outcomes:

- To provide participants an opportunity to examine a topic area from multiple perspectives.

- To provide students an opportunity to understand popular culture from a world view.

- To encourage the act of critical consumerism.

- To challenge audiences to listen, read, and look deeper into the artistic messages of hip-hop culture.

CULTURAL ENGAGEMENT PROGRAMS

These social programs typically include performances, entertainment, and social interaction activities. Festivals, multi-ethnic luncheons, and performance troupes are examples of cultural engagement programs. Here is a programmatic example:

World Cultural Festival: Aimed at promoting an increased appreciation of multiculturalism, this event—an afternoon filled with entertainment and education—is held the first week of classes each year. The event has multiple components:

(a) The Global/Community Bazaar: Tents representing the five corners of the world feature cultural displays, educational posters, food samples, cultural demonstrations, "neighborhood games," and artwork. A university community tent displays paraphernalia and information from campus departments and organizations.

(b) Cultural Entertainment: All afternoon, cultural performances on the main stage allow students to relax on the grass, enjoying and immersing themselves in cultural expression (students not only watch but also participate in the performances).

(c) Barbecue: At an "American Grill," faculty and staff serve hotdogs and burgers to students.

(d) The Passport Program. As part of a promotion to encourage student engagement in the Global Tents, mock passports are distributed and stamps given for each tent visit. Passports with all parts of the world stamped are put into a drawing at the end of the night for a semester of free textbooks.

PURPOSE AND INTENDED OUTCOMES:

- ○ To provide new and returning students an opportunity for social engagement and exposure to various forms of cultural expression.

- ○ To provide diverse forms of learning about and interacting with multiple cultures (performance, exhibits, interaction with cultural organizations).

- ○ To engage administrators socially with students in a relaxed and culturally stimulating environment.

THE WCF PLANNING COMMITTEE:

The World Cultural Festival planning committee spends five months planning this program. Committee members come from several departments that serve the student body: residence life, multicultural resource center, international students services office, LGBT student center, student activities, and fraternity and sorority life. The campus cultural center is the primary coordinator.

CULTURAL DEVELOPMENT PROGRAMS

These programs address holistic development of students, with particular attention to how culture affects leadership, professional orientation, and wellness. They also make important contributions to student understanding, connectedness, and ethos toward their personal cultures and communities (Jenkins, 2003). Here is a programmatic example:

The Diaspora Institute is a semester-long culturally focused leadership and personal development experience. Participants can explore their cultural histories and cultural values; learn about leadership models and practices; study historical and contemporary leaders of color; deepen their knowledge of critical social issues; participate in a leadership exchange with another college or university; and get seed funding to implement culturally focused community projects in their home neighborhoods.

First Program Component:

Credit-Bearing Education Sessions: Sessions meet for three hours each week. Students read texts, view films, hear guest presentations from campus officials, and participate in group activities/discussions. The sessions cover the following topics: Cultural Influences on Leadership and Personal Growth; Servant Leadership Within Communities of Color; Organizational Management; Collegiate Involvement & Cultural Leadership Post College; Community Connectedness; and Cultural Values.

Second Program Component:

Cultural Journey: Once each semester, participants travel to another university to engage in a weekend cultural community experience. The experience includes:

(a) *Cultural Leadership Swap*—meeting with other student leaders (Black Student Union, Latino Student Union, African Student Association, Caribbean Student Association, etc.)

(b) *Community Dinner*—meeting with local city leaders to establish and build relationships with professionals, and to discuss assuming community leadership in postundergraduate life

(c) *Cultural Education*—participation in a heritage tour that focuses on culture and history

(d) *Helping Home*—a civic engagement activity with an underrepresented community to further expose participants (students from both universities) to civically engaged leadership and the concept of "Helping Home."

Third Program Component:

Leadership Engagement: As part of the institute experience, the group participates in several campus-based, regional, or national leadership conferences.

FOURTH PROGRAM COMPONENT:

Cultural Engagement: As part of the institute experience, the group participates in several campus cultural performance/education programs.

FIFTH PROGRAM COMPONENT:

Education Abroad: When funding is available, the institute also includes a short-term education abroad experience to give students additional understanding of their cultural/ethnic histories and locally driven renewal in global communities.

CONCLUSION ON CULTURAL PRACTICE

Excellence in cultural programming is a well-blended mixture of cultural education, cultural engagement, and culturally focused personal development experiences. All three areas can be guided by student affairs practitioners as part of a solid portfolio of student service. To develop such a comprehensive portfolio, cultural practitioners must dedicate substantial time, thought, research, and personal commitment. Cultural practice is bold and creative. It involves students outside the classroom and puts them in touch with cultures of the world. Cultural practice is meaningful and engaging. It involves understanding that students need multiple ways to engage and to enjoy culture. Cultural practice is diverse and dynamic. It involves multiple ways of knowing, experiencing, and growing. Fortunately, cultural fulfillment is an ongoing, lifelong adventure.

REFERENCES

Garcia, M., & Smith, D. G. (1996). Reflecting inclusiveness in the college curriculum. In L. I. Rendón & R. O. Hope (Eds.), *Educating a new majority: Transforming America's educational system for diversity* (pp. 265–288). San Francisco: Jossey-Bass.

Gorski, P. (2000). A Multicultural education definition. In Multicultural education. Retrieved November 6, 2007, from http://www.edchange.org/multicultural/initial.html

Howe, N., & Strauss, W. (2000). *Millennials rising: The next great generation.* New York: Vintage Books.

Hurtado, S. (1996). How diversity affects teaching and learning. *Educational Record,* 77(4), 27–29.

Jenkins, T. (2003). The color of service. *About Campus, 8*(2), 30–32

Karenga, M. (1996) *Kwanzaa: A celebration of family, community and culture.* Los Angeles: University of Sankore Press.

Quaye, S. J., & Harper, S. R. (2007). Shifting the onus from racial/ethnic minority students to faculty: Accountability for culturally inclusive pedagogy and curricula. *Liberal Education, 92*(3), 32–39.

Sharma-Brymer, V. (2005, September). *To act or not to act: Linking 'actionable space' with human rights and education.* Paper presented at the 8th UKFIET Oxford International Conference on Education and Development, Oxford University, England.

CHAPTER SIX

○○○○○

Transforming Physical Spaces into Inclusive Multicultural Learning Environments

JILLIAN KINZIE AND SHAILA MULHOLLAND

○○○○○

The campus tour guide leads us toward the student union at Southwest University. We walk up a long series of steps leading into what appears to be one of many front doors, entering near a dining area. Five Black undergraduates are seated around a table, surrounded by an ample supply of caffeinated beverages, working on a biology lab report. Other students are eating with their peers and the few faculty or staff are mostly eating alone. The tour guide comments this is a popular place to study since the coffee shop is open until 2:00 a.m. Near the interior entrance to the busy food court are tables staffed by representatives from service organizations, all trying to recruit participants for their upcoming events.

One group, with a sign in both English and Spanish, is promoting a weekend service project painting an after-school center in a nearby Latino community. Our guide then leads us down a hallway past a section featuring students' photographs from recent study-abroad trips to France and India. He takes this opportunity to promote the darkroom in the union and the popularity of study abroad. In our rush to get to the bookstore, which closes at 5:00 p.m., we pass a bulletin board plastered with posters; the largest advertises an upcoming performance of the *Laramie Project*.

C olleges and universities have become increasingly concerned with fostering the development of students' multicultural awareness and cross-cultural skills, while also striving to create environments inclusive of a plurality of student populations. As the number of diverse students enrolling in institutions of higher education increases, the need to address inclusion issues has become more crucial (Minorities in Higher Education, 2002; Smith, 1997). The opening description of a short tour of a student union illustrates how campuses are becoming more multicultural learning environments. Many campus spaces have been altered in recognition of the broad diversity of cultures characteristic of contemporary students, faculty, and staff. Likewise, institutions have embraced multiculturalism through initiatives to diversify the curriculum, enhance delivery of new programs and services to support different populations of students, and create new efforts to celebrate diverse cultures. Even more needs to be done to create rich multicultural learning environments because the campus environment is prone to retaining the traditions, styles, and ways of behaving characteristic of only one culture (Stage & Manning, 1992).

The campus environment has an influence on college students and their experiences in higher education (Evans, Forney, & Guido-DiBrito, 1998; Kuh & Whitt, 1988; Kuh, Kinzie, Schuh, Whitt, & Associates, 2005; Pascarella & Terenzini, 1991, 2005). Environmental conditions include location (urban or rural), size, control (public or private), and curricular emphasis (e.g., liberal arts, engineering), as well as mission, physical and social environments, opportunities for engagement, and curricular and cocurricular policies and practices (Kuh, 2000; Strange & Banning, 2001). For example, the campus environment can encompass physical location, the campus grounds, architectural features of the library, student union, residence halls, and the space in the recreation centers. As innocuous as these environmental features may seem, they influence student learning and personal development. Because individual students and different populations can perceive the campus to be hospitable or unwelcoming and inclusive or exclusive, it is important to understand how various aspects of the environment influence student behaviors.

Campus facilities can play an important role in helping students develop a greater level of comfort and sense of community, which are both keys to success and retention (Hurtado, Milem, Clayton-Pedersen, & Allen, 1999; Sedlacek, 1993). According to Brazzell (2001), today's college students desire a college environment where they have a sense of belonging and connection to the overall campus community. Important to this is the inclusiveness of the environment and physical spaces. The physical environment of the campus, whether natural or constructed, shapes behavior by permitting certain kinds of activities while limiting—or making impossible—others. The ability to provide effective support to students rests largely on the extent to which the needs, interests, and backgrounds of the diverse populations on campus are reflected in its physical environment (Banning & Cunard, 1996).

This chapter presents an overview of perspectives on campus environments along with practical recommendations for making physical spaces more conducive to cross-cultural engagement and learning. Since there are so many spaces on a college campus, considering them all is beyond the parameters of a single book chapter. We primarily use the student union as an illustrative site for our examples, even though our strategies can be applied easily to other spaces. We begin by presenting three vignettes and introducing key concepts in the literature on campus environments, then describe how students interact with the campus environment, and explore the impact of campus environment on student outcomes. We assert that physical environments, such as those in student unions, can be intentionally designed to facilitate multicultural learning and inclusiveness. Though the term multicultural often describes race and ethnicity, the ideas presented in this chapter can also be extended to women; students with disabilities; lesbian, gay, bisexual, and transgender (LGBT) students; and returning adult learners. Examples illustrate how the campus environment can affect various student populations. Finally, we provide practical suggestions to encourage student affairs educators to discover how college and university cultures promote or inhibit the creation a more multicultural learning environment.

STUDENT RESPONSES TO SPACE ON CAMPUS

These short vignettes illustrate how physical spaces on three different campuses influenced student behaviors and feelings of inclusiveness.

DISCOMFORT AND THE ASPIRING BOARD MEMBER

Vanessa, a multiracial sophomore, applied for a chair position on the arts and films committee of the Campus Activities Board. The interview was conducted in the Alumni Room, a formal conference room in the student union. She and the three-member selection committee were seated around the corner of a long oak table. After the interview, Vanessa told a friend it went well, but she felt uncomfortable in the meeting room. "We're in this large meeting room, and all four walls around me are lined with photos and plaques of important alumni. The whole time I am thinking, 'Weren't there any women or people of color who were important to this college?' All of the photos except for a few were of White men! The room just oozed Whiteness." She questioned whether she deserved a position on the board, but told her friend that if she got the chair position, she would try to increase the visibility of students and alumni of color at the university.

THE CULTURALLY RESPONSIVE UNION DIRECTOR

John is director of the student union at a college with a large Latino student population. Despite the number of Latinos attending the college, cultural diversity is only minimally visible. Members of Latino Caucus, the largest campus organization for Hispanic and Latino students, approached John and the union staff with concerns of needing more personalized space and a venue on campus for their events. After a few meetings, John helped the Latino student group organize an exhibit featuring the work of regional Mexican American artists, arrange a space for the display, and later helped the student group persuade the college to buy several pieces to be permanently displayed in the union. As a result of the art exhibit, Latino student use of the union increased and additional student events were organized. The Latino Caucus began partnering with other multicultural groups to create a lecture series and a leadership conference with representation from a variety of student organizations. Subsequently, many Latinos commented to John that they appreciated having a place where they can meet together and host events, especially because they did not have a support office or center of their own on campus.

DISTRIBUTING MULTICULTURAL SPACE AT MIDWESTERN STATE

Midwestern State College has about 50 student organizations and offers opportunities for them to personalize student organization offices and bulletin boards. More than 40 bulletin boards advertising clubs and promoting events are a brilliant display of the various activities in the building and around campus. Some boards contain up-to-date announcements about programs and resources, while others act as sounding boards where students can respond to a question of interest posed by an organization. The union also has more than 30 small offices available for use by student organizations. Each office is expressive and highly personalized with decorated doors and noninstitutional furnishings. The Rainbow Educational Alliance (a newly established student group that educates the campus on issues of sexual orientation) and the Returning Women Students Association are just two examples of student organizations that have personalized space in the union to create a place of comfort and community.

These vignettes illustrate simple ways in which the physical space of the union (or any other space on campus) influence and make a difference in students' lives. In the first example, the exclusivity of the photos in the meeting room influenced Vanessa's mood during the interview, caused her to question her worth at the institution, and communicated to her that women and people of color were unimportant and less present at the university. In the second example, the exhibit of Mexican artists' work celebrated pluralism. By involving the students in the show and providing them support to personalize space, the union director communicated to the Latino Caucus that they were valued. By creating a space where Latino students felt comfortable gathering, the presence and place of this student population within the campus community was affirmed. In the final example, the arrangement and personalization of bulletin boards and office space in the student union created a lively environment centered on promoting diverse student organizations and activities. Office space drew individual students and groups into the student union, facilitated their interaction, and encouraged respect for each other's similarities and differences.

THE PHYSICAL ENVIRONMENT

To understand how physical space can reflect the needs of diverse populations and promote multiculturalism, it is important to understand the role of the physical environment. The relationship between the design and shape of physical environments and behavior can be understood from different disciplinary perspectives, including architecture, urban planning, anthropology, ecology, and cultural geography. The common link among all these perspectives is a belief in the mutually shaping effects of the environment and human behavior. The environment has important objective physical characteristics, as well as subjectively perceived and experienced qualities. By integrating objective and subjective elements, it is possible to understand the meaning of some perceptions and to discover the impact of the environment on human behavior and interaction in the physical space.

According to Moos (1976), one of the most powerful ways to influence human behavior is through the arrangement of the environment. Educational environments should be designed to create conditions that promote student learning and growth. The importance of the learning environment in college has been recognized in higher education. For example, Kuh and Whitt (1988) documented the importance of physical artifacts as communicators of college and university culture, and Strange and Banning (2001) examined the types and impacts of college campus environments. In this chapter, the influence of the physical campus environment on students will be briefly introduced from two perspectives: campus ecology and the anthropological concept of culture.

CAMPUS ECOLOGY MODEL

The *campus ecology* approach to understanding the interaction between students and the campus environment is typically associated with the work of James Banning. Banning and McKinley (1980) and Banning (1989) advanced the idea of campus ecology as the transactional relationship among students and the campus environment. This view expands the focus from the individual student to students as part of ecology, and emphasizes the goal of designing campus environments that meet the needs of students rather than imposing structures with the expectation that students will adapt (Banning, 1989). Components of the campus environment are the physical, biological, and social stimuli that impinge on students' sensory modalities. In this chapter, only the physical environment is discussed.

The physical environment, both natural and constructed, contributes to student learning and development. Features of the physical environment— buildings and architecture, signs, art, and traffic patterns—can encourage or discourage learning and development. Moreover, the process of design or redesign of physical space can also promote student development. The essence of the campus ecology model is that the physical environment produces nonverbal communications that elicit behaviors and give clues about valued social and attitudinal factors (Banning, 1989; Banning & Bartels, 1997). It can affect students' sense of well-being and identity, as well as the extent to which they feel valued by the institution (Banning, 1989). Strange and Banning (2001) believe that the nonverbal messages communicated through the physical environment may be more potent than the spoken word.

The design of buildings, space, and traffic patterns are important elements of campus ecology. If the display of paintings by Mexican American artists described in the second vignette had been in a less-traveled hallway, its benefits would have been lost. And by including the Latino student group in the redesign of the space, the union director further affirmed the group's presence, creating a space for students to come together and host other enriching learning opportunities.

Another ecological concept that elaborates the power of human interaction with the environment is the concept of *territoriality*, the acquisition or demarca tion of spatial areas with related dimensions of implied ownership, control, and personalization (Strange & Banning, 2001). This concept is particularly important for multiculturalism. In environments with a dominant culture and multiple subcultures, different groups need to demarcate space to affirm their presence. The identification of territory contributes to group identity formation as well as enabling others to identify them. The public image of the Latino student group and Mexican American culture was celebrated in defined space in the union and gave Latino students a place on campus where they felt comfortable socializing. Understanding students' views about the space is also important. Black students at an urban university identified a red couch in the student union as the main place they congregated. Although they described this space as their territory—and a visible symbol of Black students on campus—it offered little in terms of comfort or other valuable appurtenances and hardly facilitated the intermingling of students.

The depiction of the student union in the third vignette provides a more vivid example of how even small office spaces can give student groups a territorial base. The assistant director of the union and a board of student representatives determined which of the 50 organizations would be assigned one of the 30 offices. The committee based decisions on the quality of the applications received, but also had other goals: accepting fledgling organizations that might need a space to help draw members, and incorporating an intentional objective to feature a mix of diverse organizations. By situating different student organizations as neighbors, conversations among diverse groups were more likely to occur. Providing institutionally assigned office space can be particularly important to marginalized groups like LGBT student organizations. Having access to an office with resources and written information concerning LGBT issues can be a contact point for campus education and support efforts that may help combat negative attitudes and increase awareness of the LGBT population. A lively student-centered space draws individual students and groups into the union, facilitates their interaction, and encourages respect for each other's similarities and differences. The notion of territory provides a frame in which group identity may be expressed and maintained.

CULTURE

Culture, as a concept, refers to the deeply embedded patterns of behavior, values, and beliefs shared by members of an organization or community (Kuh & Whitt, 1988; Schein, 1985). Evidence of an institution's culture can be found in its various artifacts, which are largely symbols of the culture (Kuh & Whitt, 1988). While artifacts are often considered material objects representing culture, they may also include the way work is organized, decisions are made, and procedures are carried out (Kuh & Whitt, 1988; Kuh, 1993). Together these forms of artifacts represent the basic beliefs and assumptions of an institution (Kuh & Whitt, 1988) and communicate important messages about multiculturalism to the campus (Banning & Bartels, 1997). Artifacts can affect how people perceive their environment, how they feel about the institution, and how they behave (Schein, 1985).

Banning and Bartels (1997) identified four categories of physical artifacts: art, signs, graffiti, and architecture. Art includes paintings, posters, and statuary found inside and outside of campus buildings. A quick walk through a campus union reveals various types of official and unofficial signs (i.e., student organization postings). Graffiti, while categorized as "illegitimate signs" (Banning & Bartels, 1997), can send powerful messages to the campus community. For example, graffiti targeting specific groups can have damaging effects on individuals, especially when such discriminatory incidents are not carefully addressed. The fourth artifact, architecture, is particularly important because the presence of structures may prohibit accessibility for individuals with physical or visual disabilities and there may be symbols within the architecture that hold negative meanings for specific groups (Banning & Bartels, 1997). While identifying various forms of cultural artifacts is a relatively easy task, it is more difficult to determine how the assumptions and beliefs they manifest influence the behavior of individuals and groups over time (Banning & Bartels, 1997; Schein, 1985).

APPLYING ECOLOGICAL AND CULTURAL PERSPECTIVES

The vantage points of the ecological model and cultural perspective can help identify positive and problematic environmental issues for specific student populations and can also suggest ways to develop multicultural learning environments. The physical features of the student union as depicted in the campus tour story can create a critical first impression of the campus. Physical artifacts (student photography) suggest that students' art and their experiences matter, while the subject matter affirmed the value of internationalism. However, steep steps leading to a residence hall might communicate a lack of response to the needs of students, faculty, or staff with disabilities. In addition, a bookstore that closes at 5:00 p.m., coupled with a long walk from the nearest parking area, suggests the environment is less conducive to the needs of commuter and evening students. And although bulletin boards may be filled with flyers and walls decked with art, a lack of relevant and culturally appropriate pictures, posters, and other materials can leave the impression of an environment that is less than inviting.

Both the campus ecology model and cultural perspective emphasize the messages communicated through physical artifacts. Physical artifacts, such as a bronze bust of Dr. Martin Luther King Jr. located prominently in the main administration building, or murals that include positive images of people of color, are symbolic tributes and intentional affirmations of diversity. A display of flags representing the countries of all the international students on campus demonstrates a commitment to internationalism. These artifacts not only send a message of inclusion, but their mere presence can promote conversations and cross-cultural interaction. For example, prospective students and visitors who are curious about what the flags represent might ask their tour guide about their significance. Artifacts like those described in the first vignette—encoded with the message that women and Blacks are not important—suggest a less welcoming environment. A mural in the campus auditorium depicting stereotypical images of people of color conveys a message of exclusion, privileges the dominant culture, and is more likely to stifle cross-cultural communication. Because numerous studies have demonstrated that predominantly White institutions are perceived differently by students of color—sometimes as hostile environments (see Harper & Hurtado, 2007, for a synthesis of this research)—it is critical to understand these perceptions.

The display of community through posters advertising events, banners promoting important traditions, and other physical artifacts meaningful to the community, is important. However, the use of space creates a dynamic sense of community. Public lounges, dining areas, and other spaces that encourage interaction among all campus constituents are vital to campus life. They are the natural space to engage with others and foster community. The student union in the second vignette was on its way to creating a dynamic community that celebrated diversity and encouraged cross-cultural interaction. From the perspectives of both the campus ecology and cultural models, the physical environment clearly influences human behavior and plays an important role in multiculturalism on campus.

FOSTERING MULTICULTURAL LEARNING ENVIRONMENTS

Practical approaches can transform physical spaces into multicultural learning environments. Below are some key practices that student affairs educators might adopt.

BECOME MORE ANTHROPOLOGICALLY-MINDED

To understand physical spaces on campus from a cultural perspective, educators need to be more "anthropologically minded" (Tierney, 1988): adopting the attitudes of diverse learners and attempting to experience spaces from the vantage point of different student groups. To know a physical space on campus, educators and administrators need to understand how different groups view it and what they experience in its environment. For example, the program advisor working with Vanessa in her new role on the Campus Activities Board might ask her to convene a diverse group of students to describe their perception of the physical environment in the union. These students could create a perceptual map of the space. Perceptual mapping involves asking students to project their feelings or perceptions of an area onto a map of the location (Mitchell, Sergent, & Sedlacek, 1997). Students of color could be asked to map a certain building on campus by indicating where they felt most and least comfortable, their level of familiarity with the areas and how they became acquainted, and overall impressions of the climate in the space. The identification of areas that are negatively and positively perceived by students of color can help student affairs educators pinpoint physical aspects of the environment to highlight or address.

CONDUCT A CULTURAL AUDIT OF PHYSICAL SPACES

To understand campus culture and the environment, educators must go into natural settings and observe everyday activities. Educators should walk around campus on a fairly regular basis, carefully observing the spaces where students interact, with an eye toward conducting an audit of the space. Kuh and Whitt (1988) explain that an audit is essentially the process of examining features of the environment to develop a picture that is thick in description and based in the perspective of insiders (students, faculty, administrators, and others). Student affairs educators may adapt aspects of this process to discover more about the physical environment and the influence on students. The following questions are useful for conducting such observations: What kinds of people are present? Where are they located? What are they doing? What is the nature of interaction between individuals and among groups in this space? In what ways are they using the space as you expected? How are the chairs, couches, and tables arranged? How easy is it to move the furniture? Describe the physical artifacts in the space (bulletin boards, art, statues, photos, signs, etc.). Identify unique features in the space. How are students interacting with these features? How much of the space is devoted to student expression and how much is institutional? What sorts of behaviors are routine in this space?

Auditors should carefully assess their own impressions of the space, as well as attempt to evaluate those spaces through the eyes of diverse student populations. Brown and Kysilka (2002) suggest the importance of taking an objective assessment to help determine whether or not the environment could be perceived as warm and inviting from a multicultural perspective. Though it is difficult to examine something that might seem so familiar, the exercise has the potential to lend new insights about the environment.

An audit should also incorporate the perspectives of students. For example, union directors could ask students of color to show them around the building. As they tour the facility, they might ask the students to name places and features of the union, indicate some of the activities carried out in different locations, and describe in detail how they use this space. Such observations might expose locations and physical artifacts that alienate students and might also suggest areas that could easily become more sensitive to the needs of different student populations. Conducting a cultural audit will allow educators to examine the environment to assess the messages the institution is sending its students.

ARRANGE ENVIRONMENTAL CONDITIONS TO MAXIMIZE INTENDED OUTCOMES

Moos (1976) asserted that the physical environment must be arranged to create the conditions to maximize certain intended effects. Are residence halls, for example, arranged to enable students to improve their cross-cultural communication skills? It is important to assess the current set up and determine how well a particular building or space is providing services, building community, unifying the campus, and promoting student engagement and loyalty. Consider how these aspects are perceived by different populations of students. For example, it is not uncommon to find an area or symbol of the campus regularly personalized by students (a large rock, bridge, bench, etc.). Enabling students to use campus symbols to express themselves can promote enthusiastic relationships with the institution and sense of pride in it. But educators must also consider whether these opportunities are equally available to different student populations. It is a tradition at many historically Black colleges and universities (HBCUs) to allow students to decorate and paint "plots" and sitting areas with colors and artifacts associated with their sororities and fraternities. In the union at one HBCU, there are large framed portraits representing all Greek letter organizations on campus. These images, which include both men and women, were perceived by students as powerful displays of unity and positive community building. Such space and features are common at HBCUs, and together these portraits and symbolic areas enable students to identify with their organizations and feel validated in the environment.

Some campus facilities, however, do very little to build community and promote loyalty to the institution. These might have a sterile feel, with little student expression in the space. Although having comfortable chairs and space to relax is important in an ethnic culture center, the space can seem rather uninviting if it lacks ambiance and does not look like students are the intended users. Rather than giving students the ability to express themselves through the physical environment, these facilities are at best perceived as neutral spaces, or worse, as a signal that the environment is cold and unresponsive to students. Even with the most neutral and sterile of places, it is necessary to consider the messages sent to students and feelings generated as a result.

Physical facilities can exert positive effects on other educational aims. A union that provides services and offices for faculty and students can provide opportunities for meaningful out-of-class engagement between the two. One large university added a coffee bar and outfitted a large space in the union with potted plants and other sound buffers to encourage more use by commuter students. Commuter student use increased, as did the use of the space by adjunct instructors and graduate teaching assistants who found it more conducive to meetings with students than the shared offices provided by their departments.

INVOLVE STUDENTS AND MULTICULTURAL STUDENT GROUPS IN DECISION MAKING

To transform a physical space into a multicultural learning environment—beyond consideration of the physical environment—trained staff, innovative leadership, and input from students must be engaged in the entire process (Malaney, Gilman, & O'Connor, 1997). Students from majority and nonmajority groups must be given a voice in decision making (Malaney, Gilman, & O'Connor, 1997). One of the hallmarks of the campus ecology model is the role of participants in the design of the space. The success of any space design or redesign requires the involvement of students in the initiation, planning, and implementation of physical space. Returning to the vignettes, it is easy to see how by seeking Vanessa's input in the redesign of the alumni meeting room, the student union director could communicate the value of her perspective and concern for creating a space that is welcoming to and reflective of all students.

CHALLENGES TO CREATING MULTICULTURAL SPACES

Transforming physical spaces into multicultural learning environments is an exciting prospect, but not a simple undertaking. There are many aspects of the physical environment that we can do little about, but there are other things that can be changed and several questions to consider. How does the institution's historical attitude toward diversity influence the present culture and climate (Hurtado, Milem, Clayton-Pedersen, & Allen, 1999)? What are the influences from the dominant culture, including the power of the larger institution, that present challenges to students who are members of underrepresented groups (Kuh & Whitt, 1988)? While physical changes can be threatening to those with power, intentional efforts should be taken to create an environment that is inclusive of an institution's various subpopulations.

The cost of making changes to physical space is also a challenge. When one university considered removing a controversial mural, concerns were raised about the cost, possible damage to the mural, and criticism from alumni and donors. Many historical pieces (artwork, statues, etc.) around campus may have great significance to loyal alumni, but have a very different meaning in today's multicultural environment. Student affairs educators must carefully weigh the costs associated with their efforts to create more inclusive environments. In sensitive situations, it is wise to involve current students, faculty, and other important constituents to ensure a broad consideration of issues and concerns.

While there are challenges to any decision-making process that includes a variety of constituents, the overall process is likely to ensure that the transformed space will consider the various experiences of individuals on the campus. Including students in the decision-making process can promote learning and development. Meaningful engagement in the design of the physical environment allows students to simultaneously participate in leadership positions and develop collaborative work skills (Banning & Cunard, 1986, 1996). Transforming a physical space into a multicultural learning environment and involving students in the process is an opportunity to send a message to students that their ideas and input are valued by the institution.

CONCLUSION

This chapter introduced the ways that basic features of the physical environment, the seemingly mundane attributes of space, influence multiculturalism. Student affairs educators who are serious about fostering supportive campus communities for all students must observe and attend to the influence of the physical environment and what it represents. Indeed, the transformation of physical spaces into multicultural learning environments may be one possible way to change the chilly climate perceived by marginalized students (Harper & Hurtado, 2007; Milani, Eakin, & Brattain, 1992). Creating space in the union that reflects the needs and interests of a multicultural community sends important messages about acceptance—essential to creating a more positive climate for all students. Educators and administrators are encouraged to adopt an ecological or cultural lens in their work to create a more multicultural learning environment.

REFERENCES

Banning, J. H. (1989). The campus ecology manager role. In U. Delworth & G. Hanson, and Associates, *Student Services: A handbook for the profession* (2nd ed.). San Francisco: Jossey-Bass.

Banning, J. H. & Bartels, S. (1997). A taxonomy: Campus physical artifacts as communicators of campus multiculturalism. *NASPA Journal, 35*(1), 29–37.

Banning, J. H. & Cunard, M. (1986). Environment supports student development. *ACUI Bulletin, 54*(1), 8–10.

Banning, J. H. & Cunard, M. (1996). Assessment and design of the physical environment in support of student development. In N. Davis Metz (Ed.), *Student development in college unions and student activities.* Bloomington, IN: Association of College Unions-International.

Banning J. H. & McKinley, D. L. (1980). Conceptions of the campus environment. In W. H. Morrill, J. C. Hurst, and Associates (Eds.), *Dimensions of intervention for student development.* New York: Wiley.

Brazzell, J. C. (2001, January–February). A sense of belonging. *About campus: Enriching the student learning experience, 5*(6), 31–32.

Brown, S. C. & Kysilka, M. L. (2002). *Applying multicultural and global concepts in the classroom and beyond.* Boston: Allyn and Bacon.

Evans, N., Forney, D. & Guido-DiBrito, F. (1998). *Student development in college: Theory, research, and practice.* San Francisco: Jossey-Bass.

Harper, S. R., & Hurtado, S. (2007). Nine themes in campus racial climates and implications for institutional transformation. In S. R. Harper & L. D. Patton (Eds.), *Responding to the Realities of Race on Campus: New Directions for Student Services, No. 120.* San Francisco: Jossey-Bass.

Hurtado, S., Milem, J., Clayton-Pedersen, A., & Allen, W. (1999). *Enacting diverse learning environments: Improving the climate for racial/ethnic diversity in higher education.* ASHE-ERIC Higher Education Report

Volume 26, No. 8. Washington, DC: The George Washington University, Graduate School of Education and Human Development.

Kuh, G. D. (2000). Understanding campus environments. In M. Barr, M. Desler, & Associates (Eds.), *The handbook of student affairs administration* (2nd ed., pp. 50–72). San Francisco: Jossey-Bass.

Kuh, G. D. (1993). Appraising the character of a college. *Journal of Counseling and Development, 71,* 661–668.

Kuh, G. D., Kinzie, J., Schuh, J. H., Whitt, E. J., & Associates (2005). *Student success in college: Creating conditions that matter.* San Francisco: Jossey-Bass.

Kuh, G. D. & Whitt, E. J. (1988). *The invisible tapestry: Culture in American colleges and universities.* ASHE-ERIC Higher Education Research Report No. 1. Washington, DC: Association for the Study of Higher Education. (ERIC Document Reproduction Service No. ED299934)

Malaney, G. D., Gilman, D., & O'Connor, J. (1997). Assessing student opinion toward a multicultural student union. *NASPA Journal, 34*(3), 170–185.

Milani, T. E., Eakin, J. T., & Brattain, W. E. (1992). The role of the college union and the future, in T. E. Milani & J. W. Johnston (Eds.), *The college union in the year 2000: New Directions for Student Services, No. 58* (pp. 3–10). San Francisco: Jossey-Bass.

Minorities in Higher Education 2001–02: Nineteenth Annual Status Report. (2002). Washington, DC: American Council on Education.

Mitchell, A. A., Sergent, M. T., & Sedlacek, W. E. (1997). Mapping the university learning environment. *NASPA Journal, 35*(1), 20–28.

Moos, R. H. (1976). *The human context: Environmental determinants of behavior.* New York: Wiley-Interscience.

Pascarella, E. T. & Terenzini, P. T. (1991). *How college affects students: Findings and insights from twenty years of research.* San Francisco: Jossey-Bass.

Pascarella, E. T., & Terenzini, P. T. (2005). *How college affects students, Volume 2: A third decade of research.* San Francisco: Jossey-Bass.

Sedlacek, W. E. (1993). Employing noncognitive variables in admission and retention of nontraditional students. In *Achieving diversity: Issues in the recruitment and retention of traditional underrepresented students* (pp. 33–39). Alexandria, VA: National Association of College Admissions Counselors.

Schein, E. H. (1985). *Organizational culture and leadership. A dynamic view.* San Francisco: Jossey-Bass.

Smith, D. G., & Associates. (1997). *Diversity works: The emerging picture of how students benefit.* Washington, DC: Association of Colleges and Universities.

Stage, F. K. & Manning, K. (1992). *Enhancing the multicultural campus environment. A cultural brokering approach: New Directions for Student Services, No. 60.* San Francisco: Jossey-Bass.

Strange, C. C. & Banning, J. H. (2001). *Educating by design: Creating campus learning environments that work.* San Francisco: Jossey-Bass.

Tierney, W. G. (1988). Organizational culture in higher education. *Journal of Higher Education, 59*(1), 2–21.

Chapter Seven

ooooo

Making Campus Activities and Student Organizations Inclusive for Racial/Ethnic Minority Students

Kimberly A. Griffin, Andrew H. Nichols, David Pérez II, and K. Dex Tuttle

ooooo

Ana was hurrying off to buy her chemistry book when she passed the long rows of tables set up in the main quad. The tables were draped with colorful cloths and vibrant signs that read: "Get involved in student government . . . write for the campus newspaper . . . join the intramural lacrosse team!" The students staffing the tables all seemed friendly enough—smiling and waving, calling for students to sign up for the bowling team, and talking about why everyone should join this sorority or that fraternity. But she did not see other Latino students anywhere nearby. No brown faces were smiling at her from behind the tables, beckoning her over or encouraging her to join in all the fun their group was having. She saw a table for a ballroom dancing club, which sounded like fun. Ana loved to dance and had done Ballet Folklorico back home. Was that close enough? Would she fit in? And where was the Ballet Folklorico table, anyway? As Ana looked around again for something that seemed more familiar, she could not tell if anyone was *really* waving to her. Even though she had only been at college a few days, she could already tell that everything was so different from the way things were back home. Feeling a little overwhelmed and more than a little self-conscious, Ana focused her sights on the bookstore and walked away, deciding to worry about chemistry for now and getting involved later.

As students begin their experiences at colleges and universities across the country, they are often told the same things: "Get involved, find a club or organization that reflects your interests, take on opportunities to lead, and learn as much as you can outside the classroom." Much of this encouragement is based on higher education research literature that highlights the importance of participating in student groups, interacting with peers, and building relationships with faculty and staff outside the classroom (Kuh, Kinzie, Schuh, Whitt, & Associates, 2005). Purposeful engagement in social and community activities on campus improves social integration and retention for undergraduates from all groups, and can greatly enrich the academic and social experiences students have on their college campuses (Astin, 1984, 1993; Harper, 2006; Kuh, 1995; Kuh, Palmer, & Kish, 2003; Pascarella & Terenzini, 2005; Person & Christensen, 1996; Tinto, 1993).

The cry of student affairs professionals to get involved is often directed toward all students, regardless of race, ethnicity, or background. Yet despite the importance of participating in campus organizations and student groups, many scholars have found that campus involvement does not come easily to all and may be particularly challenging for students of color. Many racial and ethnic minority students report their lack of participation in campus life (Allen, 1985; Person & Christensen, 1996), and research reveals that students of color exist on the margins at their institutions in many ways. They feel alienated, unwelcome, and disinterested in participating in many of the social events and activities their campuses offer (Harper, 2006; Harper & Hurtado, 2007; Hurtado, 1992; Loo & Rollison, 1986; Person & Christensen, 1996; Turner, 1994).

This chapter explores issues of minority student engagement in campus communities, presenting the ways students of color have been excluded from meaningful participation in social activities and offering strategies to foster inclusiveness and participation. We address the barriers at predominantly White institutions (PWIs) that lead to the isolation and alienation many students of color experience. We present literature on the involvement patterns of student of color, addressing both their lack of participation in "mainstream" activities and reliance on racial/ethnic student organizations. In response to the literature and based on our collective experiences, we offer practical approaches that campus leaders can implement to encourage involvement among students of color. Finally, we offer concluding thoughts about promoting more positive outcomes for all by remaining committed to focusing on involvement for all students and fostering minority student participation in a wide array of campus activities.

MINORITY STUDENT EXPERIENCES AND ENGAGEMENT AT PWIS

Before discussing students of color and the nature of their involvement in campus activities, it is important to understand the institutional environments in which these students are often immersed. On many campuses, a historical legacy of exclusion continues to shape the experiences and outcomes of members of the campus community (Harper & Hurtado, 2007; Hurtado, Milem, Clayton-Pedersen, Walter, 1999). In 1954, the Supreme Court held that the segregation of public education was unconstitutional; yet many colleges and universities remained segregated through the 1960s and 1970s (Ogletree, 2004). Some scholars assert that a history of exclusion, if unaddressed, will continue to be reflected in current institutional policies and practices, and will also influence students' sense of inclusion in the campus community. At institutions with a historical legacy of exclusion, students of color may not see themselves or their interests reflected in campus traditions; they may feel less than full members of their institutions. Turner (1994) offers an example of how this legacy of exclusion can influence the experience of students of color, likening it to being a guest in someone else's home. She writes, "Like students of color in the university climate, guests have no history in the house they occupy. There are no photographs on the wall that reflect their image. Their paraphernalia, paintings, scents, and sounds do not appear in the house" (p. 356). Turner suggests that this sense of visitation engenders feelings of alienation and marginalization, distancing students from a sense of true belonging and community membership.

Alienation and marginalization appear to be common experiences for many students of color at PWIs, drawn out not only by an institution's history, but also by students' interactions with other members of the campus community (Bennett & Okinaka, 1990; Loo & Rolison, 1986, Malaney & Shively, 1995; Turner, 1994). Students of color are often subject to racism, prejudice, and stereotyping that can negatively influence their college experiences and outcomes. Research consistently indicates racial/ethnic minority students, especially African Americans, perceive there to be more racism and racial tension on campus than their White counterparts (Harper & Hurtado, 2007). Specifically, racial/ethnic minorities have consistently reported the advancement of stereotypes by White members of the college or university community; dissatisfaction with the inadequate representation of racial/ethnic minority peers, faculty, and staff; Eurocentric curricula; and racist interactions with White persons on campus (Cabrera & Nora, 1994; Diver-Stamnes & LoMascolo, 2001; Harper & Hurtado, 2007; Hurtado, 1992; Loo & Rolison, 1986; Rankin & Reason, 2005; Tan, 1994). These encounters only add to the students' feelings of marginality and exclusion. Various scholars report that students of color have also felt culture shock and cultural incompatibility in response to hostility on campus, and they perceive a lack of institutional support and commitment to diversity (Ancis, Sedlacek, & Mohr, 2000). Such perceptions and feelings can have dramatic effects on student outcomes and reduce overall educational satisfaction, persistence, student transition and adjustment, sense of belonging, and institutional attachment (Cabrera, Nora, Terenzini, Pascarella, & Hagedorn, 1999; Helm, Sedlacek, & Prieto, 1998; Loo & Rollison, 1986; Nora & Cabrera, 1996; Pascarella & Terenzini, 2005).

The alienation, marginalization, and isolation many students of color feel seem to go hand in hand with their lack of participation in mainstream campus activities. Students of color have been described as feeling more comfortable in their campus's academic settings than social ones (Person & Christensen, 1996). Tinto (1993) notes that students of color may be more likely than their White peers to struggle with social integration because "on all but the very largest campuses students of color have relatively fewer options as to the types of communities in which to establish membership than White students" (p. 74). Allen's (1985) work seems to confirm this, and he found that 45% of Black students in his sample felt very little, or not at all, a part of campus life, with only 12% reporting that they felt very much a part of campus activities. In a similar study, Allen (1987) found that while two thirds of African American students at HBCUs felt they were a part of campus life and 26% reported the highest level of involvement, Black students at PWIs were less involved. Only 38% of Black students at PWIs felt they were a part of campus life, and 8% reported being involved at the highest levels.

To counterbalance these harsh realities at PWIs, some students of color develop their own subcultures within the larger campus community, centering around culturally or ethnically based student organizations and support services (Chang, 2002; Guiffrida, 2003; Harper & Quaye, 2007; Hurtado et al., 1999;

Patton, 2006a). To various degrees, these racial/ethnic student organizations serve as enclaves that have been instrumental in reducing feelings of isolation, marginality, and alienation among Native American, Latino, Black, and Asian American students (Murguia, Padilla, & Pavel, 1991; Wang, Sedlacek, & Westbrook, 1992). Although these enclaves also exist for White students, Murguia et al. maintain these subcommunities may be especially critical to the social integration of racial/ethnic minority students who may have limited access to mainstream activities and communities. For students of color, these student organizations often satisfy needs that are unmet by mainstream clubs and campus activities. Racial/ethnic minority students report campus activities and organizations rarely reflect their unique cultural interests (Davis, 1991; Person & Christensen 1996; Rooney 1985). Using Black organizations as an example, research by Guiffrida (2003) and Harper and Quaye (2007) notes that among a host of other outcomes, racial/ethnic student organizations provide students with a sense of cultural connection. Racially and ethnically focused organizations and activities appear to offer minority students more social options, enhancing their integration and comfort on campus (Allen, 1985; Hurtado et al., 1999; Livingston & Stewart, 1987; Loo & Rollison, 1986; Tinto, 1993). Though these cultural niches are sometimes regarded as bastions of self-segregation, Hurtado et al. (1999) suggest these communities serve as valuable support mechanisms, social outlets, and facilitators for further involvement in more mainstream campus activities.

Because of their dissatisfaction and perceptions of cultural incongruence, students of color may deem participation in mainstream activities as inconsequential or trivial. Even so, it is important for them to be encouraged and feel welcome to participate in activities both within and outside their ethnic communities. According to Ringgenberg (1989), exclusion can cause these racial/ethnic minority students to experience feelings of marginality and lack of integration into all aspects of campus life. Constraining minority students to participation in ethnic subcommunities also limits their options, leaving them with fewer (and in many cases, less diverse) opportunities to reap the benefits of campus involvement. The lack of true incorporation of students of color into all aspects of campus life limits the potential benefits that all students can yield from interactions with their diverse peers. Having more students of color on campus does not magically produce growth and social change; students with diverse backgrounds and perspectives must interact and build friendships with one another to truly benefit from a multicultural campus community (Hurtado et al., 1999). Though racial/ethnic organizations are crucial avenues for support that must not be maligned, engaging only in ethnic subcommunities may inhibit students of color and their White peers from developing all the beneficial academic, democratic, and critical thinking skills that accompany interactions across difference.

PRACTICAL STRATEGIES FOR INCLUSIVE ENGAGEMENT

While participation in campus activities can have a positive influence on student outcomes, many students of color enrolled at PWIs are not experiencing or becoming involved in their campus communities in the same ways as their White peers. Efforts to make campus activities more culturally inclusive and welcoming to students of color will temper some of the feelings of alienation, isolation, and marginality that seem to be prevalent at PWIs. For this to occur, student affairs professionals and other campus leaders must become more culturally sensitive to the experiences, needs, fears, and cultural interests of racial/ethnic minority students (Sutton & Kimbrough, 2001).

The following approaches are intended to help educators and administrators increase engagement of underrepresented students in campus activities, clubs, and organizations. Strategies for developing inclusive programs and holding student leaders accountable for supporting these efforts are provided.

1. **Begin engaging underrepresented students in the campus community before they arrive on campus.** A welcome publication that educates students of color about a wide range leadership opportunities, both within and outside of culturally focused student organizations—sent before they arrive on campus—can help emphasize the benefits of participation in out-of-class activities. The publication should also prominently feature minority students actively involved on campus, sending the message that students of color are central, rather than marginal, members of the community. Such a publication also offers student affairs professionals and campus leaders an opportunity to engage and support organizations on campus that serve and incorporate students from diverse populations.

2. **Host orientation events to welcome new students and educate them about campus leadership opportunities.** Involvement fairs

and discussion panels that highlight the "hows and whys" of participating in campus activities provide venues to engage students in campus leadership experiences early in the year. Specific attention should be focused on planning involvement events targeted toward underrepresented student populations. Involvement events educate students about the benefits of extracurricular experiences and also present opportunities for new and returning students to engage in meaningful dialogue. Leaders from culturally focused and prominent mainstream campus organizations (i.e., Student Government Council, Residence Hall Association) should be encouraged to participate. Faculty and administrators should also be encouraged to participate in this event to demonstrate the institution's commitment to supporting underrepresented student populations.

3. **Work with engaged student leaders from underrepresented communities to personally recruit their uninvolved peers.** Students of color in leadership roles can have great influence on their peers. These students should be encouraged to reach out to their uninvolved friends and classmates and encourage their participation in campus activities. Student affairs officers and organization advisors can facilitate this by partnering with student leaders of mainstream and multicultural campus organizations to create a recruitment process for new members and leaders. In addition to encouraging students to recruit peers directly, advisors and students affairs professionals can enhance recruitment by writing personalized letters to students nominated by leaders, inviting them to assume specific leadership roles within campus organizations.

4. **Create and support groups that cater to the diverse needs of underrepresented student populations.** Student affairs professionals must recognize the importance of establishing, maintaining, and supporting organizations that serve the diverse interests of underrepresented students. These organizations not only create a supportive environment where students can exercise leadership skills, but also can lead to greater involvement in the campus community. Support for these organizations can be advisory and financial, and may include allocation of other community resources. For example, on many college campuses, organizations serving underrepresented students are grossly underfunded and lack the resources

needed to effectively engage students in meaningful programmatic experiences (Chang 2002, Patton, 2006b). Unlike mainstream student groups, minority-focused organizations often lack dedicated facilities (i.e., office space, lounge, etc.) for their student leaders. These groups should be assigned advisors who are thoughtful and well informed about issues and concerns of students of color.

5. **Hold student organization leaders accountable for reaching out to underrepresented students and fostering an inclusive community.** Student affairs professionals and organization advisors should not hesitate to draw attention to the lack of participation of underrepresented student populations in mainstream clubs and organizations. When planning campus events and activities, leaders should be held accountable for organizing programs that are open and welcoming to all students. When identifying lack of representation as a problem, campus officials should also be prepared and willing to support student leaders as they devise plans focused on intentionally engaging underrepresented student populations.

6. **Use inclusive leadership models to provide ongoing training and development opportunities for student leaders.** The Social Change Model (SCM) of Leadership Development (Higher Education Research Institute, 1996) is a framework to enhance the development of student leaders, promoting the values of equity, inclusion, citizenship, and service. The SCM examines leadership from three different levels—individual, group, and community/society—and highlights seven values critical to student empowerment. In addition to enhancing student learning and development, this model is intended to facilitate positive social change at institutions of higher education. Incorporating the SCM into leadership development and training sessions can encourage leaders of mainstream student organizations to become more inclusive. It may be even more valuable to underrepresented student leaders, providing greater opportunities to improve their leadership skills and their confidence in engaging in campus activities.

7. **Encourage and support student leaders to organize programs that raise the consciousness of their peers and inspire activism.**

Advisors of student organizations should encourage leaders to coordinate programs and activities that encourage dialogue, interaction, and sharing perspectives across differences. Intergroup dialogues, for example, can raise awareness about issues that negatively affect minority students and improve the campus climate by engaging students to create and sustain inclusive communities (Nagda & Zuniga, 2003). To support these initiatives, administrators could consider providing grants to organizations for programs that address discrimination, privilege, or inclusion. To bridge the gap between minority and White students, student organizations can be encouraged or even required by the institution to collaborate on such initiatives each year.

8. **Establish mentoring programs to connect new students with faculty members and administrators.** Mentors can provide much more than academic support; they can facilitate students' integration into their campus community and encourage students to become more involved in extracurricular activities (Freeman, 1999; Nagda, Gregerman, Jonides, von Hippel, & Lerner, 1998; Pascarella, 1980). Mentors can advise minority students on how to best negotiate the academic and social challenges they may encounter as student leaders. These relationships may also increase mentors' interest in serving as advisors for minority student organizations. While any mentor has the potential to connect with students of color, institutions should make an effort to recruit minority faculty and administrators to serve as mentors whenever possible. Underrepresented students often feel more comfortable with and seek support from members of their own community based on their shared culture and experiences at PWIs (Loo & Rollison, 1986; Tan, 1995; Tinto, 1993).

9. **Encourage collaboration between faculty, student affairs professionals, and other campus administrators committed to the successful involvement of underrepresented student populations.** Faculty and administrators should be encouraged to collaborate to create new ways of fostering student involvement. Residential learning communities and service–learning opportunities may be useful strategies to encourage student participation, creating seamless learning environments that ensure the successful inclusion of all students. Residential

learning communities focused on educating students about diversity can promote student development, inspire students to foster positive change on campus, and demonstrate an institution's commitment to supporting inclusive learning environments (Pike, 2002). Service–learning experiences can also be pivotal, instilling the value of civic responsibility and giving students an opportunity to interact with diverse populations in the broader community (Bringle & Hatcher, 1996; Myers-Lipton, 1998).

10. **Communicate with parents throughout the year about the involvement of minority student leaders.** Harper (2006) noted the importance of making parents aware of the challenges that underrepresented students encounter at PWIs. Institutions should educate parents about the benefits of extracurricular experiences: forming meaningful relationships with administrators; successfully competing for scholarships, internships, and jobs; and acquiring transferable skills that can be applied in other settings. Institutions should consider ways to communicate this information to parents throughout the year—not just during orientation. With this information, parents can be engaged in their students' lives in new ways. They can be another voice encouraging students to branch out and get involved, reminding them that participating in campus activities is important and will enhance their learning.

11. **Celebrate the contributions of minority student leaders.** Institutions should consider organizing celebratory events and opportunities to acknowledge minority student leaders publicly, such as awards or end-of-year recognition events. This can be a transition event for student leaders, demonstrating an institution's commitment to serving underrepresented student populations. Members of the broader campus community should be invited, and a highly regarded faculty member or administrator should address award recipients, parents, advisors, and others in attendance. Newly elected student leaders should be acknowledged and encouraged to maintain their commitment to enhancing the broader campus community.

CONCLUSION

When we engage in dialogues about the importance of diversity and its influence on student outcomes, the conversation often turns to the benefits produced by interactions across difference. With race-conscious programs and policies facing repeated challenges, higher education scholars have rallied, developing empirical literature showing that diverse campus communities provide their students with a wide array of benefits. Diversity and interactions across difference have been linked to gains in a wide array of positive outcomes, including cognitive development and critical thinking ability, academic and social self-concept, academic skill development, and tolerance (Gurin, Dey, Hurtado, & Gurin, 2002; Gurin, Lehman, & Lewis, 2004; Hurtado, 2001; Milem, 2003).

Researchers have also noted these positive outcomes do not simply appear. Integrating multiculturalism into the curriculum and engaging in constructive conflict during class yields benefits, but many of the interactions with the greatest potential for influence take place outside the classroom (Hurtado et al., 1999; Kuh et al., 2005). It has been widely suggested that students from different backgrounds and with diverse perspectives must be given opportunities to interact outside of the classroom through cocurricular workshops and programs, clubs, and campus activities.

The evidence that diversity has an enriching effect on students' college experiences and outcomes is conclusive. Now, it is up to student affairs professionals and other campus leaders to facilitate interactions outside the classroom, allowing students to benefit from the diverse perspectives of their peers. A crucial question presents itself: How do we empower students of color to take on leadership roles and truly immerse themselves in the social environment of their campus? We must consider how to go beyond superficially involving students of color in mainstream activities, assuring that students from all racial and ethnic backgrounds feel important and integrated into the campus and its community.

This chapter offers guidance for addressing these issues, suggesting practical ways faculty, administrators, and campus leaders can work to increase levels of minority student involvement. By reaching out to students of color in thoughtful and intentional ways, informing them about the wide range of opportunities available on campus, and encouraging more organizations to embrace multiculturalism and participation from a wide range of students, we can support potentially great change in how students of color view participation in campus activities. When students of color feel more comfortable on campus, less alienated, and less marginalized, the likelihood of their retention and satisfaction with their college experiences increases.

As institutional leaders work toward better incorporating students of color into mainstream campus organizations, they cannot ignore the importance of creating opportunities for students of color to interact with and support one another. While some may perceive a tension between encouraging students of color to engage in mainstream versus culturally focused activities, participation in these activities does not have to conflict. Maintaining and fostering racially and culturally focused activities can play a critical part in both supporting students of color and encouraging them to become involved in other activities—including those with opportunities to interact across difference. So when working with a student like Ana, we can tell her she doesn't have to choose between ballroom dancing and Ballet Folklorico; she can do both. Participating in activities that reflect her Latino background will encourage her and give her confidence to try something new and outside her comfort zone, perhaps making campus feel a little bit more like home.

REFERENCES

Allen, W. R. (1985). Black student, white campus: Structural, interpersonal, and psychological correlates of success. *Journal of Negro Education, 54*(2), 134–147.

Allen, W. R. (1987). Blacks in higher education: The climb toward equality. *Change,* 28–34.

Ancis, J. R., Sedlacek, W. E., & Mohr, J. J. (2000). Student perceptions of campus cultural climate by race. *Journal of Counseling & Development, 78,* 180–185.

Astin, A. (1984). Student involvement: A developmental theory for higher education. *Journal of College Student Personnel, 25,* 297–308.

Astin, A. (1993). *What matters in college? Four critical years revisited.* San Francisco: Jossey-Bass Publishers.

Bennett, C., & Okinaka, A. M. (1990). Factors related to persistence among Asian, Black, Hispanic, and White undergraduates at predominantly White university: comparison between first and fourth year cohorts. *The Urban Review, 22*(1), 33–60.

Bringle, R. G., & Hatcher, J. A. (1996). Implementing service learning in higher education. *Journal of Higher Education, 67*(2), 221–239.

Cabrera, A. F., Nora, A., Terenzini, P. T., Pascarella, E., & Hagedorn, L. S. (1999). Campus racial climate and the adjustment of students to college: A comparison between White students and African American students. *The Journal of Higher Education, 70*(2), 134–160.

Cabrera, A. F., & Nora, A. (1994). College students' perceptions of prejudice and discrimination and their feelings of alienation. *Review of Education, Pedagogy, and Cultural Studies, 16,* 387–409.

Chang, M. J. (2002). Racial dynamics on campus: What student organizations can tell us. *About Campus, 7*(1), 2–8.

Davis, R. (1991). Social support networks and undergraduate student academic-success-related outcomes: A comparison of Black students on Black and White campuses. In W. R. Allen, E. G. Epps, & N. Z. Haniff (Eds.), *College in black and white: African American students in predominantly white and in historically black public universities* (pp. 143–160). Albany: State University of New York Press.

Diver-Stamnes, A., & LoMascolo, A. F. (2001). The marginalization of ethnic minority students: A case study of a rural university. *Equity & Excellence in Education, 34*(1), 50–57.

Freeman, K. (1999). No services needed? The case for mentoring high-achieving African American students. *Peabody Journal of Education, 74*(2), 15–26.

Guiffrida, D. A. (2003). African American student organizations as agents of social integration. *Journal of College Student Development, 44*(3), 304–319.

Gurin, P., Dey, E., Hurtado, S., & Gurin, G. (2002). Diversity and higher education: Theory and impact on educational outcomes. *Harvard Educational Review, 72*(3), 330–366.

Gurin, P., Lehman, J. S., & Lewis, E. (2004). *Defending diversity: Affirmative action at the University of Michigan.* Ann Arbor, MI: University of Michigan Press.

Harper, S. R. (2006). Enhancing African American male student outcomes through leadership and active involvement. In M. J. Cuyjet (Ed.), *African American men in college* (pp. 68–94). San Francisco: Jossey-Bass.

Harper, S. R., & Hurtado, S. (2007). Nine themes in campus racial climates and implications for institutional transformation. In S. R. Harper & L. D. Patton (Eds.), *Responding to the Realities of Race on Campus: New Directions for Student Services, No. 120.* San Francisco: Jossey-Bass.

Harper, S. R., & Quaye, S. J. (2007). Student organizations as venues for Black identity expression and development among African American male student leaders. *Journal of College Student Development, 48*(2), 127–144.

Helm, E. G., Sedlacek, W. E., & Prieto, D. O. (1998). The relationship between attitudes toward diversity and overall satisfaction of university students by race. *Journal of College Counseling, 1,* 111–119.

Higher Education Research Institute. (1996). *A social change model of leadership development.* Los Angeles: University of California, Los Angeles.

Hurtado, S. (1992). The campus racial climate: Contexts of conflict. *The Journal of Higher Education, 63*(5), 539–569.

Hurtado, S. (2001). Linking diversity and educational purpose: How diversity affects the classroom environment and student development. In G. Orfield (Ed.), *Diversity challenged: Evidence on the impact of affirmative action* (pp. 187–203). Cambridge, MA: Harvard Education Publishing Group.

Hurtado, S., Milem, J., Clayton-Pedersen, A., & Walter, A. (1999). Enacting diverse learning environments: Improving the climate for racial/ethnic diversity in higher education. *ASHE/ERIC Higher Education Report Series, 26*(8). Washington, DC: The George Washington University, Graduate School of Education and Human Development.

Kuh, G. D. (1995). The other curriculum: Out-of-class experiences associated with student learning and personal development. *Journal of Higher Education, 66*(2), 123–155.

Kuh, G. D., Kinzie, J., Schuh, J. H., Whitt, E. J., & Associates (2005). *Student success in college: Creating conditions that matter.* San Francisco: Jossey-Bass.

Kuh, G. D., Palmer, M., & Kish, K. (2003). The value of educationally purposeful out-of-class experiences. In T. L. Skipper & R. Argo (Eds.), *Involvement in campus activities and the retention of first-year college students. The First-Year Experience Monograph Series* (No. 36, pp. 19–34). Columbia: University of South Carolina, National Resource Center for the First-Year Experience and Students in Transition.

Livingston, M. D., & Stewart, M. A. (1987). Minority students on a White campus: Perception is truth. *NASPA Journal, 24*(3), 39–49.

Loo, C. M., & Rolison, G. (1986). Alienation of ethnic minority students at a predominantly White university. *Journal of Higher Education, 57*(1), 58–77.

Maleney, G. D., & Shively, M. (1995). Academic and social expectations and experiences of first-year students of color. *NASPA Journal, 33*(1), 3–18.

Milem, J. (2003). The educational benefits of diversity: Evidence from multiple sectors. In M. J. Chang, D. Witt, J. Jones, & K. Hakuta (Eds.), *Compelling interest: Examining the evidence on racial dynamics in colleges and universities* (pp. 126–169). Stanford, CA: Stanford University Press.

Murguia, E., Padilla, R. V., & Pavel, M. (1991). Ethnicity and the concept of social integration in Tinto's model of institutional departure. *Journal of College Student Development, 32*, 433–439.

Myers-Lipton, S. J. (1998). Effect of a comprehensive service–learning program on college students' civic responsibility. *Teaching Sociology, 26*, 243–258.

Nagda, B., Gregerman, S. R., Jonides, J., von Hippel, W., & Lerner, J. S. (1998). Undergraduate student-faculty research partnerships affect student retention. *The Review of Higher Education, 22*(1), 55–72.

Nagda, B. R. A., & Zuniga, X. (2003). Fostering meaningful racial engagement through intergroup dialogues. *Group Processes and Intergroup Relations, 6*(1), 111–128.

Nora, A., & Cabrera, A. F. (1996). The role of perceptions of prejudice and discrimination on the adjustment of minority students to college. *Journal of Higher Education, 67*(2), 119–148.

Ogletree, C. J. (2004). *All deliberate speed: Reflections on the first half century of Brown v. Board of Education.* New York: W.W. Norton & Company.

Pascarella, E. T. (1980). Student-faculty informal contact and college outcomes. *Review of Educational Research, 50*(4), 545–595.

Pascarella, E. T., & Terenzini, P. T. (2005). *How college affects students. A third decade of research.* San Francisco: Jossey-Bass.

Patton, L. D. (2006a). The voice of reason: A qualitative examination of Black student perceptions of Black culture centers. *Journal of College Student Development, 47*(6), 628–644.

Patton, L. D. (2006b). Black culture centers: Still central to student learning. *About Campus, 11*(2), 2–8.

Person, D. R., & Christensen, M. C. (1996). Understanding Black student culture and Black student retention. *NASPA Journal, 34*(1), 47–56.

Pike, G. R. (2002). The differential effects on- and off-campus living arrangements on students' openness to diversity. *NASPA Journal, 39*(4), 283–299.

Rankin, S. R., & Reason, R. D. (2005). Differing perceptions: How students of color and White students perceive campus climate for underrepresented groups. *Journal of College Student Development, 46*(1), 43–61.

Ringgenberg, L. J. (1989). Expanding participation of student subgroups in campus activities. In D. C. Roberts, (Ed.), *Designing Campus Activities to Foster a Sense of Community: New Directions for Student Services, No. 48.* San Francisco: Jossey-Bass.

Rooney, G. D. (1985). Minority students' involvement in minority student organizations: An exploratory study. *Journal of College Student Personnel, 26*(5), 450–456.

Suarez-Balcazar, Y., Orellana-Damacela, L., Portillo, N., Rowan, J. M., & Andrews-Guillen, C. (2003). Experiences of differential treatment among college students of color. *The Journal of Higher Education, 74*(4), 429–444.

Sutton, E. M., & Kimbrough, W. M. (2001). Trends in Black student involvement. *NASPA Journal, 39*(1), 30–40.

Tan, D. L. (1994). Uniqueness of the Asian American experience in higher education. *College Student Journal, 28,* 412–421.

Tan, D. L. (1995). Perceived importance of role models and its relationship with minority student satisfaction and academic performance. *NACADA Journal, 15*(1), 48–51.

Tinto, V. (1993). *Leaving college: Rethinking causes and cures of student attrition* (2nd ed.). Chicago: The University of Chicago Press.

Turner, C. S. V. (1994). Guests in someone else's house: Students of color. *The Review of Higher Education, 17*(4), 355–370.

Wang, Y., Sedlacek, W. E., & Westbrook, F. D. (1992). Asian Americans and student organizations: Attitudes and participation. *Journal of College Student Development, 33,* 214–221.

CHAPTER EIGHT

ooooo

Collaboration for Cultural Programming: Engaging Culture Centers, Multicultural Affairs, and Student Activities Offices as Partners

LORI D. PATTON AND MICHAEL D. HANNON

ooooo

P romoting diversity and multiculturalism on college and university campuses is
a challenging yet attainable goal that can be met through collaborative efforts
among students, faculty, and staff. Offices within student affairs—multicultural
programs, student activities, and residence life—play a significant role in facilitating
the educational, out-of-class experiences of college students. Ensuring that students
learn to communicate and interact across racial and cultural boundaries is important
in enhancing these experiences and promoting student engagement. Student
affairs educators must create cross-cultural learning experiences for students and
encourage them to move beyond their spaces of comfort. Various offices on campus
can collaborate, pooling resources to offer programs and services that cater to the
needs of a diverse student body, while also creating a welcoming environment that
embraces diversity and multiculturalism.

A major challenge in creating these cross-departmental collaborations is the
unspoken and often unchallenged assumption that multicultural affairs offices
or centers should bear the brunt of the responsibility for cultural education and
programming. While such offices certainly have staff who are trained and skilled in

this functional area, the responsibility of creating cross-cultural learning opportunities should be a collaborative one with various campus entities engaged in meaningful partnerships. Shuford and Palmer (2004) contend that multicultural affairs professionals should work with allies throughout campus to ensure that diversity is woven into the fabric of the institution—including policies, human resources, programming, and curricula. This chapter describes how collaboration between multicultural affairs/culture centers (MACCs) and the student activities office (SAO) can advance institutional goals for cross-learning and multiculturalism. We chose SAOs because of their programming function and emphasis on out-of-class student engagement. Certainly, there are collaborative possibilities for MACCs and other offices/departments in student affairs and academic affairs. But for the sake of focus, we concentrate solely on SAOs.

This chapter provides both rationale and encouragement for enhanced relationships between SAOs and MACCs to help create an atmosphere that embraces and celebrates different cultures and students from various backgrounds. In this discussion, MACC refers to an administrative office or space that focuses on supporting and integrating target populations. Through programming, advisement, leadership development, and other forms of student involvement, MACCs support students from underrepresented racial/ethnic groups and those who have been historically disenfranchised, including women as well as lesbian, gay, bisexual, and transgender (LGBT) students. Several colleges have established women's centers, international student centers, and culture centers for racially underrepresented populations. Such facilities allow students who share common histories, cultures, customs, and challenges to support each other in an environment designed to meet their specific needs. These centers can also promote cross-cultural interactions among students.

This chapter provides a clearer understanding of MACCs and how their collaboration with other campus entities, particularly SAOs, could enhance college experiences for multicultural and ethnic students through educational and social programming. We first explore factors that contributed to the establishment of MACCs at predominantly White institutions (PWIs), and how these factors have influenced missions and operating philosophies. We interpret the current mission and values espoused by MACCs, and explore barriers that hinder collaboration between SAOs and MACCs. Finally, we offer programmatic ideas for SAO and MACC collaboration.

HISTORICAL DEVELOPMENT OF CULTURE CENTERS
AND MULTICULTURAL AFFAIRS

To effectively discuss the collaboration between SAOs and MACCs, we must understand the historical context in which they were established, as well as the role students played in seeking greater societal and educational equality. Shuford and Palmer (2004) and Patton (2005) contend that many minority affairs offices were established when large numbers of students of color, primarily African American students, were allowed mass admission into PWIs in the 1960s. Several pivotal moments in history precipitated this.

MACCs can trace their roots primarily to two periods: the Civil Rights Movement (mid-1950s to early 1970s) and the Multicultural Movement in higher education (early 1970s to present). The Civil Rights Movement illustrated the extent to which the United States confronted challenges to its social and philosophical paradigm of segregation and inequality, including educational policy. Examples of the struggle to embrace a more progressive social paradigm were demonstrated through the *Brown v. Board of Education* (1954) decision; the March on Washington (1963); the assassinations of John F. Kennedy (1963), Malcolm X (1965), and Martin Luther King Jr. (1968); and the Vietnam War (1959–1975). These events manifested themselves on college campuses the same way they did in the broader American population, through sit-ins, marches, protests, hunger strikes, and other forms of civil disobedience. These events, combined with a more liberal approach to higher education, gave birth to the Multicultural Movement in higher education, discussed later.

CIVIL RIGHTS AND BLACK STUDENT MOVEMENTS

In the late 1950s, college students began to play a critical role in the Civil Rights Movement. The sit-in at Woolworth's lunch counter in Greensboro, North Carolina, may be the most notable demonstration because it brought public attention to Black student involvement in the Civil Rights Movement. Students also formed activist organizations such as the Student Non Violent Coordinating Committee (SNCC). By the mid-1960s, amid continuing societal unrest, Black student involvement in the Civil Rights Movement began to dissipate; students were influenced by the Black Panther Party and newly elected SNCC leader, Stokely Carmichael, who espoused the idea of "Black Power" (Patton, 2005; 2006a). The focus moved from the larger society onto the college campus where student unrest was steadily rising. Federal legislation gave Black students greater access to PWIs, and their numbers increased significantly.

Despite the swelling Black enrollment at these institutions, campus administrators had done very little to prepare for the arrival of these students. African American students were expected to assimilate into the White racial fabric of PWIs and accept the existing institutional culture—a culture plagued by racism, oppression, and discrimination. Unwilling to assimilate or forfeit their own cultural values and identity, African American students and their allies began to protest and conduct sit-ins, demanding that PWIs hire more African American faculty, admit more African American students, include African American topical areas in the curriculum, and provide offices and facilities where they could meet and commune in a safe, nonhostile environment (Patton, 2005).

Patton (2004) noted, "Following their entrance into PWIs, which were not prepared to meet their needs, Black students galvanized to have their voices heard and their presence recognized" (p. 22). Their goal was to make universities more relevant to Black students and the larger Black community. By the late 1960s, several colleges and universities acquiesced to Black student demands and established minority affairs offices and Black culture centers. Young (1991) wrote: "The first Black cultural centers were viewed by students and staff as safe havens in an alien environment . . . minority centers were viewed as a necessary and just alternative to this environment" (p. 18). The efforts of Black students and their supporters were pivotal in the creation of Black culture centers and minority affairs offices at PWIs. By the early to mid-1970s, ethnic culture centers for Latino and Asian students were established, stemming from similar protests and requests from students. Culture centers and multicultural affairs offices on many campuses handled multiple functions and in some ways resembled a "mini student affairs division" by recruiting, overseeing precollege enrichment programs, advising, and planning social or educational programs (Shuford & Palmer, 2004).

MULTICULTURAL MOVEMENT

Around the late 1970s and early 1980s, the Multicultural Movement began to surface in higher education. It became abundantly clear during this movement that diversity and multiculturalism were values that should be reflected in higher education. This period was marked by a commitment from the federal govern-

ment and university leadership to increase the successful enrollment, matriculation, and graduation of racial minorities to be at least congruent with the racial
minority population in the United States. Policy initiatives such as the Higher
Education Act of 1965 helped increase racial minority enrollment by 56% between
1971 and 1981 (Office of Minority Concerns, 1985).

Another important indicator of the Multicultural Movement was the
Commission on Minority Participation in Education and American Life's publication of *One Third of a Nation* (1988). The commission's report documented the
American Council on Education's (ACE) estimates of the rising racial minority
populations. It also documents the federal government's concern about minority
populations' full participation in American life, including postsecondary educational opportunities. The report challenged American educational leaders to
renew and strengthen efforts toward recruitment, retention, and graduation of
racial minority students. Among the report's recommendations were creating an
academic atmosphere that nourishes minority students, creating a campus culture
that values the diversity minority students bring to campus life, and enhancing
the academic curriculum to reflect the experiences of non-European cultures
(Commission on Minority Participation in Education and American Life, 1988).

One result of the Multicultural Movement was the establishment of African/
Black Studies academic programs at PWIs. Ethnic and gender studies programs
also began to emerge. The curriculum was expanded to reflect a more interdisciplinary perspective in course offerings, research, and scholarship. Some colleges
even added multicultural courses to their graduation requirements for all students.
The impact could be seen in more than the curriculum; what is recognized today
as the office of multicultural affairs was established. Some Black culture centers
and other dedicated ethnic support facilities remained intact, while other institutions collapsed their culture centers and minority affairs offices into multicultural
affairs offices or multicultural centers. In some cases, college and university
administrators were demonstrating their desire to connect with the larger campus
community. Their actions were viewed as an attempt to become politically correct.
Much of the progress of the Multicultural Movement has been (and still is) challenged and thwarted by opponents of diversity.

Opponents argued that colleges and universities were simply appeasing
groups who considered themselves to be victims of oppression; doing so, they said,
lowered standards and created double-standards that were crippling students,

under the guise of diversity. Such opposition was disguised as a politically correct effort toward diversity issues; no true commitment or belief in the value of diversity and multiculturalism existed underneath. Patton (2006b) also highlighted the misconceptions that often plague race-specific support services, such as perceptions of self-segregation, erroneous assumptions that such services are geared *only* toward one particular group, and the flawed notion that these offices or centers *only* serve a social mission. She challenged these ideas and asserted that MACCs (Black culture centers in particular) validated students' experiences, served as a springboard for their involvement in larger campus activities, created a sense of community, and facilitated identity development. Despite the challenges and backlash against diversity and multiculturalism, MACCs still provided a great deal of service to racially underrepresented students and their outreach extended to the broader campus community (Shuford & Palmer, 2004). Also, offices and services geared toward women, GLBT students, and other populations were established, expanding the definition of campus diversity and multiculturalism.

CULTURE CENTER MISSIONS AND OPERATING PHILOSOPHIES

To date, no published work documents the first culture center or minority/multicultural affairs office. Young (1991) stated the earliest culture centers can be traced specifically from the mid-1960s to the early 1970s, and several of these still exist today. The Institute of Black Culture at the University of Florida was founded in 1972; the Paul Robeson Cultural Center at Penn State University and the J. D. O'Bryant African-American Institute at Northeastern University were founded in 1969; and the University of Maryland, College Park's Nyumburu House was established in 1971. While culture centers and minority affairs offices continue to exist, they have at times been criticized as promoting separatism on campus. Patton (2004) asserted that a clearer understanding of these centers might lend some clarification to their actual programs, student uplift, and their missions. Most MACCs have mission statements that include a directive to provide opportunities for experiencing and learning about the value of racial/ethnic diversity on their respective campuses. Na'im Akbar (1993) articulated four functions of the culture center:

1. The culture center must contribute to identity development and validation.

2. The culture center must provide programs and services that encourage the broader university community to increase its knowledge of ethnic identity.

3. The culture center must be student-centered and serve as an advocate for students.

4. The culture center, through programs and services, must bridge the gap between disciplines and administrative areas by encouraging collaboration.

Similarly, Shuford and Palmer (2004) offer the following mission of minority/multicultural affairs offices:

1. The office should provide support to underrepresented ethnic groups.

2. The office should provide multicultural education for all students.

3   The office should promote systemic change that fosters a multicultural perspective across the campus.

As one might interpret, these functions could very easily be found within the missions of many college unions and student activities offices. As a result, the culture center and multicultural affairs office are typically found within the student affairs division.

UNDERSTANDING HOW LOCATION AND OPERATIONAL PHILOSOPHIES AFFECT THE LARGER CAMPUS PERCEPTION OF MULTICULTURAL AFFAIRS AND CULTURE CENTERS

Young (1991) has discussed how the MACC and its location, structure, and operating philosophy contribute to its perception by the broader campus community. Young (1991) recommends that under ideal circumstances the MACC should be located in a freestanding, highly visible facility close to the center of campus. Though this may be the ideal, student life administrators recognize that promoting diversity has not always been perceived as an important institutional value. The MACCs on some campuses are still functioning in their original facilities, having undergone little or no major renovation, and in some cases, far from the daily traffic of campus. The perception of the MACC as separatist and unwelcoming is heightened by this isolation from the mainstream of campus life. Young (1991) categorized the operating philosophy of MACCs into two distinct approaches that also can have an impact on campus perception: the fortress philosophy and the oasis philosophy.

The fortress approach argues that students from racially underrepresented populations use the MACC as a safe haven. It suggests that allowing perceived outsiders to infiltrate the MACC dilutes its authenticity (Hannon, 2001). For example, continued use of a Black culture center by White students could impact the number of Black students who use the facility; they may not feel comfortable with White students in a space they perceive and believe is designated specifically for Black students. Young (1991) wrote:

> . . . the cultural center is a safe haven for students who, feeling . . . under attack adopt the *laager* mentality . . . If the . . . others . . . are allowed in, they will take everything . . . In the safe haven model, every effort is made to preserve the self-perceived purity of the culture. (p. 52)

In the second philosophy, the MACC operates as an oasis. The MACC welcomes anyone who wants to participate in what it has to offer. The facility is "shared willingly with everyone and the property of all who seek [it] out . . . the ethnic minority center is viewed as a place of relief from the surrounding sameness . . . where cultures meet, exchange, interact, and then emerge renewed . . . made stronger by the sharing" (Young, 1991, p. 52).

Under ideal circumstances, the MACC should operate under the oasis model, but given the ever-changing climate of campuses, it may use elements of either approach at different times. The adaptability of the MACC to meet different students' needs once again makes it an ideal department for collaborative efforts with other campus entities. The MACC can also serve as a supplementary resource in the student academic and social experience, for example by providing advisors and cosponsoring social and educational programs. MACCs also can enhance student enrollment by participating in recruitment.

It is common for the MACC to have a formal relationship with student organizations that have similar missions. Cosponsored activities between the MACC and student organizations often include cultural festivals, sorority and fraternity step shows, lectures, and art exhibits. In addition, multicultural affairs offices and culture centers have traditionally sponsored major campus programs such as Kwanzaa and ethnic commemorative months (i.e., Black History Month) that solicit volunteers and cosponsorship from student organizations. Staff members of MACCs provide important advising and support to student organizations, which often have difficulty finding suitable advisors who understand their goals, mission, and culture; this is especially true for Greek-letter organizations. These organizations seek advisory leadership from MACCs because they perceive the staff to be more open and willing to assist them.

MACCs also can play a strong role in recruitment initiatives. Hefner's article (2002) "Black Cultural Centers: Standing on Shaky Ground?" discussed the possible future of cultural centers at PWIs: "Cultural centers are a critical part of recruiting and retaining students of color at White colleges and universities" (p. 26). Many admissions offices, guided by university policies to diversify the incoming first-year student cohort, will seek to build a partnership with the multicultural affairs or ethnic centers. Admissions office employees can benefit from the cultural resources available: input from MACC staff on factors that attract this population; brochures and materials that can be sent to prospective students; and programs for students during campus visits. For MACCs, this partnership provides early outreach to targeted populations, giving them a sense of the resources available to them at the institution. Students who have a keen awareness of the support systems in place may find it easier to choose which college to attend.

MACCs can also play a significant role in student retention. Career services, academic advising offices, residential life, and academic affairs are all departments that can benefit from partnerships with MACCs. Shuford and Palmer (2004) asserted that MACCs were instrumental in helping faculty members create courses, establishing academic departments, and promoting interdisciplinary curricula such as ethnic studies. Moreover, MACCs made advisors and counselors aware of the issues facing racially underrepresented students so they could effectively help the students. While these examples certainly demonstrate the possibilities of collaboration, there are also barriers to building partnerships—especially with student activities offices, which often compete with MACCs for the attention and participation of racially underrepresented students in out-of-class activities.

BARRIERS TO COLLABORATION BETWEEN MACCS AND SAOS

Several factors might hinder collaborative efforts between SAOs and MACCs. Generally, SAOs provide a breadth of services that include educational, recreational, and leisure programming; consultation services to student organizations (i.e., program planning, budget management, officer training); and leadership education programs. MACC and SAO administrators must be willing to identify and overcome hindrances to effective collaboration if they are to maximize student engagement. Hindrances include, but are not limited to, institutional climate; inaccurate campus perception of the MACC; policies and procedures specific to the MACC or SAO; and fear of consolidation.

One major obstacle that can prevent meaningful collaboration is institutional culture, which can either support or discourage collaboration. The extent to which MACC and SAO staff believe upper-level administrators are sincere about collaboration can determine the extent to which they reach out to collaborate with one another. When MACC, SAO, or other student life administrators believe that positive outcomes for their respective units result from sole ownership of programming initiatives, they are less likely to initiate collaborative programs. Another potential obstacle for collaboration is campus perception of the MACC and the SAO. As students become more engaged with the activities of the MACC, a sense of ownership naturally evolves. This may send an overt or covert message to White students, for example, that their presence at the MACC is not welcomed or valued. This is the epitome of the fortress mentality.

Likewise, racially underrepresented students can very easily perceive the SAO as catering only to White students. As a result, they may perceive that mainstream activities are not welcoming of diverse participants or perspectives. For example, traditional university events that are rooted in Whiteness, such as homecoming or Greek Week, may be perceived as unwelcoming and to some degree boring by racially underrepresented students. Such perceptions of these administrative areas can prevent meaningful engagement and exchange.

A third hindrance to collaboration between the SAO and the MACC is separate policies and procedures for each. Because the MACC targets a specific community of students, faculty, and staff in its outreach, its policies may cater specifically to that population. The MACC may have its own events management processes, allocation procedures for student organizations, and even cosponsorship guidelines. The SAO may have difficulty working within the boundaries and guidelines of the MACC operation.

One last hindrance to collaboration is fear of consolidation, particularly for MACCs. MACC administrators often find themselves justifying the existence, outreach, impact, and rationale of their programs to campus and community critics. Other administrative units whose target population and services are specialized—women's centers, LGBT student support centers, religious or interfaith centers—must also balance the task of meeting the needs of their target audience and justifying why specialized services are needed. When the MACC cannot clearly justify its existence to the satisfaction of influential critics, the fear of consolidation becomes relevant. Hefner's (2002) article quotes one MACC administrator as saying, "We . . . get caught up in a zero-sum game because they think resources are scarce" (p. 25). Another administrator noted, "Tensions have occurred essentially on campuses where there is only one center—and . . . students are fighting for a bigger piece of the pie" (p. 25). All these factors can inhibit collaboration between the MACC and the SAO.

RECOMMENDATIONS FOR COLLABORATION BETWEEN SAOs AND MACCs

These recommendations may help increase collaboration between multicultural affairs and culture centers and various offices within student affairs divisions.

COLLABORATION THROUGH ORIENTATION

On many campuses, SAOs coordinate orientation activities, where students learn about opportunities for involvement in student government, programming boards, community service, and Greek life. This is a prime opportunity for the MACC to become a visible partner in meaningful engagement to the incoming first-year and transfer class. Patton (2006a) suggests that Black culture centers play a crucial role in reaching out to Black first-year students, letting them know they have a space and a support system. She notes that Black culture centers often provide welcome week and orientation activities that do not undermine similar universitywide programs, but instead provide more detailed information not necessarily covered in the broader program (i.e., finding hair products, ethnic food, and churches). The MACC can present information on involvement opportunities in partnership with the SAO and broadly discuss the potential for student life enrichment through both special interest and mainstream campus organizations. Patton (2006) wrote, "Because first-year programming is so critical to student adjustment, BCC directors and staff should work toward fostering collaborative relationships with other campus offices . . ." (p. 642).

COLLABORATION FOR LEADERSHIP DEVELOPMENT

Many SAOs engage student leaders in some form of leadership education. This presents at least two opportunities for collaboration. The first is involving the MACC in planning and coordinating the classes, perhaps by including diversity issues. Topics such as *Multicultural Competencies for Effective Leadership* or *Understanding Diversity's Place in Leadership* could significantly contribute to any leadership education course.

The second area for potential collaboration in leadership education is student leadership retreats. How often do ethnic minority student leaders, primarily loyal to the MACC, attend SAO leadership retreats? Patton (2006b) noted that without involvement in their culture center, students were less likely to get involved in larger, more mainstream campus activities. Through their involvement with cultural centers, these students gained valuable skills that would easily transfer to leadership roles on campus. Where resources permit, the MACC might sponsor its own student leadership retreat as well. The MACC and the SAO might consider appointing student leaders to attend each other's retreats to become familiar with issues important to each community. This undoubtedly can open up possibilities for increased collaboration, not only between the offices, but also among the student organizations advised by these offices.

PROGRAMMING BOARD COLLABORATION

For effective student input and advocacy, both MACCs and SAOs commonly use programming boards. Through these boards, students can voice their opinions on programs and activities, and coordinate the events they deem most appealing to their peer constituency groups. With collaboration between the MACC and SAO programming boards, the potential for engaging more of the student body is greater. Collaboration can take the form of broader campus programming such as the Dr. Martin Luther King Jr. Celebration or various heritage months, or it could consist of late-night programming, lecture series, bus trips, movie series, plays, and other functions typical of both the SAO and the MACC.

COLLABORATION FOR DIVERSITY EDUCATION

As institutions of higher education seek greater diversity and multiculturalism, they must ensure their students have greater opportunities to interact cross-culturally in settings that welcome challenging dialogue. The SAO and MACC are in an optimal position to collaborate on diversity education programming that introduces students to general concepts and allows them to learn about and from one another. While many students participate in organizations based upon commonalties and comfort, a diversity education program can encourage them to move beyond their comfort zones to learn about other cultures, and accept and embrace difference. Through partnering for diversity education, students of all backgrounds gain a higher level of consciousness.

Such an effort might be best spearheaded by the SAO and the MACC. Both offices stand to gain from this effort because students affiliated with the offices individually can come together collectively for diversity education training. The SAO and MACC would be modeling the way for their students, helping them understand the possibilities of collaboration. Because MACCs have the trust and respect of racially underrepresented students, their staff can encourage students to understand the importance of interacting with students beyond the office. They can help students understand that collaboration does not erase their uniqueness, but rather enhances their ability to connect with others. The SAO, which often has a larger budget, can enhance marketing and provide facilities for a diversity education program, while the MACC can lend great resources for formulating the diversity education components. Encouragement from the SAO is crucial for getting majority-culture students involved—especially because of the often misconstrued notion that diversity means only Black students or other racially underrepresented populations.

COLLABORATION FOR OVERALL ENGAGEMENT

Many students find affiliation with the SAO or the MACC and rarely go beyond those boundaries to explore other opportunities offered elsewhere on campus. When the SAO and the MACC collaborate by cosponsoring organizational fairs and workshops, they can bring students into a setting that exposes them to other forms of involvement. It may be helpful to have highly involved students from both entities tell audiences how their collegiate experiences have been enhanced as a result of participating in SAO and MACC activities. Equally important for increasing overall involvement is to create informational brochures or Web sites with SAO and MACC information linked or cross-referenced. The content should highlight benefits for all students of greater involvement in the SAO and MACC. The MACC and the SAO also can create a joint student ambassador team to reach out to the campus community and encourage all students to get involved with the programs and services of the MACC and SAO.

CONCLUSION

These examples are not a complete list of collaborative opportunities for the SAO and MACC, but rather are a springboard for a discussion about collaborative efforts. As student life administrators become more creative in finding ways to contribute to the student experience, the SAO and the MACC can and should be integral to that effort. The opportunities for collaboration and meaningful engagement are increased when these administrative areas can combine forces for the good of student development. Indeed, these suggestions might assist in the effective promotion of diversity and multiculturalism in college unions and student activities offices.

REFERENCES

Akbar, N. (1993). *The centering of Black culture* [Video lecture]. Tallahassee, FL: Mind Productions & Associates.

Commission on Minority Participation in Education and American Life. (1988). *One-third of a nation*. Washington, DC: American Council on Education & Education Commission on the States.

Hannon, M. D. (2001). *Hostel Robeson 2000–2001: The African/African-American cultural center's role during black student activism & unrest at Penn State University*. Position paper presented at 11th Annual Association of Black Cultural Centers Conference, Urbana, IL.

Hefner, D. (February 2002). Black cultural centers: Standing on shaky ground? *Black Issues in Higher Education, 18*, 22–29.

Office of Minority Concerns. (1985). *Fourth annual status report on minorities in higher education*. Washington, DC: American Council on Education.

Patton, L. D. (2004). From protest to progress? An examination of the relevance, relationships and roles of black culture centers in the undergraduate experiences of black students at predominantly white institutions (Doctoral dissertation, Indiana University, 2004). *Dissertation Abstracts International, 65*, 292.

Patton, L. D. (2005). Power to the people!: A literature review of the impact of black student protest on the emergence of black culture centers. In F. Hord (Ed.), *Black culture centers and political identities*. Chicago: Third World Press.

Patton, L. D. (2006a). The voice of reason: A qualitative examination of black student perceptions of the black culture center. *Journal of College Student Development, 47*(6), 628–646.

Patton, L. D. (2006b). Black culture centers: Still central to student learning. *About Campus 11*(2), 2–8.

Shuford, B. C., & Palmer, C. J. (2004). Multicultural affairs. In F. J. D. MacKinnon (Ed.), *Rentz's student affairs practice in higher education* (3rd ed., pp. 218–238). Springfield, IL: Charles C. Thomas.

Young, L. W. (1991). The minority cultural center on a predominantly white campus. In H. E. Cheatham (Ed.), *Cultural pluralism on campus.* Alexandria, VA: American College Personnel Association.

CHAPTER NINE

ooooo

Understanding the Difference Diversity Makes: Faculty Beliefs, Attitudes, and Behaviors

JEFFREY F. MILEM AND PAUL D. UMBACH

ooooo

I nstitutional mission statements at colleges and universities across the country increasingly reflect affirmations that diversity enhances higher education (Alger, 1997). Administrators, academics, and national educational associations (e.g., see recent initiatives and statements from the Association of American Colleges and Universities, American Association of University Professors, American Council on Education, and other organizations) offer compelling arguments about diversity's ability to expand and enrich the educational enterprise through the benefits it provides to individual students, to colleges and universities, and to our society and our world.

At the same time, the momentum on campuses for diversity is reaching unprecedented levels. Institutional leaders often find they must respond to attacks against an essential part of their educational missions. Opponents of affirmative action argue that increased racial and ethnic diversity on campus is not a compelling interest for colleges and universities, and assert that increased diversity leads to less vibrant educational communities (e.g., see recent statements by the National Association of Scholars).

Faculty members may be the campus constituency best positioned to assess how diversity influences teaching and affects student learning. Milem (1999) argues that faculty members serve as "human bridges" between an institution and its students, playing an integral part in helping colleges and universities achieve their educational goals, particularly in the classroom. A significant body of research examines different facets of faculty life, but relatively little of it examines how faculty view diversity on the campuses and in the classrooms. There are a few notable exceptions. Milem's (2003) and Milem and Hakuta's (2000) descriptions of faculty views of diversity are derived from a faculty survey conducted by the Higher Education Research Institute at the University of California, Los Angeles and a monograph published by the American Council on Education and the American Association of University Professors, *Does Diversity Make a Difference?* (2000). antonio (2002) found that faculty of color are more likely than their White colleagues to show "a higher commitment to research activities, stronger support for educational goals that encompass the affective, moral, and civic development of students, and in the more explicit connection they make between the work of their profession and service to society" (p. 594). Others have found that faculty of color more frequently use diversity in instruction, employ a broader range of pedagogical techniques, and interact more frequently with students than their White counterparts (Umbach, 2006).

The Student Learning Imperative (ACPA, 1994) called for student affairs educators to assume a central role in bridging the divide between the classroom and out-of-class experience of students. To be successful in this role, student affairs educators must know more about faculty members and what makes them tick—especially as it relates to their attitudes and behaviors about campus and classroom diversity. This chapter endeavors to do just that. In the following sections, we describe the different aspects of faculty and how their backgrounds and socialization influence their views and behaviors regarding the role of campus diversity.

THE SALIENCY OF DISCIPLINE

Earlier studies of faculty provide important insights into how faculty view diversity in their institutions, but they do not consider how these views vary by academic discipline. Disciplines play a critical role in the socialization of graduate students and college faculty, so any study of faculty views and behaviors must consider the influence of disciplinary affiliation in these views. Becher (1987) proposes a system for classifying academic disciplines derived from the earlier work of Biglan (1973a, 1973b). Becher's modification of the Biglan system proposes there are four major groupings of faculty: (a) the pure sciences or *hard-pure* fields, (b) the humanities or *soft-pure* fields, (c) the technologies or *hard-applied* fields, and (d) the applied social sciences or *soft-applied* fields. These categories are based on the nature of knowledge as viewed in the group and by the nature of the group's disciplinary culture.

The hard-pure group includes physicists and faculty in the physical sciences. They tend to view knowledge as cumulative and atomistic. This group is concerned mostly with universals, quantities, and simplification. They often believe that knowledge should result in further discovery or explanation. These faculty tend to be politically well organized. They usually have a high publication rate and are very task-oriented.

The soft-pure group includes historians, anthropologists, and other social science disciplines. These faculty view knowledge as reiterative and holistic, and are concerned with particulars, qualities, and complication. They think that knowledge should result in understanding and interpretation. Their culture is characterized as very individualistic and pluralistic; it is very loosely structured and person-oriented.

The hard-applied group includes engineers and faculty from other science technology fields. They tend to view knowledge as very purposive and pragmatic. These faculty are mainly concerned with mastering the physical environment, resulting in the development of new products or techniques. The culture is very entrepreneurial and cosmopolitan; it is dominated by professional values. In this group, patents can be substituted for publications.

Finally, the soft-applied group views knowledge as highly functional and utilitarian. They are concerned with the enhancement of professional practice. Discovery results in protocols or procedures. Education is an example of a soft-applied discipline. The culture is very outward looking and uncertain in its status. There is a tendency to be dominated by intellectual fashions and the group tends to be very power-oriented. Publication rates for this group tend to be reduced because so many of these faculty serve as consultants (Becher, 1987; Biglan, 1973a, 1973b).

OTHER FACTORS INFLUENCING FACULTY ROLE PERFORMANCE

Discipline is not the only factor that influences how faculty approach their work. Research on factors influencing the teaching methods used by faculty indicates that faculty background characteristics contribute greatly to the learning process (Easton & Guskey, 1983; Kozma, Belle, & Williams, 1978). Milem and Astin (1992) and Milem and Wakai (1996) found gender to be a positive predictor of student-centered teaching practices. Milem and Astin investigated science faculty's teaching techniques and found that female faculty in the sciences were more likely than male faculty to use active learning techniques such as class discussion, student-selected topics, and student-developed learning. Similarly, Milem and Wakai found race and gender to be important predictors of the likelihood that faculty would use a student-centered approach to teaching and learning in the classroom. Women as well as African American, Native American, Mexican American, and Puerto Rican faculty were more likely than their other colleagues to report using feminist pedagogy in the classroom, for example. Milem (2001) found a similar pattern of relationship between race and gender and using active learning techniques in the classroom, including the perspectives of women and racial/ethnic minorities in the curriculum, engaging in research on issues of race and ethnicity, and attending workshops designed to help them incorporate the perspectives of women and racial/ethnic minorities into their curricula. Statham, Richardson, and Cook (1991) examined gender and university teaching and found female professors to be more likely than their male colleagues to encourage student input and independence, and to view students as active collaborators in the learning process.

Other faculty characteristics that may influence teaching methods include academic rank and social status. Statham, Richardson, and Cook (1991) found that assistant professors were more likely than full professors to adopt participatory teaching practices. Mulkay's (1972) study on social status and innovation among scientists found that low-status or young scientists were more likely to be academically innovative because deviation from social norms posed little threat to their careers. In researching social status, Merton (1973) considered "outsiders" of an institution to be those having lower status and being frequently frustrated by the social system. Merton asserted that outsider status provides individuals with special perspectives and insights, which may compel them to inquire into problems relevant to their group and cause them to develop unique solutions. Similarly, Hill Collins (1986) wrote persuasively about the insights and perspectives offered by those who have outsider status within colleges and universities.

As teachers, outsiders may be more sensitive to classroom dynamics taken for granted by insiders. Gumport's (1987) study of the emergence of feminist scholarship supports the notion that personal status (being new, marginal, or an outsider to a field of study) may influence reform efforts. The group Gumport identified as *pathfinders* were feminist scholars politically active during the women's movement. They tended to remain peripheral to mainstream academic life because the institution's traditional values were contrary to their own political and intellectual agendas. Outsider status may have given the pathfinders a unique perspective that enabled them to work for innovative reform. This same tendency may also apply to faculty from other underrepresented groups, such as professors of color.

The nature of the organizational climate at colleges and universities can also shape the teaching and learning enterprise (Austin, 1996; Berger, 1997; Berger and Milem, 2000; Bowen, 1977; Finkelstein, 1984; Milem, 2001). Because they are proximal to individual experiences, organizational climates have the potential to influence personal behaviors (Dey, 1991). Mauksch (1980) suggested that institutional climate is linked to teaching practices because it provides faculty with the social norms for teaching. Astin (1993) found that student-oriented climates produce more positive student outcomes than almost any other environmental variable. Milem (2001) found that measures of the institutional climate for diversity at colleges and universities were significant predictors of the likelihood that faculty would employ more student-centered methods in the classroom, modify their curriculum to ensure the perspectives of women and racial/ethnic minorities are represented, attend faculty development sessions designed to help them incorporate these issues into their course content, and engage in research on issues of race/ethnicity.

A Study of Faculty Views and Behaviors

The remainder of this chapter is based on findings from our research study using data gathered by ACE and AAUP as part of a project to understand faculty views about diversity on campus. With the support of these organizations, a team of researchers developed the Faculty Classroom Diversity Questionnaire to address several constructs related to faculty beliefs about campus diversity. The sample included 1,210 randomly selected faculty at Carnegie Classified Research I institutions. The final survey response rate was 47%.

The study focuses on the relationship between academic discipline and faculty beliefs and behaviors related to classroom diversity; we used Becher's modification of Biglan's classification of disciplines. We placed faculty into four categories along two dimensions (hard/soft and pure/applied) of the Biglan classification of disciplines.[1] The four disciplinary groupings included 74 hard-applied faculty, 81 hard-pure faculty, 87 soft-applied faculty, and 193 soft-pure faculty. An "other" group included 95 faculty who did not fall into any of the categories.

RESULTS

We analyzed data in two stages. First, we explored the data using descriptive statistics (see Table 9.1). These data suggest that discipline is quite salient in predicting faculty beliefs about the effect of diversity in the classroom. For example, 54% of the hard-pure and 44% of the hard-applied faculty said that diversity never or rarely allows for variety in the classroom; in contrast, 21% of faculty in the soft-applied and 16% in the soft-pure disciplines responded that diversity never or rarely allows for variety in the classroom. When asked how often students in racially and ethnically diverse classrooms challenged racial stereotypes, 56% of the hard-pure faculty and 53% of the hard-applied faculty responded never or rarely; only 25% of the soft-applied and 22% of the soft-pure responded never or rarely.

Table 9.1. Select descriptive statistics.

	Taught ethnic studies course	Taught racial issues	Conducted res. on race	Taught women's studies	Taught women's/ gender issues	Conducted res. on women's issues
Biglan/Becher Categories						
Hard-Applied (N=74)	1.4	22.2	8.3	0.0	15.3	4.2
Hard-Pure (N=81)	2.5	17.5	12.5	8.8	27.5	12.5
Soft-Applied (N=87)	5.8	55.2	33.3	4.7	53.5	22.1
Soft-Pure (N=193)	15.4	60.0	30.4	10.6	60.6	40.0
Other (N=95)	11.6	55.8	29.5	12.8	59.6	34.4
All (N=530)	9.6	50.0	27.9	10.9	50.9	26.9
Race Ethnicity						
White (N=451)	5.9	49.8	23.8	12.2	51.0	27.5
African American (N=26)	38.5	69.2	61.5	7.7	61.5	26.9
Chicano/Latino (N=19)	36.8	57.9	63.2	21.1	68.4	31.6
Asian Pacific American (N=31)	12.9	41.9	38.7	6.5	35.5	26.7
All (N=530)	9.2	50.7	28.4	11.9	51.3	27.8

	Minorities raised issues	Diversity allows for variety	Interaction w/diversity expose different perspectives	Challenged stereotypes- racial issues	Challenged stereotypes- social issues
Biglan/Becher Categories					
Hard-Applied (N=74)	21.3	36.1	27.6	38.1	39.2
Hard-Pure (N=81)	9.7	28.7	22.2	24.6	30.4
Soft-Applied (N=87)	39.6	59.7	45.0	49.3	35.8
Soft-Pure (N=193)	34.7	57.8	39.1	44.2	47.4
Other (N=95)	34.8	58.2	41.6	41.1	45.2
All (N=530)	30.1	51.2	36.7	36.7	43.2
Race Ethnicity					
White (N=451)	28.1	40.7	35.5	32.4	41.0
African American (N=26)	61.6	61.6	50.0	66.6	62.9
Chicano/Latino (N=19)	47.4	73.7	33.3	64.7	64.7
Asian Pacific American (N=31)	30.7	40.0	46.1	50.0	47.7
All (N=530)	30.7	51.3	36.9	44.3	43.6

As we would expect based on earlier studies, race is another factor that is useful in predicting faculty beliefs about the effect of diversity in the classroom. White faculty were twice as likely as African American or Latino faculty to indicate students of color do not bring diverse perspectives to their classes. Almost half the White faculty (46%) responded that students of color never or rarely raised issues/perspectives not raised by White students in their classes, compared to 23% of the African American faculty and 21% of the Latino faculty. Similarly, when asked how often students in racially and ethnically diverse classrooms challenged racial stereotypes, 30% of the White faculty responded never or rarely, while 15% of the African American faculty and 17% of the Latino faculty responded never or rarely.

When we examined whether faculty were engaged in a selection of activities related to diversity, we also found differences between racial/ethnic groups and Biglan categories. Only 22% of the hard-pure faculty and 18% of the hard-applied faculty indicated they had taught a course that included racial or ethnic issues. In comparison, 69% of the soft-pure and 55% of the soft-applied faculty indicated they had included racial or ethnic issues in a course they had taught. When we examined whether faculty had conducted research focused on race we saw similar patterns. Only 13% of the hard-pure faculty and 8% of the hard-applied faculty indicated their research focused on race, while 38% of the soft-pure faculty and 33% of soft-applied faculty stated that they had done research focused on race.

The descriptive findings are consistent with earlier research indicating that race is a predictor of faculty behaviors related to diversity. Only 6% of White faculty indicated they had taught an ethnic studies class compared to 39% of African American faculty, 37% of Latino faculty, and 13% of Asian Pacific American faculty. Moreover, White faculty were more than 2.5 times *less* likely than African American and Latino faculty to indicate they were involved in research that addressed racial/ethnic issues. Among White faculty, 24% indicated their research focused on race, compared to 62% of African American faculty, 63% of Latino faculty, and 39% of Asian Pacific American faculty.

To further test these relationships, we constructed a series of regression models that predicted faculty attitudes, beliefs, and behaviors. See Table 9.2 for a summary of the regression results.

Table 9.2. Faculty attitudes, beliefs, and behaviors.

	Attitudes and Beliefs			Behaviors		
	Prepared to Teach	Benefits Classroom	Benefits White Students	Diversity Activities	Address in Teaching	Affects Research
Race/ethnicity and gender						
Asian/Pacific American	+					
Latino	+	+	+	+	+	+
African American	+		+			
Female		+	+	+	+	+
Academic discipline						
Hard-Applied						
Soft-Applied		+	+		+	
Soft-Pure		+	+	+	+	
Other		+		+	+	
Institutional emphasis						
Institutional priority		+	+			+

Note: A "+" indicates a statistically siginificant positive effect (p<.05). Models also include controls for whether the faculty member was born and educated outside of the United States, attended a historically Black college or university, percentage minorities at baccalaureate institution, percentage minorities at graduate institution, faculty rank, part-time/full-time status, age, years teaching, years in rank.

FACULTY ATTITUDES AND BELIEFS

We constructed three scales to represent faculty attitudes and beliefs about diversity and regressed each measure on a series of individual faculty measures. The first scale measures *how prepared faculty believed they were to teach about issues of diversity* and includes two items assessing perceived preparation and comfort. Faculty of color reported higher levels of preparedness to teach about diversity: African American, Latino, and Asian Pacific American faculty felt more prepared than White faculty to teach about diversity. The greater the emphasis an institution placed on diversity, the more prepared faculty report they felt to teach about diversity, regardless of race or ethnicity. Contrary to our hypothesis, discipline was not a significant predictor of faculty beliefs about their preparedness and comfort with teaching about diversity.

The second scale represented faculty beliefs about *how diversity benefits the classroom*. Some of the items in this scale include the frequency with which classroom diversity caused the class to be challenged by racial issues, challenged by social issues, and allowed for variety. When predicting faculty beliefs about the benefits of diversity in the classroom, several factors appear important. Compared with their male colleagues, female faculty indicated higher levels of perceived benefits. The racial/ethnic background of faculty appears to be less salient in predicting perceptions about the benefits of classroom diversity, as only Latino faculty indicated greater benefits of classroom diversity than White faculty. Academic discipline had a significant impact on faculty beliefs about the benefits of diversity. Both the soft-pure and soft-applied faculty were more likely than hard-pure faculty to report the benefits of diversity in the classroom. Faculty who perceived that their institutions placed a high priority on diversity were more likely to believe that diversity was beneficial than those who perceived their institutions to be less committed.

The third measure represents faculty beliefs about *whether diversity benefits White students*. Four items included in this scale solicited faculty views about how increased classroom diversity affected the issues White students considered in their coursework and the issues they addressed in their research for classes. Several individual characteristics were significantly related to the belief that diversity benefits White students. Women were more likely than men to report they believed that diversity benefits White students. African American and Latino faculty were more likely than White faculty to report they believe diversity benefits White students. As with the model predicting beliefs about the benefits of diversity in the classroom, the Biglan/Becher categories served as significant predictors of faculty beliefs about the benefits of diversity for White students. Faculty in both soft categories were more likely than hard-pure faculty to report that diversity is beneficial to White students. Institutional commitment to diversity significantly predicts faculty beliefs about the benefits of diversity for White students. Faculty who believed their institutions were committed to diversity were more likely to endorse the view that diversity benefits White students than faculty from other institutions.

Faculty Behaviors

We also constructed three measures to represent faculty behaviors related to diversity. The first of the scales, *faculty engaged in diversity related activities*, includes responses to items such as whether they had engaged in teaching an ethnic studies course, conducted research focused on race, taught a women's studies course, and attended a diversity awareness workshop. In the regression predicting engagement in diversity activities, a scale that includes two measures representing the frequency with which faculty had initiated discussions about diversity as well as their efforts to have students work together across race and gender served as significant predictors; women participated in diversity activities more frequently than men. Compared with White faculty, Latino faculty engaged more frequently in diversity activities. One Biglan/Becher category was a significant predictor of frequency of participation in diversity-related activities: faculty in soft-pure disciplines were more likely to participate in diversity activities.

Addressed diversity in teaching includes two measures of the frequency with which faculty initiated discussions about diversity as well as their efforts to have students work together across race. The model predicting whether faculty addressed diversity in their teaching is similar to the model predicting engagement in diversity activities. Women were more likely than men to include diversity-related information in their teaching. Latino faculty were more likely than White faculty to address diversity in their teaching. The Biglan/Becher categories were significant predictors of addressing diversity in teaching. Faculty from both the soft disciplines were more likely to address diversity in their teaching than faculty from the hard disciplines.

The final scale measured the extent to which faculty reported that *diversity affected their own research*. This scale included items such as whether diversity led to different research topics and whether classroom diversity affected faculty research. Again, women were more likely than men and Latino faculty were more likely than White faculty to have their research affected by diversity. None of the disciplinary variables were significantly related to diversity affecting research, but the perceived institutional commitment to diversity was positively related to diversity affecting research.

DISCUSSION OF RESEARCH FINDINGS

The analysis of factors related to faculty beliefs, attitudes, and behaviors about diversity suggest a complexity that is difficult to capture in a quantitative analysis. Even so, several themes emerge when we look across the models. First, consistent with findings of earlier research examining faculty attitudes and behaviors toward campus diversity, gender, and race/ethnicity serve as significant predictors of diversity-related faculty outcomes. Faculty of color and women faculty tend to hold more positive beliefs about the impact and benefits of diversity and are more likely to engage in research and teaching activities related to diversity. Using a nationally representative sample of faculty from four-year colleges and universities in a study of faculty role performance, Milem (1999) and antonio (2001) reported similar findings. There is one interesting caveat in our study of research university faculty. In our analyses, we see that the predictive power of being an African American faculty member appears to be confounded substantially by the inclusion of measures of HBCU attendance and of disciplinary grouping in the regression equations. More than one in four African American faculty reported they had attended an HBCU. In addition, of the African American faculty in our sample, 40% were in soft disciplines.

Our findings suggest that discipline is highly salient in predicting faculty views and behaviors regarding campus diversity. Specifically, faculty from the soft fields, and in particular, the soft-pure disciplines, are more likely to engage diversity in their work and to see the benefits of diversity in higher education.

We also found that institutional climate is a significant predictor of faculty attitudes and behaviors regarding diversity. Consistent with a previous study by Milem (2001), the findings of this study reinforce the effect of faculty perceptions of their institution's diversity climate in shaping their views and behaviors. Faculty from institutions they believed were committed to diversity were more likely to report that diversity benefited the teaching and learning environment in their classrooms and were more likely to incorporate diversity-related issues into their own scholarship. It is not clear whether this finding suggests that institutions with a climate supporting diversity are better able to recruit faculty who are more likely to believe that diversity is beneficial, or whether by creating a supportive environment for diversity, institutions can create pressures that encourage faculty to change their beliefs and behaviors. We suspect it is probably a combination of both.

Conclusion and Implications

The findings of our research have implications for theory and practice, as well as for informing the legal debate on diversity in higher education. The results extend our understanding of the influence of personal characteristics, career-related measures, disciplinary affiliation, and perceptions of institutional climate on the diversity-related views and behaviors of college and university faculty. Evidence of this is found in the descriptive and multivariate analyses we conducted.

As with findings from previous research, this study identifies the important contributions of women and people of color to their roles as faculty members. They are much more likely to understand how diversity benefits teaching and learning, to incorporate diversity-related information into the content of their courses, and to examine diversity-related themes in their own research. Moreover, this study speaks to the valuable insight and commitment that faculty who were educated in diverse educational settings bring to our campuses.

Given the significant disciplinary differences in faculty views about diversity in the classroom, our findings suggest that faculty from selected disciplines (the hard-pure and hard-applied fields) could benefit from development activities designed to help them use the increasing diversity of their classrooms. Our analyses suggest these faculty members are much less likely to recognize or to place value on the ways diversity can be used to enhance teaching and learning in their classrooms. Working with other campus constituencies to reach out to faculty in these disciplines, student affairs educators can play an important role in helping faculty understand the opportunities for teaching and learning that campus diversity provides, and help them develop the skills they need to achieve these benefits in their classrooms.

With the many legal challenges to race-conscious policies and practices on college campuses, there is clearly a need for more empirical research like this study. The diversity of our college and university campuses will continue to grow because our population is becoming increasingly diverse. Sometime around the middle of this century, we will become a "majority minority" nation. It is crucial that we better understand the impact of diversity on the teaching and learning process. By understanding how to maximize opportunities for teaching and learning and minimize the challenges increased diversity presents, we can work to create campus environments that enhance learning outcomes for all students. By expanding their knowledge about what makes faculty tick and using this information to reach out and create academic and student affairs partnerships, student affairs educators can play an important role in this process.

References

American College Personnel Association (1994). *The student learning imperative: Implications for student affairs.* Washington, DC: Author.

antonio, a. l. (2002). Faculty of color reconsidered: Reassessing contributions to scholarship. *Journal of Higher Education, 73*(5), 582–602.

Astin, A. W. (1993). *What matters in college? Four critical years revisited.* San Francisco: Jossey-Bass.

Austin, A. (1996). *Institutional and departmental cultures: The relationship between teaching and research: New Directions for Institutional Research, No. 90* (pp. 57–66). San Francisco: Jossey-Bass.

Becher, T. 1987. The disciplinary shaping of the profession. In B. R. Clark (Ed.), *The academic profession.* Berkeley, CA: University of California Press

Berger, J. B., & Milem, J. F. (2000). Organizational behavior in higher education and student outcomes. In J. C. Smart (Ed.), *Higher education: Handbook of theory and research* (Vol. XV, pp. 268–338). New York: Agathon Press.

Berger, J. B. (1997). *The relationship between organizational behavior at colleges and student outcomes: Generating a quantitatively grounded theory.* Unpublished doctoral dissertation, Vanderbilt University, Nashville.

Biglan, A. 1973a. The characteristics of subject matter in different academic areas. *Journal of Applied Psychology, 57,* 195–203.

Biglan, A. 1973b. Relationships between subject matter characteristics and the structure and output of university departments. *Journal of Applied Psychology, 57,* 204–213.

Bowen, H. (1977). *Investment in learning.* San Francisco: Jossey-Bass.

Dey, E. L. (1991). *Perceptions of the college environment: An analysis of organizational, interpersonal, and behavioral influences.* Unpublished doctoral dissertation, University of California, Los Angeles.

Easton, J., & Guskey, T. (1983). Estimating the effects of college, department, course, and teacher on course completion rates. *Research in Higher Education, 19*, 153–158.

Finkelstein, M. (1984). *The American academic profession. A synthesis of social scientific inquiry since World War II.* Columbus, OH: Ohio State University Press.

Gudeman, R. H. (2000). College missions, faculty teaching, and student outcomes in a context of low diversity. In *Does diversity make a difference? Three research studies on diversity in college classrooms.* Washington, DC: American Council on Education and American Association of University Professors.

Gumport, P. (1987). *The social construction of knowledge: Individual and institutional commitments to feminist scholarship.* Unpublished doctoral dissertation, Stanford University, Stanford, CA.

Hill Collins, P. (1986). Learning from the outsider within: The sociological significance of Black feminist thought. *Social Problems, 33*(6), 514–532.

Kozma, R., Belle, L., & William, G. (1978). *Instructional techniques in higher education.* Englewood Cliffs, NJ: Educational Technology Publications.

Marin, P. (2000). The educational possibility of multi-racial/multi-ethnic college classrooms. In *Does diversity make a difference? Three research studies on diversity in college classrooms.* Washington, DC: American Council on Education and American Association of University Professors.

Maruyama, G. and Moreno, J. F. (2000). University faculty views about the value of diversity on campus and in the classroom. In *Does diversity make a difference? Three research studies on diversity in college classrooms.* Washington, DC: American Council on Education and American Association of University Professors.

Mauksch, H. (1980). What are the obstacles to improving quality teaching. *Current Issues in Higher Education, 2*(1), 49–56.

Merton, R. (1973). *The sociology of science: Theoretical and empirical investigations*. Chicago: The University of Chicago Press.

Milem, J. F., & Astin, H. S. (April, 1992). *Science faculty: Culture, roles and pedagogy*. Paper presented at the annual meeting of American Educational Research Association.

Milem, J. F. (1999, January). *The importance of faculty diversity to student learning and to the mission of higher education*. Paper presented at A Symposium and Working Research Meeting on Diversity and Affirmative Action, American Council on Education, Washington, DC.

Milem, J. F. (2001) Diversity is not enough: How campus climate and faculty teaching methods affect student outcomes. In G. Orfield (Ed.), *Diversity challenged: Legal crisis and new evidence* (pp. 233–249). Cambridge, MA: Harvard Education Publishing Group.

Milem, J. F., & Hakuta, K. (2000). The benefits of racial and ethnic diversity in higher education. In D. J. Wilds (Ed.), *Minorities in higher education, 1999-2000* (pp. 39-67). Washington, DC: American Council on Education.

Milem, J. F., & Wakai, S. (1996, November). *Understanding how faculty teach: Facilitators and inhibitors of student-centered pedagogy*. Paper presented at the annual meeting of the Association for the Study of Higher Education, Memphis.

Milem, J. F. (2003). The educational benefits of diversity: Evidence from multiple sectors. In M. J. Chang, D. Witt, J. Jones, & K. Hakuta (Eds.), *Compelling interest: Examining the evidence on racial dynamics in higher education* (pp. 126-169). Palo Alto, CA: Stanford University Press.

Mulkay, M. (1972). *The social process of innovation: A study in the sociology of science*. London: Macmillan Press.

Statham, A., Richardson, L., & Cook, J. (1991). *Gender and university teaching: A negotiated difference*. Albany, NY: SUNY.

Umbach, P. D. (2006). The contribution of faculty of color to undergraduate education. *Research in Higher Education, 47*(3), 317–345.

NOTES

[1]Hard-pure disciplines included biology, geology, math, and chemistry. Hard-applied disciplines included engineering and agriculture. Soft-pure disciplines included English, history, philosophy, and foreign languages. Soft-applied disciplines included business, education, and economics.

Chapter Ten

○○○○○

Framing the Effect of Multiculturalism on Diversity Outcomes among Students at Historically Black Colleges and Universities

Brighid Dwyer[1]

○○○○○

H istorically Black colleges and universities (HBCUs) have been a tremendous asset for African Americans seeking higher education over the past 150 years (Anderson, 1988). Before 1950, traditionally Black institutions educated more than 75% of African American college students (Anderson, 1984). Although the percentage of African Americans educated at HBCUs has decreased to 20% since that time (U.S. Department of Education, 2005), retention rates among Black students at HBCUs are significantly higher than at traditionally White institutions (TWIs) (Redd, 1998). In addition, HBCUs reported better outcomes in student learning and self-confidence (Allen, 1992; 1996; Fleming, 1984). For example, compared to Black students at TWIs, Black students at HBCUs are more likely to report higher grade point-averages, better psychological development, greater satisfaction with campus activities and cultural support, and academic growth and maturity (Allen, 1987, 1992, 1996; Fleming, 1984). Moreover, students have better relationships with faculty and staff and are more likely to aspire to an advanced degree (Allen, 1996; Harvey & Williams, 1996). Furthermore, because of racially hostile campus climates at TWIs (Hurtado, 1996), HBCUs provide students with an alternative to predominantly White campuses wherein African American students may spend much of their time feeling alienated, frustrated, and unsupported (Oliver, Rodriguez, & Mickelson, 1985; Smith, 1989; Watson & Kuh; 1996).

However, greater numbers of African American students are choosing to attend TWIs over HBCUs (Allen & Jewell, 2002; Harvey & Williams, 1996; Redd, 1998). Harvey and Williams (1996) suggest that this shift has occurred because African American students now have a large array of institutions to choose from. As a result of the school desegregation acts of the 1950s (i.e., *Brown v. Board*, etc.) and the desegregation of higher education in the 1970s through the 1990s[2], HBCUs must now contend not only with being one of several institutions, historically Black or otherwise, from which African American students choose to attend, but must also consider admitting greater numbers of non-Black students into their institutions (Allen & Jewell, 2002; Blake, 1991; Brown, 2002). As a result of the greater numbers of White, Hispanic, Asian American, and Native American students attending HBCUs (Brown, 2002), the already existing international student population, and the diverse faculty that teach at these institutions (Anderson, 1988), HBCUs are becoming more racially diverse institutions.

The diversification of HBCUs has emerged as a result of factors specific to these institutions, yet despite the contributing factors, their bent toward diversity aligns with the recent push in higher education toward greater diversity, inclusion, and multiculturalism. Although diversity outcomes and multicultural curricula have been a part of an important discourse within mainstream higher education, these conversations have in large part neglected discussing multiculturalism and diversity outcomes at HBCUs. This investigation addresses this gap by examining the multiculturalism literature, as well as the literature specific to HBCUs, in an attempt to answer the question: *What is the effect of multiculturalism on diversity outcomes of HBCU students?*

DEFINING DIVERSITY OUTCOMES

Before progressing with the discussion, it is important to define the way in which the term *diversity outcomes* will be employed. In a 2002 research investigation conducted by Gurin, Dey, Hurtado, and Gurin, the concept *diversity experiences* was used to describe both the classroom and informal interaction with college students from diverse experiences. This term describes most closely the phenomenon that is investigated in this study. However, I use *diversity outcomes* as a way of capturing the experiences students have as they interact with diverse others within their college environment; as well as the ways in which these experiences shape the interactions students will have with the world once they graduate from college. This term has been chosen in order to shift the focus away from the broad term "learning outcomes," and a more specific term, "democracy outcomes." *Diversity outcomes* describes more specifically the learning that occurs from exposure to diversity. Furthermore, it is an attempt to intentionally highlight students' facility with diversity and draw closer connections between diversity experiences and multiculturalism.

CONTEXTUALIZING MULTICULTURALISM AND MULTICULTURAL EDUCATION

Multiculturalism within education is defined and contextualized in different ways depending on the specific educational field. The literature within higher education discusses multiculturalism in terms of democratic outcomes and the ways in which exposure to diverse others in college provides individual and societal benefits (e.g., Bowen & Bok, 1998; Gurin, et al., 2002; Hurtado, 2003; Milem, 1994). In comparison, the literature in educational studies on multiculturalism is described as, "a nonhierarchical approach that respects and celebrates a variety of cultural perspectives on world phenomena" (Asante, 1991b, p. 172). Furthermore, most often in educational studies, the topic of multiculturalism is discussed by using the term multicultural education (Banks, 1993). I have included literature from K-12 research in order to provide an additional perspective on multiculturalism in education and to discuss how these approaches may inform work in higher education, particularly the ways in which they contribute to a conceptual framework for understanding multiculturalism in HBCUs.

MULTICULTURALISM

The higher education literature contextualizes multiculturalism in two main ways, as democratic outcomes the ways in which exposure to multiculturalism in college provides benefits to the greater U.S. society (Bowen & Bok, 1998; Gurin, et al., 2002; Hurtado, 2003; Hurtado, Engberg, Ponjuan & Landreman, 2002);

and through curricular means (Clayton-Pedersen & Musil, 2003). Democratic outcomes are discussed first within the context of learning outcomes students acquire in college, and secondly in terms of the benefits to society attained as students are exposed to diverse others (antonio, 2001; Greene & Kamimura, 2003; Gurin, Dey, Gurin, & Hurtado, 2004; Gurin, et al., 2002; Hurtado, 2003; Hurtado, et al., 2002; Hurtado, Bowman, Dwyer, & Greene, 2004; Milem, 1994). These different discussions of multiculturalism, most often occur concurrently within studies and cumulatively demonstrate that diversity experiences influence students' learning in college, their sense of civic responsibility once they graduate, and better equip them to work in this increasingly diverse society (AAC&U, 2002; Carnevale & Fry, 2000; Gurin, et al., 2004; Gurin et al., 2002; Hurtado, 2003).

Some of the educational outcomes associated with interactions between students with diverse backgrounds include: cognitive skills (e.g., cognitive flexibility, socio-historical thinking, and critical thinking); socio-cognitive outcomes (e.g. leadership skills, social, and cultural awareness); democratic outcomes (e.g., propensity to vote in elections, a belief that conflict enhances democracy, and a concern for the public good), prejudice reduction, cultural awareness and cultural acceptance (antonio, 2001; Astin, 1993a; 1993b; Chang, 2001; Hurtado, 2003, Milem, 1994).[3]

Although all of the previously mentioned learning outcomes occur on college campuses, they each occur in different ways, and as a result of various campus circumstances. Research shows that structural diversity, or a critical mass of students from underrepresented groups, impacts students' interaction with diverse others on campus (Gurin, et al., 2002; Hurtado, Carter, & Kardia, 1998). Additionally, the literature is rich with quantitative studies that analyze the curricular, cocurricular, and informal experiences students have interacting with diverse peer groups (antonio, 2001; Hurtado, 2003; Hurtado, et al., 2002; Hurtado, et al., 2004; Greene & Kamimura, 2003; Pascarella, Edison, Nora, Hagedorn, & Terenzini, 1996).

Moreover, further literature on multiculturalism within higher education indicates that multiculturalism is found, practiced and implemented through the curriculum—either through required courses that meet what has been termed a "diversity requirement" (AAC&U, 1995a; AAC&U, 1995b; Levine & Cureton, 1992), or through departmental infusion of multiple perspectives into the curriculum (Levine & Cureton, 1992). While the departmental infusion is haphazard, the more common method of implementing multiculturalism into the curriculum has been through university-wide diversity requirements which expose students to experiences different from their own. These curricular experiences include courses on gender studies, ethnic studies, institutional or societal racism, religion, ethnicity, intolerance, and social class (Butler & Walter, 1991; Humphreys, 1997; Hurtado, Milem, Clayton-Pedersen, & Allen, 1999). In addition, diversity requirements may also take a more social justice orientation and analyze systems of inequality and discrimination (Humphreys, 1997).

MULTICULTURAL EDUCATION

The K–12 literature uses the term multicultural education and addresses it in a multifaceted way. Banks (1993) model of multicultural education considers several dimensions including: *content integration*, knowledge construction, prejudice reduction, equity pedagogy, and empowering school culture. Banks' (1993) *content integration* explains the extent to which teachers use "examples, data, and information from a variety of cultures and groups to illustrate key concepts, principles, generalization and theories" (p. 5). Furthermore, it pertains to Gay's (1997) discussion about multicultural infusion through the curriculum. *Knowledge construction* refers to the frames of reference and the cultural experiences that inform thinking and produce knowledge. Loewen (1995) and hooks (1990) purport that the knowledge constructed is dependent upon the frame of reference from which it is taught. *Prejudice reduction* describes strategies that can be used to enhance democratic values among students (Lynch 1987). Furthermore, prejudice reduction occurs not only through exposure to diversity within the curriculum, but is also affected by the racial awareness of children and occurs when youth have greater interaction with others of different racial and cultural backgrounds (Milner, 1983).

Equity pedagogy occurs when teachers utilize instructional techniques that are beneficial to students of various racial, ethnic, and socio-economic backgrounds. Banks' concept of *empowering school culture* builds off the previously discussed dimensions of multicultural education. Banks (1993) suggested that while content integration, knowledge construction, and equity pedagogy occur within the school, "the school itself can also be conceptualized as one social system that is larger than its interrelated parts (e.g., its formal and informal curriculum, teaching materials, counseling programs, and teaching strategies)," (p. 33) and schools are cultural systems with specific values, traditions, customs, and shared meanings (Willis, 1977).

The literature within higher education, as well as with educational studies, offer specific notions about what multiculturalism and multicultural education are and how they apply to specific settings. However, they do not address the way in which multiculturalism exists at HBCUs, nor the way multicultural education in K-12 settings relates to or prepares students for HBCUs. As a result, there is only a small collection of works that discuss aspects of multiculturalism at HBCUs.

MULTICULTURALISM AT HBCUs

Sims (1994) posited that multiculturalism should accessible to all students regardless of the institutional type they attend. Furthermore, she stated that experiences with diversity are just as important to foster at HBCUs as in other institutions of higher education. She echoed the majority of literature on diversity in higher education, stating that diversity promotes awareness, respect for difference, and a variety of cultures. In addition, Bey (2004) indicated the importance of multiculturalism at HBCUs by highlighting the 71% increase in White student enrollment at HBCUs between 1976 and 1994. Willie (1991) imparted that exposure to non-African American students is beneficial for African Americans as this helps disconfirm stereotypes. This exposure is particularly important due to highly segregated high school environments from which both African American and White college students come (Orfield, Frankenberg, & Lee, 2003).

With this in mind, multiculturalism at HBCUs is an important topic that warrants attention. The limited literature that is present on multiculturalism at HBCUs does not define itself as such, nor is it comprehensive. Rather, separate and unrelated pieces have been published covering various aspects of HBCUs including: curricular multiculturalism at HBCUs, White students at HBCUs, diverse faculty at HBCUs, identity development of students at HBCUs, and a single study on diversity outcomes at HBCUs. Within this article I will to bring this literature together forming a portrait of multiculturalism at HBCUs, and to identify areas for future research. Although these disparate studies relate to multiculturalism at HBCUs, they do so indirectly and some perhaps address it unintentionally. However, they are useful in this discussion because, as I will argue, they inform a conceptual framework for research that can directly address diversity outcomes and multiculturalism at HBCUs.

CURRICULAR MULTICULTURALISM AT HBCUs

In a mixed methods study conducted by Bey (2004), multicultural education at two HBCUs in Virginia was investigated. In her study, Bey sought to understand the ways in which multiculturalism is situated within the general education curriculum of HBCUs, how faculty and administrators defined it, and the extent to which there was an institutional responsibility to promote multicultural education. In this examination she found that in all of the general education courses with titles that suggest inclusion of underrepresented persons, only two of them included multiple perspectives, and according to her index, provided a moderate amount of multicultural education. Furthermore, both courses concentrated on people of African descent. However, in 45% of her interviews with faculty, respondents indicated that diversity was promoted not by the structure of the general education curriculum, but by the faculty within the classroom.

The chief academic officer at one of the institutions studied by Bey (2004) indicated that multiculturalism was at the core of their institution because of their diverse faculty and student population, as well as the "large number of multicultural and diversity courses taught throughout the curriculum" (p. 178). However, additional findings indicated that definitions of multicultural education included: appreciation of cultural differences, integration of cultural material, expanding knowledge, and valuing difference. Within these definitions, more than 50% of respondents at both institutions defined multiculturalism in terms of African American or Black experiences; thus indicating a very narrow definition of multiculturalism. Bey (2004) suggested that these definitions may indicate that respondents did not understand the multidimensional aspects of multiculturalism, or that the HBCU setting influenced the definition of the term.

Bey's (2004) research also found that faculty and administrators were split approximately 50-50 as to whether or not a multicultural education perspective should be included in discipline specific requirements, or be made a part of the general education requirements. Yet faculty suggested that they employed multicultural teaching tactics by encouraging students to insert their own experiences into educational contexts, allowing sources other than the instructor serve as information centers, and encouraging students to challenge conventional notions of knowledge. They also believed that multicultural education was an important empowerment tool for the well being of students. However, respondents indicated that issues pertaining to multiculturalism and the curriculum were not the most pressing ones at these institutions.

Bey's research finds that multicultural education does exist within the core curriculum at HBCUs, but not in the traditional sense. She suggests that HBCUs affinity toward African American centered multiculturalism is rooted in the history and mission of HBCUs to serve and prepare the African American community.

WHITE STUDENTS AT HBCUS

Brown (2002) indicates that in 1994 White students comprised 16.5% of the HBCU enrollment and that there have been significant demographic shifts within the HBCU student population since 1976. During this 18-year period there was a 19% decrease in African American enrollment, a 70% increase in White student enrollment, a 45% increase in Hispanic enrollment, a 274% increase in Asian student enrollment, and a 139% increase in the Native American student enrollment at HBCUs. Despite this growing diversity among the student body at HBCUs, research has focused almost exclusively on the experiences of White students on these campuses. This dearth in scholarship on other non-African American students at HBCUs is problematic and needs to be addressed; however, because of the nature of this review, I am limited to discussing existing research.

The growing number of White and other minority students at HBCUs has added an aspect of multiculturalism to HBCUs. By virtue of diverse students being present on campus, they are creating greater structural diversity (as defined in Hurtado, et al., 1999) at HBCUs which helps inform Banks (1993) dimensions of knowledge construction and prejudice reduction. However, as Hurtado, et al. (1999) and Gurin, et al. (2002) insisted, structural diversity is not enough. Simply because student bodies are more diverse on HBCU campuses it does not mean that a multicultural climate is being fostered. In fact, according to Conrad, Brier, & Braxton (1997), many White students choose to attend HBCUs not with the intension of diversifying HBCU campuses or interacting with African American students, but rather for specific reasons such as to enroll in particular majors or due to scholarships and financial aid. Conversely, Conrad and associates (1997) also found that some White students do attend HBCUs because of the welcoming environment they perceive on theses campuses and because they view them as multi-racial institutions that are supportive and inclusive.

However, while the above mentioned examples may speak to the reasons White students choose to attend HBCUs, the experiences they have on campus can be quite different than anticipated. One White student on Howard's campus explained that he "experienced pressure to remember that [he] was a guest and not challenge the campus culture" (Ruffins, 1999, p. 22). Furthermore, Sims (1994) found that African American students do not see White students as peers due to the historical experiences of slavery Whites have not endured.

Although the experiences White students have at HBCUs may be uncomfortable and challenging for them, studies have shown that the experiences they have interacting with diverse peers develops their sense of understanding and learning. Brown (2002) and Willie (1983) both stated that White students who attend HBCUs have greater ease communicating with people of different backgrounds. Furthermore, in her quantitative dissertation White (2000) highlighted this learning that White students obtain as she states:

> it is important that White students possess an opportunity to enhance their learning experience by developing an awareness and sensitivity to the Black student's experience, as well. Efforts in this direction may serve to counteract the pervasiveness of racial and ethnic stereotypes within the college environment. (p. 13)

Although White students seem to benefit from attending HBCUs, there is some concern about the ways in which greater numbers of White students at HBCUs will lead to changes in campus climate HBCUs and specifically to a decrease in service to African American students. Bluefield State University (BSU) is often presented as a case in point of such shifts. Once an institution with a large majority of African American students, in 1994 the student enrollment of BSU was 92% White as was the percentage of White faculty (Brown, 2002). Today, many argue that BSU bears very little resemblance to a traditional HBCU because its Black Greek organizations are absent, as is its marching band, and the president of this institution is White (Brown, 2002).[4] Because climate and culture are the primary contributors to African American student success at these institutions (Allen, 1992; 1996; Brown, 2002) there is great concern over the possibility of a changing climate at HBCUs.

Furthermore, although Brown (2002), White (2000), and Willie (1983) indicated the benefits White students experience from their attendance at HBCUs, direct connections are not drawn between the benefits White students obtain, the benefits Black students gain, and the campus contributions that can occur as a result of White student attendance at HBCUs. Overall the research was primarily concerned with the experiences of White students at HBCUs. However, the focus of this area of literature is either on the individual benefits White students experience from attending HBCUs, or the fear associated with White students' HBCU attendance. Thus, because of their growing and diversifying campuses, HBCUs do not appear to be promoting multiculturalism through interactions between their students from diverse backgrounds.

DIVERSE FACULTY AT HBCUs

Although the literature on democracy outcomes has focused almost exclusively on the peer to peer interactions of students, literature on structural diversity (see Gurin, et al., 2002; Hurtado, et al., 1998; Hurtado, et al., 1999) and learning outcomes states the important role faculty play in student learning and persistence (Tinto, 1997). Additionally, Bey (2004) indicated that a chief financial officer she interviewed stated that presence of a diverse faculty contributed to their institution being multicultural in nature. Furthermore, Allen (1992) noted that at HBCUs students have more positive relationships with faculty. Moreover, Harvey and Williams (1996) explained the importance of students interacting with diverse faculty by stating:

> Black colleges have always served as welcoming forums for visiting scholars, political statesmen, and business leaders, irrespective of their race, creed, or religion . . . Black colleges' students receive wide exposure to a variety of racial and ethnic groups, and they benefit from the exchange of diverse opinions and views. (p. 236)

In addition to being historically welcoming, HBCUs have attracted a diverse group of Latino, Asian American, and international scholars in more recent years. Yet, despite these shifts in population, the literature on non-African American HBCU faculty focuses on White faculty (Anderson, 1988; Jewell, 2002). Due to their White missionary founding, HBCUs have a history of having White as well as African American faculty members. Bey (2004) found that the presence of such faculty on HBCU campuses created a multicultural setting by which African

American students took classes from White professors and interacted with White faculty outside of class. However, Drewry and Doermann (2001) offered that during the 1980s as African American students began to choose to attend TWIs, African American faculty were heavily recruited to these institutions to help them become more diverse and supportive for African American students. In some cases HBCU faculty were recruited to TWIs and wooed by larger salaries. Although there has been a resurgence of African American students to HBCUs, acquiring African American faculty and retaining them still remains a struggle for HBCUs.

Despite this challenge some argue that HBCUs must retain an African American faculty and that having a multi-racial faculty composition on campus can be detrimental to the Afrocentric perspectives some HBCUs teach to their students (Johnson, 1971, as cited by Foster & Guyden, 2004). Johnson (1971) suggested that some White faculty teach at HBCUs out of convenience and never fully understand the culture of African Americans and HBCUs. However, as illustrated below, this is not the case for all White faculty members at HBCUs.

Foster and Guyden (2004) present a case study of a White male faculty member who worked at two HBCUs. Although this individual did not seek out employment at an HBCU he found that the experiences he had at these institutions was one from which he benefited tremendously. He was aware of the racial difference between himself and his students, and took advantage of situations in which racial identity was broached to create teaching moments for his students. Furthermore, he learned a great deal about himself, race, and the way in which he could teach history from multiple perspectives. Moreover, a study conducted by Willie, Grady, and Hope (1991) found that White faculty who left HBCUs to teach at TWIs were not satisfied because of the lack of faculty diversity and negative race relations on campus.

The few findings on faculty at HBCUs suggest that the environment is welcoming for African American and White faculty alike, and students at HBCUs benefit tremendously from the close interactions they have with these faculty members. However, other opportunities, including higher salaries at TWIs, draw instructors away from HBCUs.

IDENTITY DEVELOPMENT AT HBCUS

The present social and psychological conditions of African Americans are distinct from those of other racial and ethnic backgrounds, specifically due to the impact of slavery upon them (Merelman, 1993; White, 2000). Arnold (1997, as cited by White, 2000) found that environment plays a significant role in the adjustment of students to college. He stated that "students enter college with their own personalities, attributes, values, skills, and needs based on their prior experience in their homes, families, communities, and peer groups" (White, 2000, p. 23). Similar findings have been noted by many education scholars including Dey and Hurtado (1994) who found that "students bring values and attitudes associated with larger social forces into academe, thereby creating change within the higher education system" (p. 249).

In White's (2000) quantitative study of racial identity development at HBCUs and TWIs she coupled the research of Arnold (1997) with the historical experiences of African Americans. In doing so she indicated that African American students come to college not only with their family experiences, but embedded within these are historical experiences of being a descendent of enslaved people. In her study, White (2000) measured the racial identity brought to college by African American students who attended HBCUs and African American students who attended TWIs. Her findings suggested that this identity related to historical oppression brought to college by students is salient. Furthermore, White (2000) found that African American students at HBCUs reported greater gains in internal racial identity and cultural awareness than African American students at TWIs. Although her findings indicated positive racial identity outcomes for African American students at HBCUs, she also found that students at HBCUs reported that there was less of an emphasis on racial diversity.

Additionally, Sleeter (1991) believed it is imperative that African American students develop a sense of group identity because it helps them navigate the racialized educational and societal hardships they will face in school settings. Furthermore, Merleman (1993) stated that African American students come to school with "the makings of a strong sense of group identity on which the teaching of black history can build" (p. 336). He further suggested that African American students' excellence in African American history is a demonstration of group loyalty. Together these studies suggest the importance of identity and identity development among African Americans at HBCUs.

DIVERSITY OUTCOMES AT HBCUS

Through investigating literature on diversity outcomes at HBCUs only one study was found which dealt specifically with interracial interaction among students at HBCUs. This single study was Wathington's (2004) dissertation in which she examined the "relationship between pre-collegiate experiences, attitudes, and behaviors and the amount of interracial interaction students engage in before entering college" in four public research institutions, one of which was an HBCU (p. 11). The HBCU in Wathington's study was homogenous with 95% of students identifying racially as African American. Her research focused on specific pre-college characteristics of students including background characteristics, values, beliefs, and prior interracial interaction.

Wathington's findings indicated that of the entering HBCU students, the only background characteristic that predicted interracial interaction was race. Moreover, African American students beginning at this HBCU were more likely to interact with other African American students and less likely to interact with students of different racial backgrounds. Finally, Wathington determined that the values students perceive other groups to have are strong deterrents for cross-racial interaction.

Wathington's study established the pre-college effects of cross-racial interaction among students attending one public HBCU. Her introduction to this literature is valuable, yet it alone does not tell the story of cross-racial interaction or multiculturalism at HBCUs. However, together with Bey's (2004) research on multiculturalism in the HBCU curriculum, White's (2000) study on identity development at HBCUs, the research studies on White students and diverse faculty at HBCUs, a portrait of multiculturalism at HBCUs begins to emerge. It is the collective of these studies that informs my conceptualization of multiculturalism and diversity outcomes at HBCUs presented below.

CONCEPTUAL FRAMEWORK

As discussed, the literature related to multicultural issues at HBCUs is rather scarce, disparate, and largely unconnected. However, after reviewing this research, I believe that synthesizing the various areas of study can inform the construction of a conceptual framework that examines diversity outcomes and multiculturalism at HBCUs. Through this effort five components of multiculturalism at HBCUs have emerged which create diversity outcomes: (1) classroom multiculturalism, (2) structural diversity, (3) pre-college experiences, (4) internal development, and (5) empowerment. They can be grouped more specifically into two sub-categories—HBCU institutional factors and the individual factors brought to the HBCU by students. A diagram of this conceptual framework appears as Figure 10.1. In the following sections, I will discuss each of the five components of the framework in greater detail.

Figure 10.1. **Conceptual framework.**

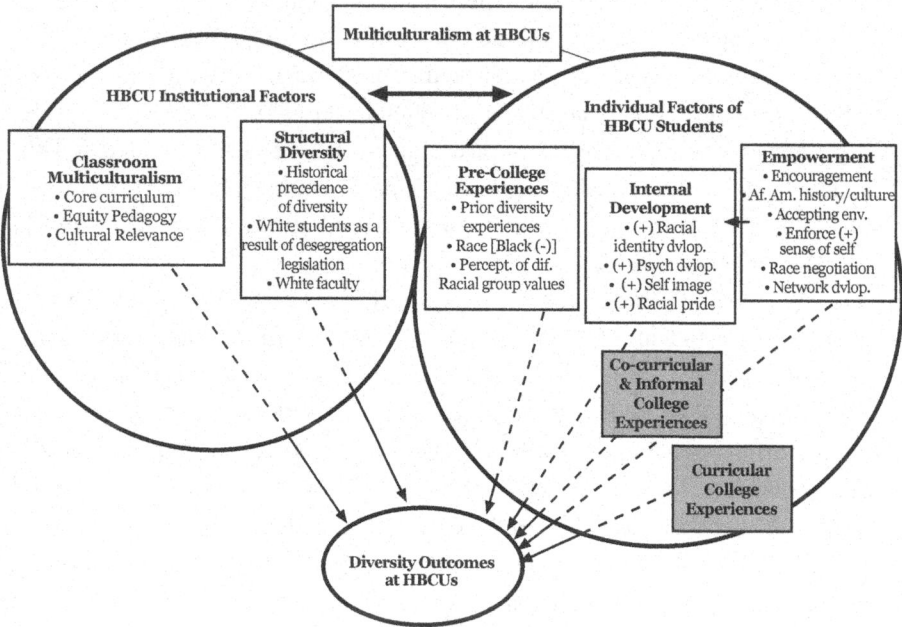

INSTITUTIONAL FACTORS

Classroom multiculturalism. This dimension is informed by the contributions of Bey's (2004) research on the core curriculum at HBCUs, Banks' (1993) study that addresses equity pedagogy, and a concept I have labeled "cultural relevance" which combines the work of both Bey (2004) and Banks (1993). Bey's (2004) research on multiculturalism at HBCUs is an introduction to literature in this area. Bey's findings indicated the presence of multiculturalism within the core curriculum of the two institutions in her study. Furthermore, she found that the teaching methods employed in classrooms are considered to be inclusive of diverse perspectives, and finally that the most frequently used "diverse perspective" at the HBCUs in her study is an African American one.

Banks (1993) presents equity pedagogy as one of the dimensions of multicultural education that is transformative for students' education. He describes this dimension as one which takes into consideration the cultural or ethnic background of the students in order to better assist their learning. This dimension can be applied to HBCUs as Bey's (2004) research indicated that HBCU instructors invoke the African American perspective within their classrooms.

The use of equity pedagogy by HBCUs to employ an African American perspective that is taught in the HBCU curriculum is what I have chosen to call cultural relevance in the curriculum. Within the study conducted by Bey (2004) the HBCUs she examined were institutions with a large majority of African American students. As a result, the employment of education that utilized an African American perspective takes into account the cultural background of the majority of students in the classroom. Collectively, the findings of Bey (2004), Banks (1993) and classroom cultural relevance, form a component of multiculturalism at HBCUs: *classroom multiculturalism.*

Structural diversity. The other HBCU institutional dimension that comprises multiculturalism at Black colleges is structural diversity. In addition to the developmental benefits accrued by African Americans in the above-mentioned studies, African American students may also receive benefits from the increasing structural diversity at many HBCUs. As a result of the desegregation legislation (i.e., *Adams v. Richardson, Ayers v. Mabus, United States v. Fordice*) that brought more White students to public HBCUs (Blake, 1991; Brown, 1999; Williams, 1988), the history of inclusion at HBCUs (Anderson, 1988; Jewell, 2002), and the greater numbers of White faculty to HBCUs (Anderson, 1988; Bey, 2004; Foster & Guyden, 2004; Jewell, 2002), many of these campuses are more structurally diverse.

Due to this additional diversity, students have greater opportunities to interact across racial groups. However, Wathington's (2004) research found that upon entering an HBCU, African American students have a very low likelihood of interacting cross-racially. Furthermore, Gurin, et al.,'s (2002) study found structural diversity in and of itself is not enough to promote cross-racial interaction; rather, institutions must take an active role to create opportunities for diverse interactions. Yet there is not existing research that investigates the extent to which HBCUs promote cross-racial interactions between students let alone research that measures the benefits of these interactions. Additionally, it should be noted that many HBCUs are already structurally diverse; therefore, many institution may already promote cross-racial interaction. However, without further exploration we cannot know the extent of institutional initiatives and programs.

INDIVIDUAL FACTORS

Pre-college experiences. The *pre-college experiences* dimension is grounded in the research studies conducted by Hurtado (2003), Hurtado, et al., (2004), and Wathington (2004). This dimension consists of four components—prior diversity experiences, interactions with diverse others, Black students being less likely to interact cross-racially, and perceptions of different racial group values.

The research conducted by Hurtado (2003), Hurtado, et al. (2004), and Wathington (2004) all found that students have predispositions to diversity prior to college attendance. Although the research conducted by Hurtado et al. (2004) did not explicitly focus on African American students, nor on HBCUs, it found that a student's racial background, their gender, SAT score, mother's education, experience with discrimination, previous participation in diversity related activities, and social identity awareness are determinants of "whether or not students developed cultural awareness during their first two years of college" (p. 24). Furthermore, the portion of Wathington's (2004) study that focused on HBCUs found that incoming Black HBCU students were less likely to interact across racial lines. Moreover, she determined that the lack of interaction across racial lines was the result of Black students' perceptions that non-Black students had different values from them.

This last finding of Wathington's indicates that Black HBCU students are predisposed not to cross-racially interact. Although not explicitly stated, nor a part of Wathington's research, this finding, coupled with Hurtado and her colleagues' research, suggests that African American HBCU students could also be positively predisposed to interact cross-racially depending on their pre-college experiences. Furthermore, depending on their pre-college experiences, African American HBCU students may also be positively or negatively predisposed to other pre-college dimensions of multiculturalism in addition to cross-racial interaction. However, other pre-college dimensions of multiculturalism among HBCU students have not been researched and therefore were unable to be included in this model.

Internal development. *Internal development* includes four main concepts that have emerged from the research of White (2000), Allen (1992, 1996), and Gurin and Epps (1975). White's (2000) research on the identity development of African American students at HBCUs and TWIs found that more positive racial identity outcomes are obtained for African American students at HBCUs than at TWIs. White's findings align with results from other studies on students learning and internal development outcomes at HBCUs, such as Allen (1992, 1996) and Gurin and Epps (1975). The studies conducted by Allen found that African American students on Black campuses fare better in terms of psychological development. Furthermore, Gurin and Epps (1975) determined that African American students at HBCUs had a strong positive self-image, racial pride, and high aspirations. Collectively these studies present a comprehensive picture of the dimensions of the internal development of HBCU students. Finally, the addition of the internal development dimension contributes to the individual factors that make up multiculturalism at HBCUs.

Empowerment. In her study Sleeter (1991) indicated that when multicultural education and empowerment are combined they make for a very effective education for African American students. The literature on empowerment that relates to HBCUs and multiculturalism has led me to determine that there are five aspects that comprise this dimension: (1) African American history and culture, (2) an accepting environment, (3) the enforcement of a positive sense of self, (4) race negotiation, and (5) networks of support. These aspects have emerged as the result of the literature from Asante (1988, 1991a, 1991b), Banks (1993), Freeman and Cohen (2001), Ginwright (2004), and Merleman (1993). Additionally, as a collective they create a diverse view of empowerment. However, more than any of the other dimensions of multiculturalism at HBCUs previously discussed, empowerment is the most complex. Not only is its literature diverse, but the concepts overlap. Furthermore, this dimension as a whole, acts on another dimension of multiculturalism—internal development—creating dynamic interactions within the conceptual model.

Banks (1993) suggested that creating an empowering school culture centered on multicultural education does not come solely from the curriculum, but rather from the formal and informal curriculum, teaching materials, counseling programs, and teaching strategies. However, Ginwright (2004) took a different approach to empowerment and suggested that an Afrocentric curriculum is the way to empower African American students. Although all of the concepts from Banks' research do not explicitly appear in the visual depiction of my conceptual model, his research along with Ginwright's set the stage for empowerment as a dimension of multiculturalism at HBCUs.

Freeman and Cohen (2001) align with Ginwright (2004) in their determination that empowered African American students are created by providing them with African American history and culture. However, where Ginwright's research focuses on Black high school students and Afrocentric education, Freeman and Cohen specifically address issues at HBCUs. In addition, Freeman and Cohen found that HBCUs create empowered students through the existence of a welcoming atmosphere, a reinforced sense of self, providing students with the tools necessary to confront race in academic and work environments, and assisting with the development of personal as well as professional relationships and networks.

Finally, in his study of empowerment in predominantly African American schools that have a multicultural curriculum, Merleman (1993) found that students were not empowered to create change, but rather acted as followers as changed occurred. Based on this finding he suggested that students needed more encouragement in order to be empowered and create change without simply following others.

CROSS-DIMENSIONAL CONNECTIONS

In addition to the connections made between the researchers within the dimension of empowerment, Asante's (1988; 1991a; 1991b) research creates links between the empowerment dimension and the internal development dimension. Furthermore, his work highlights the reciprocal relationship between the institutional and individual factors of multiculturalism at HBCUs.

Asante (1991a, 1991b) believes that for African Americans to have higher achievement levels they must be empowered and centered in their classrooms.

Furthermore, he deemed that "by 'centering' their students of color, teachers can reduce feelings of dislocation engendered by our society's predominantly 'White self-esteem curriculums'" (Asante, 1991a, p. 28). To Asante, centering allows African Americans to see themselves in their education and it makes learning more intimate as well as interesting for students. This concept relates to Banks' (1993) notion of equity pedagogy. Thus, these researchers draw connections between individual and institutional factors of multiculturalism at HBCUs.

In addition to connecting internal and institutional dimensions, Asante's research also illustrates the connections between two internal factors—internal development and empowerment. In one of his 1991 articles Asante (1991b) indicated that seeing themselves within the curriculum created a "renewed sense of purpose and vision" in the lives of African American students (p. 177). Moreover, in his 1988 book on Afrocentricity, Asante described that the way in which one becomes more Afrocentric has much to do with focusing on personal identity. Therefore, this focus on personal identity as a component of empowerment can promote self reflection among students, thereby allowing them to delve into another dimension of multiculturalism at HBCUs presented in this framework—internal development. Asante's research leads me to believe that while empowerment is in and of itself a dimension of multiculturalism at HBCUs, it also informs this second dimension—internal development.

ADDITIONS TO THE CONCEPTUAL MODEL

Up to this point, the discussion of the conceptual framework has focused on the aspects that have been included within the model and substantiated by existing research. However, there are additional components that may in fact be relevant to this framework, but have yet to be researched. One such component is college experiences with diversity, specifically, interactions with diverse peers in cocurricular and informal settings. As was noted in the discussion of pre-college experiences, African American HBCU students in Wathington's (2004) study did not interact cross-racially. Although this may be the case for students entering HBCUs, it is possible that students interact with diverse others in their later college years. Despite the possibility that these interactions may occur, there is no existing research that covers the experiences of racial interactions among HBCU students in their later years of college. Thus, the insertion of a sixth dimension of multiculturalism at HBCUs, *college experiences*, has been included as a possibility, but its specific components have not been detailed as it should be examined in future studies.

Similarly, the inclusion of *cocurricular* and *informal experiences* with diversity have been added in this model. The historical literature on HBCUs indicates that cocurricular learning opportunities have been incorporated into Black colleges and universities (Drewry & Doerman, 2001). Additionally, higher education literature found that cocurricular learning and informal interactions are ways in which students can obtain benefits from interactions with diverse others (antonio, 2001; Hurtado et al., 2004; Milem, 1994). However, there is no empirical research that specifically focuses on the outcomes associated with exposure to the HBCU cocurriculum or informal settings. Therefore, like college experiences, these dimensions are included in this model as components that should be tested in future studies.

This review and framing of the literature has utilized the term *diversity outcomes* as a way to highlight the learning students obtain as a result of their experiences in college with diversity. However, undergoing this investigation has revealed that at HBCUs, little research reports on the interactions students have with diverse others. Without information on the college experiences HBCU students have in relation to diversity, the outcomes they will obtain are unable to be determined. Thus, in order to gain an understanding of this concept, additional research must be conducted on the college diversity experiences of HBCU students. Additionally, because limited research exists on this topic, the conceptualization of the term *diversity outcomes* is in its infancy and its definition deserves further consideration in future studies.

Furthermore, structural diversity along with the presence of curricular multiculturalism at HBCUs, the history of inclusion of diverse faculty and students, the sense of empowerment cultivated at HBCUs, and the internal development of African American HBCU students (including: racial identity development, positive psychological development, positive self image, and racial pride), suggests that despite HBCU students' predisposition not to interact cross-racially, I suggest that HBCUs have the potential to promote diversity outcomes among their students. Finally, credence should be given to the possibility that HBCUs may already be promoting diversity outcomes among their students; however, the lack of research in this area does not allow for this conclusion to be definitively drawn.

Expanding Current Conceptual Models. Through the organization of this literature on multiculturalism at HBCUs I have found that the ways in which the pieces fit together differs from the organization employed by previous studies that address multiculturalism and exposure to diversity within higher education. Specifically, Hurtado (2003) discussed that context, pre-college experiences, college experiences, and some internal characteristics contribute to students' formation of democratic outcomes related to diversity. Similarly, Gurin, et al., (2002) examined students interactions with diverse others, classroom diversity, and informal interaction in college environments. However, due to a lack of literature on diversity outcomes and because Hurtado's (2003) research along with Gurin et al.,'s (2002) research was not designed to specifically consider the diversity experiences of HBCU students, the framework presented in this review expands previous conceptualizations in order to create one that more adequately reflects the needs of HBCUs. Unique factors in this framework that do not appear in Hurtado's (2003) research, nor Gurin et al.,'s (2002) research, but contribute to diversity outcomes at HBCUs include the presence of empowerment and the prominence of structural diversity.

FUTURE RESEARCH ON MULTICULTURALISM AND HBCUs

The work of Bey (2004), Wathington (2004), and White (2000) is valuable to the research on multiculturalism and diversity outcomes at HBCUs. They provide new information about the HBCU curriculum, predispositions to diversity, and identity development, all of which are previously undocumented. However, three studies cannot adequately comprise an entire area of research. Their work provides an important foundation and suggests areas that need to be studied further. Furthermore, future research on HBCU curricular multiculturalism should address the HBCU curriculum from the vantage point of students to determine their perceptions about multicultural education, as well as to determine the types of diversity outcomes these students obtain from their attendance at HBCUs. Additionally, there are aspects of campus in addition to the curriculum life that contribute to multiculturalism and diversity outcomes that warrant examination. Thus, future research should investigate the multiple dimensions of multicultural education on HBCU campuses.

Further investigation of students' experiences is greatly needed. For example, Wathington (2004) looked at students' pre-college experiences at a single public research institution. Future research should examine the types of cross-racial interactions students have at various types of HBCUs. It is also important to expand upon White's (2000) comparison of identity development among African American students at HBCUs and TWIs. White's findings indicate that the greater gains in identity development of HBCU students is largely due to the environment, however, the specific environmental effects that contribute to this development are not specified. Additional studies in this area should tease out the specific environmental forces that contribute to positive gains in identity development of HBCU students.

Furthermore, Sims' (1994) model of diversification at HBCUs could be expanded. Her depiction of diversity at HBCUs confronted only the experiences of African Americans and White students which omits out the experiences of other ethnic and racial groups. Although Sims indicates that she has omitted other groups from this study due to the history of Black-White relations in this nation, the experiences of Latinos, Native Americans, and Asian American students are necessary components to this country's racial composition which need to be explored.

Moreover, future research on multiculturalism at HBCUs should look beyond the Black-White paradigm to better understand the experiences of students, faculty, and staff on HBCU campuses that are neither African American, nor White. Statistical projections indicate that by 2015, 8% of college student will be Asian American, and 13% will be Hispanic in addition to the 15% of African American students, and the 63% that will be White (Carnevale & Fry, 2000). With these changing college student demographics it is increasingly likely that more non-African American students will be attending HBCUs in years to come (Allen & Jewell, 2002; Brown, 2002; Sims, 1994). Additional benefits can be achieved from surveying and interviewing students of various racial and ethnic backgrounds in order to determine the experiences of various students on HBCU campuses. Moreover, Bey (2004) suggests, further research on multiculturalism should be conducted at other minority-serving institutions to investigate the ways in which diversity and multicultural education exists within these contexts. Specifically, she suggested that research should investigate the definitions other HBCUs have for multicultural education and the pedagogy of instructors at these institutions.

Through employing the conceptual framework presented in this piece and embarking on the future research suggested above, a more cohesive picture of multiculturalism at HBCUs should be able to be developed. By further developing literature we should then be able to better understand the role multiculturalism plays in relation to diversity outcomes. Furthermore, it is from these developments that the question posed at the beginning of this article should be able to be answered. That is, we should be able to better understand *what the effects are of multiculturalism on diversity outcomes among HBCU students.*

Conclusion

Although there is limited research that explicitly addresses multiculturalism or diversity outcomes at HBCUs, there is existing research relating to HBCUs that embodies multiculturalism. HBCUs have a clearly established mission of serving African American students, and providing opportunities for students that they may not have at TWIs. Because of increasing diversity at HBCUs and the continuing debates about desegregation and equality in education, HBCUs continue to occupy an interesting yet contentious role in the U.S. In a nation that simultaneously values colorblindness and multiculturalism, these institutions must answer to a mainstream society that views them as primarily single race institutions, and so called relics of the past that have out lived their purpose and mission (Jewell, 2002).

Further research is necessary to inform these conversations about the changing roles and social contributions of HBCUs. Bey's (2004) dissertation should not remain as the sole research study that directly examines multiculturalism at HBCUs, rather as she states, "the limited amount of multicultural research generated by HBCUs needs explanation in light of a 71% increase in white enrollment at such institutions between 1976 and 1994" (p. 3). Additionally, HBCUs must individually decide the ways in which their institutions will promote diversity and multiculturalism on their campuses. However, in order to be colleges and universities that fully embrace multiculturalism HBCUs must ensure that:

> their institutions' diversity efforts help all members learn to see phenomena through others' eyes as well as their own and that each institutional member has the opportunities to find his or her place within the institution and create more tolerance and understanding of those who are different. (Sims, 1994, p.17)

The literature examined within this paper reveals that HBCUs are clearly still needed within the higher education context. Over the course of their existence

HBCUs have maintained their mission to serve African American students by creating social mobility for those who have been left out of higher education. Not only do HBCUs diversify the college choice pool, they still provide educational opportunities for students that may not otherwise be able to afford college (Sims, 1994), and provide learning environments which benefit African American students more than White schooling environments (Allen, 1992,1996; Fleming, 1984; Gurin & Epps, 1975). Furthermore, HBCUs have shown themselves to be institutions committed to creating and maintaining supportive learning atmospheres and valuing difference while educating the disenfranchised (Jewell, 2002).

REFERENCES

Allen, W. R. (1992). The color of success: African–American college student outcomes at predominantly white and historically black public colleges and universities. *Harvard Educational Review, 62*(1), 26–44.

Allen, W. R. (1996). Improving black student access and achievement in higher education. In C. Turner, M. Garcia, A. Nora, L. I. Rendon (Eds.), *Racial & ethnic diversity in higher education. ASHE Reader Series.* Needham Heights, MA: Simon & Schuster.

Allen, W. R. & Jewell, J. O. (2002). A backward glance forward: Past, present, and future, perspectives on historically black colleges and universities. *The Review of Higher Education, 25*(3), 241–261.

Anderson, J. D. (1984). The schooling and achievement of black children: Before and after Brown. Topeka, 1900–1980. *Advances in Motivation and Achievement, 1,* 103–122.

Anderson, J. D. (1988). The education of blacks in the south, 1860–1935. Chapel Hill, NC: University of North Carolina Press.

antonio, a. l. (2001). The role of interracial interaction in the development of leadership skills and cultural knowledge and understanding. *Research in Higher Education, 42*(5), 593–617.

Arnold, M. (1997). *The environmental factor.* Unpublished manuscript. Graduate Student and Faculty Forum, University of Florida.

Asante, M. K. (1988). *Afrocentricity.* Trenton, NJ: Africa World Press.

Asante, M. K. (1991a). Afrocentric curriculum. *Educational Leadership, 49*(4), 28–31.

Asante, M. K. (1991b). The Afrocentric idea in education. *Journal of Negro Education, 60*(2), 170–180.

Association of American Colleges and Universities. (1995a). *American pluralism and he college curriculum: Higher education in a diverse democracy*. Washington, DC: Association of American Colleges and Universities.

Association of American Colleges and Universities. (1995b). *Integrity in the college curriculum: A report to the academic community*. Washington, DC: Association of American Colleges and Universities.

Association of American Colleges and Universities. (2002). *Greater expectations: A new vision for learning as a nation goes to college*. Washington, DC: Association of American Colleges and Universities. Retrieved on October 20, 2002, from: http://www.greaterexpectations.org/

Banks, J. A. (1993). Multicultural education: Historical development, dimensions, and practice. *Review of Research in Education, 19*, 3–49.

Banks, J. A., & Ambrosio, J. (2003). Multicultural education. In Guthrie, J. W. (Ed.) Encyclopedia of Education Second Edition. New York: Thomson Gale.

Bey, F. J. (2004). *A study of multicultural education in the general education programs at two historically black colleges in Virginia*. Unpublished doctoral dissertation, George Mason University.

Blake, E. (1991). Is higher education desegregation a remedy for segregation but not educational inequality?: A study of the Ayers v. Mabus desegregation case. *The Journal of Negro Education, 60*(4), 538–565.

Bowen, W. G., Bok, D. C. (1998). *The shape of the river: Long term consequences of considering race in college and university admissions*. Princeton, NJ: Princeton University Press.

Brown, M. C. (1999). *The quest to define collegiate desegregation black colleges, title VI compliance, and post-Adams litigation*. Westport, CT: Bergin & Garvey.

Brown, M. C. (2002). Good intentions: Collegiate desegregation and trans-demographic enrollments. *The Review of Higher Education, 25*(3), 263–280.

Butler, J. E. & Walter, J. C. (1991). *Transforming the curriculum: Ethnic studies and women's studies*. Albany, NY: State University of New York.

Carnevale, A. P., & Fry, R. A. (2000). *Crossing the great divide: Can we achieve equality when generation Y goes to college?* Princeton, NJ: Educational Testing Service.

Chang M. J. (2001). Is it more than about getting along? The broader educational relevance of reducing students' racial biases. *Journal of College Student Development, 42*(2), 93–105.

Clayton-Pedersen, A. R. & Musil, C. M. (2003). Multiculturalism in higher education. In Guthrie, J. W. (Ed.) Encyclopedia of Education Second Edition. New York: Thomson Gale.

Conrad, C. F., Brier, E. M., & Braxton, J. M. (1997). Factors contributing to the matriculation of white students in public HBCUs. *Journal for a Just and Caring Education, 3(1)*, 37–62.

Drewry, H. N. & Doermann, H. (2001). *Stand and prosper: Private black colleges and their students*. Princeton, NJ: Princeton University Press.

Fleming, J. (1984). *Blacks in college*. San Francisco: Jossey-Bass.

Freeman, K., Cohen, R. T. (2001). Bridging the gap between economic development and cultural empowerment: HBCU's challenges for the future. *Urban Review, 36*(5), 585–596.

Foster, L. & Guyden, J. A. (2004). Colleges in black and white: White faculty at black colleges. In C. M. Brown & K. Freeman (Eds.), *Black colleges: New perspectives on policy and practice*. Westport, CT: Praeger Publishers.

Gay, G. (1997). The relationship between multicultural and democratic education. *The Social Studies*.

Ginwright, S. A. (2004). *Black in school: Afrocentric reform, urban youth, and the promise of hip–hop culture*. New York: Teachers College Press.

Greene, S. R., & Kamimura, M. (2003). *Ties that bind: Enhanced social awareness development through interactions with diverse peers.*

Presented at the annual meeting of the Association for the Study of Higher Education. Portland, Oregon, November 2003.

Gurin, P. Dey, E. L., Gurin, G. & Hurtado, S. (2004). The educational value of diversity. In P. Gurin, J. S. Lehman, E. Lewis (Eds.), *Defending diversity: Affirmative action at the University of Michigan.* Ann Arbor, MI: University of Michigan Press.

Gurin, P., Dey, E. L., Hurtado, S. & Gurin G. (2002). Diversity and higher education: Theory and impact on educational outcomes. *Harvard Educational Review, 72*(3), 330–66.

Gurin, P., Epps, (1975). *Black consciousness, identity, and achievement: A study of students in historically black colleges.* New York: Wiley.

Harvey, W. B. & Williams, L. E. (1996). Historically black colleges. Models for increasing minority representation. In C. Turner, M. Garcia, A. Nora, L. I. Rendon (Eds.), *Racial & ethnic diversity in higher education. ASHE Reader Series.* Needham Heights, MA: Simon & Schuster.

hooks, b. (1990). *Yearning: Race, gender, and cultural politics.* Boston: South End Press.

Humphreys, D. (1997). *General education and American commitments: A national report on diversity courses and requirements.* Washington, DC: Association of American Colleges and Universities.

Hurtado, S. (1996). The campus racial climate. Contexts of conflict. In C. Turner, M. Garcia, A. Nora, L. I. Rendon (Eds.), *Racial & ethnic diversity in higher education. ASHE Reader Series.* Needham Heights, MA: Simon & Schuster.

Hurtado, S. (2003). Preparing college students for a diverse democracy: Final report to the U.S. Department of Education, OERI, Field Initiated Studies Program. Ann Arbor, MI: Center for the Study of Higher and Postsecondary Education.

Hurtado, S. Bowman, J. Dwyer, B., Greene, S. (2004). Undergraduate Students and Cultural Awareness: Examining the Relationship between Interaction with Diverse Peers and Cultural Awareness Development.

Presented at the annual meeting of the Association for Institutional Research. Boston, Massachusetts, June 2004.

Hurtado, S., Carter, D. F. & Kardia, D. (1998). The climate for diversity: Key issues for institutional self-study. *New Directions for Institutional Research*. San Francisco: Jossey-Bass.

Hurtado, H., Milem, J., Clayton-Pedersen, A., Allen, W. (1999). *Enacting diverse learning environments: Improving the climate for racial/ethnic diversity in higher education*. ASHE-ERIC Higher Education Report 26, Number 8. Washington, DC: George Washington University, Graduate School of Education and Human Development.

Hurtado, S., Engberg, M. E., Ponjuan, L., Landreman, L. (2002). Students' precollege preparation for participation in a diverse democracy. *Research in Higher Education, 43*(2), 163–86.

Jewell, J. O. (2002). To set an example. The tradition of diversity at historically black colleges and universities. *Urban Education, 37*(1), 7–21.

Johnson, T. (1971). The black colleges as system. *Daedalus, 100*(3), 798–812.

Levine, R. & Cureton, J. (1992). The quiet revolution: Eleven facts about multiculturalism and the curriculum. *Change, 24*(1), 24–29.

Loewen, J. (1995). *Lies my teacher told me: Everything your American history textbook got wrong*. New York: Simon & Schuster.

Lynch J. (1987). *Prejudice reduction and the schools*. New York: Nichols.

Merelman, R. M. (1993). Black history and cultural empowerment: A case study. *American Journal of Education, 101*(4), 331–58.

Milem, J. F. (1994). College, students, and racial understanding. *The NEA Education Journal*.

Milner, D. (1983). *Children and race. Ten years on*. London: Ward Lock Educational.

Oliver, M. L., Rodriguez, C. J., Mickelson, R. A. (1985). Brown and black in white: The social adjustment and academic performance of chicano and black students in a predominantly white university. *The Urban Review: Issues and Ideas in Public Education, 17* 3–24.

Orfield, G., Frankenberg, E. D., Lee, C. (2003). The resurgence of school segregation. *Educational Leadership, 60*(4), 16–20.

Pascarella, E., Edison, M., Nora, A, Hagedorn, L.S., & Terenzini, P.T. (1996). Influence on students' openness to diversity and challenge in the first year of college. *The Journal of Higher Education, 67*(2), 174–195.

Redd, K. E. (1998). Historically black colleges and universities: Making a comeback. In J. P. Merisotis & C. T. O'Brien (Eds.), *Minority–serving institutions: Distinct purposes, common goals.* San Francisco: Jossey-Bass.

Ruffins, P. (1999). In a society that is increasingly diverse, what's an HBCU to do? *Black Issues in Higher Education, 15*(23), 22.

Sims, S. J. (1994). *Diversifying historically black colleges and universities: A new higher education paradigm.* Westport, CT: Greenwood Press.

Sleeter, C. (1991). *Empowerment through multicultural education.* Albany, N.Y.: State University of New York Press.

Smith, D. G. (1989). The challenge of diversity: Involvement or alienation in the academy? *ASHE–ERIC Higher Education Report 5.* Washington, DC: George Washington University.

Tinto, V. (1997). Classrooms as communities: Exploring the educational character of student persistence. *The Journal of Higher Education, 68*(6), 599–623.

Taylor, M., Dwyer, B., and Pacheco, S. (2005). "Mission and community: The culture of community engagement and minority serving institutions." In P. Pasque, R. Smerek, B. Dwyer, N. Bowman, & B. Mallory (Eds.), *Higher Education Collaboratives for Community Engagement and Improvement* (pp. 32–37). Ann Arbor, MI: National Forum for Higher Education for the Public Good.

U.S. Department of Education, Office for Civil Rights. (2005). Retrieved on November 8, 2005, from: http://www.ed.gov/about/offices/list/ocr/docs/hq9511.html

Wathington, II. D. (2004). *In search of the beloved community: Understanding the dynamics of student interaction across racial and ethnic communities*. Unpublished doctoral dissertation, University of Michigan.

Watson, L. W. & Kuh, G. D. (1996). The influence of dominant race environments on student involvement, perceptions, and educational gains: A look at historically black and predominantly white liberal arts institutions. *Journal of College Student Development, 37*(4), 415–24.

Williams, L. E. (1988). Public policies and financial exigencies: Black colleges twenty years later, 1965–1985. *Journal of Black Studies, 19*(2), 135–149.

Willie, C. V. (1983). *Race, ethnicity and socioeconomic status*. Dix Hills, NY: General Hall.

Willie, C. V., Grady, M. K., Hope, R. O. (1991). *African Americans and the doctoral experience: Implications for policy*. New York: Teachers College Press.

White, V. Y. (2000). *Racial identity development among black students at a historically black and a predominantly white university in Florida*. Unpublished doctoral dissertation, University of Florida.

NOTES

[1] The author published a previous version of this chapter in the Winter/Spring 2006 issue of *Educational Foundations* (Volume 20, Number 1/2). Reprinted with permission.

[2] Higher education desegregation cases include, but are not limited to: Adams v. Richardson, 1972, Ayers v. Mabus I, 1987, Ayers v. Mabus III 1990, and United States v. Fordice 1992.

[3] A majority of the literature on diversity outcomes originates from Hurtado and her associates work on the Diverse Democracy Project at the University of Michigan. This project was a two-year longitudinal study of students from 10 Research I institutions located throughout the United States.

[4] Greek organizations and marching bands are traditional markers of HBCUs and are often integral components to the culture of these institutions (see Taylor et al., 2005).

Chapter Eleven

○○○○○

Focusing on Institutional Fabric: Assessing Campus Cultures to Enhance Cross-Cultural Engagement

Samuel D. Museus

○○○○○

I n the written opinion of the U.S. Supreme Court in the landmark case *Regents of the University of California v. Bakke* (1978), Justice Lewis Powell asserted that diversity is critical to the purpose that higher education serves in our society and declared it a "compelling state interest." The 2003 Supreme Court decisions in *Gratz v. Bollinger* and *Grutter v. Bollinger* reinforced Justice Powell's conclusion that diversity is an adequately compelling justification for considering race in admission policies and practices. The 2003 decisions also highlighted the urgency of higher education's role in realizing the benefits of diversity. If diversity is, in fact, important enough to constitute a compelling state interest, higher education administrators have the duty and obligation to understand the nature of diversity and create the conditions to allow it to flourish.

Higher education scholars have published several reviews of literature focused on the importance of diversity in higher education (see, for example, Chang, Witt, Jones, & Hakuta, 2003; Hurtado, Dey, Gurin, & Gurin, 2003; Hurtado, Milem, Clayton-Pedersen, & Allen, 1999; Milem & Hakuta, 2000; Smith, Gerbrick, Figueroa, Levitan, Moore, et al., 1997). Chang and his colleagues (2006) asserted that there was *remarkable consistency* among those reviews in concluding that the potency of an educational institution is largely dependent on the composition of its student, faculty, and staff bodies. While most of the literature in this area has focused on racial diversity, the educational experience is also enhanced by socioeconomic, gender, and religious diversity; all are important in discussion of campus diversity. In this chapter, the term *minority* encompasses individuals belonging to racial/ethnic, socioeconomic, gender, and religious groups who have historically been marginalized in higher education.

Indeed, evidence indicates that diverse campus communities constitute environments rich with educational opportunity (antonio, 2001b; Astin, 1993a; Bowen & Bok, 1998; Chang, 1999; Chang, Witt, Jones, & Hakuta, 2003; Gurin, Dey, Hurtado, & Gurin, 2002; Hurtado, 2001; Milem, 1994; Pascarella, Edison, Nora, Hagedorn, & Terenzini, 1996; Sax & Astin, 1997). Higher education researchers have asserted that structural diversity (i.e., the presence of diverse communities), while necessary, might not be a sufficient condition to promote the positive educational outcomes attributed to diversity (Chang et al., 2005; 2006). Rather, it appears that realization of the benefits of diversity, in part, depends on the extent to which institutions can create structured opportunities for their students to interact across cultural differences in sustained and meaningful ways (antonio, 2001a, 2001b; Chang, 1999; Chang, Astin, & Kim, 2004; Chang et al., 2006; Gurin et al., 2002). Put another way, the quality and quantity of engagement in cross-cultural activities matters. Evidence that meaningful and sustained cross-cultural engagement can promote desirable educational outcomes abounds. Among the positive outcomes researchers associate with cross-cultural interaction, for instance, are higher levels of cognitive development, self-confidence, motivation, intellectual and civic development, educational aspirations, cultural awareness, openness to diversity, and commitment to equity (antonio, 2001a, 2001b; Chang, 1999; Chang, Astin, & Kim, 2004; Chang et al., 2006; Gurin et al., 2002).

In 1954, Gordon Allport published *The Nature of Prejudice*, asserting that interactions across racial lines must occur under particular environmental conditions to result in positive outcomes. Allport's *Intergroup Contact Theory* suggests that the environment within which cross-racial interaction occurs is as important as the contact itself. Unfortunately, a considerable body of knowledge indicates that, on many campuses, interracial interactions intertwined with unwelcoming campus climates have a negative impact on the experiences of minority groups

(Cabrera et al., 1999; Feagin, 1992; Feagin, Vera, & Imani, 1996; Lewis, Chesler, & Forman, 2000; Nora & Cabrera, 1996). If higher education administrators are to maximize the development of their students, it is critical for them to understand how to intentionally and effectively foster campus environments that support sustained and educationally meaningful cross-cultural engagement.

Chang and his colleagues (2005) have applied the concept of *magical thinking* to characterize Justice Powell's thoughts about diversity in the context of the *Bakke* opinion. The concept of magical thinking is often used by child psychologists to describe a level of children's intellectual development: the child believes thoughts and expectations can affect what actually happens. Chang et al. (2005) make the argument that Justice Powell's opinion in *Bakke* exhibits a dose of magical thinking about the benefits of diversity. Specifically, they assert that Powell's argument for defending diversity as a compelling state interest highlighted the reality of the potential educational benefits of diversity but lacks any conceptualization about how the benefits can be realized. Higher education administrators may also consciously or subconsciously adopt these magical ways of thinking about diversity on their campuses.

To understand the nature of cross-cultural engagement—as well as how meaningful and sustained cross-cultural engagement can be realized on their campuses—college and university administrators must be aware of the extent of their own expectations that such engagement will occur without intentional, strategic administrative action. The burden of investing energy in efforts to promote meaningful and sustained cross-cultural engagement is often placed on the shoulders of minority students. Given the possibility that particular environments must be created to maximize the benefits of cross-cultural engagement (Allport, 1954; Chang et al., 2006), administrators *must* consider and underscore the importance of fostering environments where students feel safe and comfortable engaging meaningfully across cultural, ethnic, racial, socioeconomic, gender, and sexual orientation differences.

This chapter provides a discussion of how cultural perspectives and campus culture assessments can be used to understand cross-cultural engagement. First, I provide an overview of the concepts of campus cultures and campus cultural properties. Then, building on Festinger's (1957) *Theory of Cognitive Dissonance* and Bourdieu and Passeron's (1977) concept of *habitus*, I discuss a useful way of thinking about how deeply embedded elements of campus cultures can facilitate or impede cross-cultural engagement. Finally, I describe some methodological issues and concerns that can help administrators and institutional researchers develop and conduct effective campus culture assessments focused on understanding cross-cultural engagement.

Defining Campus Cultures and Subcultures

Critics of the diversity rationale for race-conscious admissions policies and programs have claimed that racial segregation and tense campus racial climates are actually producing college graduates with higher levels of racial intolerance (Chang, 2002). Research by antonio (2001a) suggests that segregation does not exist, at least on diverse college campuses, to the extent that critics have asserted. There is some evidence that students of color view racial segregation as an important problem on predominantly White campuses with small racial/ ethnic minority student populations (Museus, in press). This may be intuitive, considering that the absence of a critical mass of racial minority students on a college campus may inevitably limit the extent to which cross-racial interaction can occur there. In other words, on campuses that lack structural diversity, there are not enough students of color to go around. The question, then, is not whether structural diversity is a desirable condition on campus, but rather the question of whether the level of structural diversity on a particular campus is sufficient and, if so, how institutions can ensure they are using it to maximize positive educational outcomes. Adopting a cultural perspective can give university leaders valuable insight into how they can achieve this.

Culture is one of the most powerful forces within organizations (Schein, 1996); it has been said that culture affects everything that happens on a college campus (Kuh, 2001/2002). Despite the salience of culture in shaping individual and group behavior at institutions of higher education, inadequate attention has been given to how cultural perspectives can be used to understand campus racial dynamics and to promote and sustain productive cross-cultural engagement. If institutional leaders hope to holistically understand cross-cultural engagement on their campuses, they must comprehend the influence of institutional culture in shaping their students' behaviors and experiences.

Because of its elusive, multifaceted, and perplexing nature, discussions of campus cultures often begin with attempts to define the concept of organizational culture and delineate its numerous, elusive, ambiguous, and interactive elements (Kuh & Hall, 1993; Kuh & Whitt, 1988; Manning, 1993; Museus, in press; Whitt, 1996). Unpacking the concept of campus cultures is difficult, if not seemingly impossible, because the culture of each individual campus is complex and unique in its histories, traditions, and contexts. Any discussion of campus cultures should be prefaced with a framework for viewing and understanding those cultures because of the complexity and context-specific nature of the phenomenon.

While institutional culture has been defined in many different ways (for discussion, see Kuh & Whitt, 1988), few have discussed it in depth in the context of higher education (Kuh & Hall, 1993; Kuh & Whitt, 1988; Museus, in press; Tierney, 1999; Whitt, 1996). One of the most comprehensive definitions of campus culture is provided by Kuh & Hall (1993):

> The collective, mutually shaping patterns of institutional history, mission, physical settings, norms, traditions, values, practices, beliefs, and assumptions which guide the behavior of individuals and groups in an institution of higher education and which provide frames of reference for interpreting the meanings of events and actions on and off campus. (p. 2)

This definition highlights the complexity of the concept of culture as well as its utility for understanding the behavior and experiences of individuals and groups on college campuses (Whitt, 1996).

The increasing structural diversity of student bodies entering institutions of higher education has contributed to the progressive complexity of campus cultures by fostering of an ever-increasing array of subcultures. Campus subcultures are cohesive environments that develop within a dominant campus culture; their members' common interests are often incongruent with the interests and values of the dominant majority culture. Bolton and Kammeyer (1972) defined subculture as a "normative-value system held by some group of persons who are in persisting interaction, who transmit the norms and values to newcomers by some communicated process, and who exercise some sort of social control to ensure conformity to the norms," and highlighted that "the normative-value system of such a group must differ from the normative-value system of the larger, the parent, or the dominant society" (pp. 381–382). These definitions of campus cultures and subcultures provide a useful framework for understanding the formation and behavior of groups within an institutional culture. Having a definition of campus cultures and subcultures is important, but understanding the various elements that create a campus's cultures is also important.

CAMPUS CULTURAL PROPERTIES AND CROSS-CULTURAL ENGAGEMENT

In their seminal monograph on culture in higher education, "The Invisible Tapestry," Kuh & Whitt (1988) began their discussion of the wide variety of definitions of the concept of culture with the following quote from Becher (1984):

> If there were any word to serve the purpose as well, I would unhesitatingly use it in preference to one that seems at times downright slippery and at other times impossibly vague and all-embracing. But although "culture" has uncomfortably many denotations, it is the only term that seems satisfactorily to combine the notions . . . of a shared way of thinking and a collective way of behaving. (p. 166)

This quote illustrates the ambiguity and complexity inherent in the concept of culture as well as its all-encompassing nature. Accordingly, institutional cultures are so complex that any attempt to understand or disentangle such cultures would probably be futile without a framework to help make sense of the culture's various dynamic and interactive elements. Higher education scholars have identified four primary properties of campus cultures (Kuh & Whitt, 1988; Manning, 1993; Schein, 1992): cultural artifacts, values, perspectives, and assumptions.

ARTIFACTS

Cultural artifacts are the most noticeable elements of culture. They are "the visible products of the group" (Schein, 1992, p. 17). Manning (1993) outlined three types of cultural artifacts: physical, verbal, and behavioral. Physical artifacts include written documents, memorials, buildings, and physical spaces on campus. Verbal artifacts include myths and stories that get passed down through generations, as well as common language. Finally, behavioral artifacts are rituals, cultural performances, and traditions that carry symbolic cultural meaning.

An understanding of cultural artifacts can provide valuable insight into the nature of cross-cultural interaction on campus. Physical spaces, in particular, are pervasive influences on college campuses and are frequently designated for specific purposes, to communicate particular messages, and to increase or decrease the probability that individuals will exhibit certain behaviors. Administrators can learn much by questioning how physical structures might facilitate or impede cross-cultural engagement. For example, are cultural awareness events and celebrations held in closed spaces in a back corner of the campus student union, or are they held in high-traffic areas with high levels of exposure to students who would not actively seek out such events? Asking such questions can reveal much about how artifacts shape cross-cultural engagement.

VALUES

Institutional values are "espoused as well as enacted ideals of an institution or group and serve as a basis on which members of a culture or subculture judge situations, acts, objects, and people" (Kuh & Hall, 1993, p. 6). Athletic success, educational excellence, social justice, and diversity are all examples of values espoused by some institutions of higher education. While all these values may be important to students, the level of their importance is likely to vary from individual to individual. Manning (1993) explains that cultural artifacts, such as traditions, can remind historically marginalized groups of institutionalized beliefs about their lack of worth and status within that culture. Much like artifacts, decisions about which values are espoused and enacted can send signals of exclusion and devaluation to minority students.

Many institutions of higher education publicize their valuing of diversity and tout their own efforts to diversify their campuses. Even at institutions at which nine tenths of the student body is White, recruitment materials display an equal representation of various racial and ethnic groups. The messages that university administrators send to external constituents, however, is not always congruent with whether diversity is actually an enacted institutional value (Museus, in press). Students' perceptions of whether diversity is valued by their institutions is an intricate function of their own experiences, their knowledge of other minority students' experiences, institutional action and inaction to incidents of racism and discrimination, their knowledge of campus environments, and so on. If administrators hope to understand how they can facilitate the engagement of minority students in mainstream cultural activities, they must understand how the values of their institution might create feelings of devaluation among members of historically marginalized groups.

PERSPECTIVES

Cultural perspectives are the rules and norms shared by members of a particular cultural group (Kuh & Hall, 1993). The perspectives of students often clash with the values of faculty and administrators (Manning, 1993). Many campuses, for example, have grappled with the issue of excessive drinking on campus. While this type of behavior is contradictory to the academic values of some institutions, the student culture perpetuated at many colleges and universities teaches new students that such excess is appropriate, and sometimes necessary, to become an accepted member of the mainstream culture.

Cultural perspectives are especially useful for understanding why students do not interact across cultures. At cafeterias across the country, the racial segregation of college students is readily apparent and, in the eyes of many students, is considered the norm. This separation may not always be negative; evidence shows that affinity groups and formal subcultures filled with like-minded students can provide important sources of support for students on college campuses (Gonzalez, 2003; Guiffrida, 2003; Harper & Quaye, 2007; Kuh & Love, 2000)—a point to which I will return. The problem emerges, however, when this segregation permeates an entire college campus and is readily apparent in informal social interactions; discussion and group formation in the classroom; cultural celebrations and performances; extracurricular discussions of race and politics; and living arrangements. When the norms of an institution perpetuate the pervasiveness of such segregation, it is difficult for institutions and their students to produce the benefits of diversity. Higher education administrators, therefore, should be conscious of students' views of what is *normal* and how such notions of normality can be challenged to achieve the most positive educational outcomes.

ASSUMPTIONS

Cultural assumptions are the most basic and tacit level of culture and consist of the beliefs on which institutional policies and practices are based (Kuh & Hall, 1993; Schein, 1992). College and university administrators learn which practices are appropriate as a function, in part, of the assumptions perpetuated within an institutional culture. Moreover, sometimes external cultural assumptions (e.g., stereotypes) become intertwined with or drive institutional cultural assumptions. One example of this is the impact of *the model minority stereotype* on the practices of college administrators. The model minority stereotype refers to the belief that Asian and Asian American students are highly likely to achieve academic success and, therefore, do not need the support of institutional programs and services (Suzuki, 2002). The stereotype constitutes a pervasive and powerful cultural assumption that can result in the exclusion of Asian American students from consideration in the administration of support services. This is particularly detrimental to particular Asian American subgroups, such as Southeast Asian Americans, who face many of the same or similar challenges as other historically underrepresented minorities. Of course, not all institutions and administrators espouse this viewpoint. But Asian American students who do not fit the model minority stereotype may suffer from inadequate levels of academic and social support if they are enrolled on campuses whose administrators espouse this belief.

Evidence suggests that such cultural assumptions about particular groups can have a substantial impact on the behaviors and experiences of students who belong to the stereotyped group (Steele, 1999). Steele demonstrated that students who perceive that a stereotype exists about them can experience increased levels of anxiety that have negative effects on their academic performance. Museus (in press) reports that the engagement of students who were interviewed as part of a campus culture assessment was hindered by their fear of reinforcing or disproving stereotypes about their respective races. Knowledge about the extent of cultural stereotype influence is limited. Nevertheless, knowing how such stereotypes influence the behavior of students on a particular campus can provide invaluable information, guiding administrators to stimulate dialogues about cultural beliefs that can alleviate the negative influence of such assumptions. The next section focuses on developing an understanding of how these properties might influence students' experiences and behaviors interacting across cultures.

Moving from Cognitive to Cultural Dissonance: A Source of Conflict and Tension

After a series of hate crimes targeting Black students at a predominantly White university, a Black student leader becomes frustrated at the university's lack of responsiveness to the acts of hate. He begins to wonder whether the administration values the diversity he and other Black students bring to the educational experience on his campus.

A first-year White college student from an economically disadvantaged background wakes up in his sweatpants and T-shirt. He heads toward campus to attend a meeting held by the business student organization. When he arrives at the meeting, he notices that everyone else is dressed in business attire, the organization's normal dress on meeting days, and everyone at the meeting stares at him with a confused countenance. He suddenly feels a rush of anxiety and embarrassment.

Out of curiosity, a Hispanic student walks into ballroom where administrators are hosting the alumni association's social gathering. She immediately notices that she is the only Hispanic person in the room. After a few minutes, she perceives that people are giving her strange looks because she is out of place and decides to leave.

These three scenarios have at least two things in common. First, all three students experience a noticeable level of internal conflict or tension resulting from their respective situations. Second, the resulting conflict or tension is, in part, a result of cultural factors. The Black student, for example, is troubled by his institution's failure to enact the *value* of diversity on campus. The White student is a victim of his lack of awareness of cultural *perspectives* or *norms* that drive behavior in the business student organization. And the Hispanic student enters a *symbolical space* in which she believes people espouse *assumptions* that she does not belong because of her ethnic background. Anyone who has come in contact with a group and its foreign culture for the first time has experienced discomfort, albeit at varying levels of intensity.

While these three students' experiences might happen on any campus, they are likely to be less salient at campuses whose cultures support openness to diversity and cross-cultural engagement. In the first scenario, the institutional leaders might have reacted to the incidents of racial discrimination if they understood their inaction could cause feelings of devaluation and resentment among their racial minority students. Their actions would have promoted social cohesion rather than further alienating their minority students. Similarly, if the business students in the second scenario had been more open-minded about cultural nuances, the White student probably would have received a friendlier greeting and not been as embarrassed. In the third scenario, people in the alumni meeting could have made an effort to engage the Hispanic student in conversation and integrate her into the social function if they understood her feelings and beliefs. This section focuses on developing a framework for higher education administrators to understand how cultural factors on their campuses might influence cross-cultural engagement, and how cultural perspectives can be used to foster environments conducive to productive cross-cultural engagement.

How can knowledge of campus cultures enhance our understanding of racial dynamics and the various ways institutions can promote sustained and meaningful cross-cultural interaction? This question is difficult to answer, because of the complexity of the concept of culture and the common missing linkages between institutional cultures and human behavior. Most discussions of institutional culture in the context of higher education focus on describing the nature of campus cultures and how institutional leaders might use cultural perspectives to understand actions and events on a college campus (Kuh & Hall, 1993; Kuh & Whitt, 1988; Manning, 1993; Museus, in press; Whitt, 1993, 1996). Discussion and understanding of how cultures—or various elements of those cultures—actually shape individual or group behavior, experiences, and outcomes are sparse. While some may disagree with this assertion, we need only look at a single cultural element to see the disproportionate focus on *describing*, as opposed to *understanding*, the impact of cultural factors. There is a plethora of evidence, for example, that racial/ethnic minority students face pressure to conform to or disprove racial stereotypes (see, for example, Fries-Britt & Turner, 2002; Lewis, Chesler, & Forman, 2000; Steele, 1999). Discussion of the impact of those stereotypes on students' behavior and outcomes, however, is limited. Discussions (Fries-Britt, 2002; Museus, in press; Steele, 1999) focused on the impact of stereotypes—have only begun to unravel the importance of stereotypes in the college experience. By and large, the influence of campus cultures on student outcomes remains a *black box* (Kuh, 1994, cited in Whitt, 1996).

The lack of attention to understanding the effects of campus cultures could be due, in part, to the overwhelming complexity of the concept of campus culture, the difficulty in transferring knowledge of culture from one institution to another, or predicting the consequences of cultural phenomena in their specific contexts. Indeed, every institutional culture is different; a particular cultural element may affect the same individual's behavior and experience in drastically disparate ways at different institutions. In this section, I offer the concept of cultural dissonance as a conceptual lens for understanding the relationship between cultural elements and students' desire or willingness to engage in particular activities (e.g., cross-cultural interaction). This concept will also be useful for administrators and institutional researchers who hope to conduct culture assessments of their campuses to better understand how they can foster sustained and meaningful cross-cultural interaction.

In 1957, Leon Festinger published *A Theory of Cognitive Dissonance*—one of the most influential theories ever to emerge in the social sciences. Festinger posited that elements of knowledge can be either consonant (i.e., relevant to one another) or dissonant (i.e., irrelevant to one another). When two elements of knowledge are dissonant it can lead to psychological discomfort, to which individuals can respond in multiple ways. First, they can adapt old schemas, or structures of knowledge, to accommodate the new information. An alternative response is to avoid similar future situations to minimize cognitive dissonance and seek out situations that increase cognitive consonance. Reflections of the underlying conceptual foundations of this theory can be seen in many stage theories of student development and learning (Cross, 1971; Kohlberg, 1975; Perry, 1970, 1981). A common theme among such theories is the development that occurs when individuals are exposed to, adopt, and integrate diverse perspectives.

Inherent in Festinger's theory is the idea that cognitive dissonance or consonance within a particular individual is, in part, a function of (a) that person's prior knowledge and experiences in the environments to which the individual has previously been exposed, and (b) the new experience and knowledge to which that individual is exposed in the current environment. The level of incongruence between those two elements induces psychological discomfort within an individual. Thus, higher levels of incongruence between a person's cultures of origin and cultures of immersion lead to greater cognitive dissonance. Combining the concept of cognitive dissonance with the concept of cultural habitus provides a useful framework for viewing the decisions of individuals to interact across cultures. Bourdieu & Passeron's (1977) concept of habitus refers to internalized systems of culturally-based beliefs and dispositions that develop as a result of past experiences. In other words, habitus can be viewed as internal structures of learned skills, styles, habits, and knowledge that develop within the minds and bodies of individual actors and, in part, determine their future behavior and experiences.

By applying the concepts of cognitive dissonance and habitus, one can construct a more complete picture of how cultural factors can stimulate certain psychological reactions and shape future behavior among individuals. For purposes of illustration, consider the experiences of a recently matriculated college student who was raised in cultures in which aggressive or competitive behavior is frowned upon and it is impolite to question authority or talk frequently. Imagine that this hypothetical student attends the first day of an introductory sociology course. During that first class session, as the instructor is going over the syllabus, the student realizes that her grade is partially determined by her participation in classroom discussions and debates. She experiences some anxiety as a function of anticipating the discomfort she will feel when engaging in debates with her peers. If we employ the two aforementioned concepts to analyze this situation, we can hypothesize that the individual might react in one of two ways. First, she might accommodate the new experience and knowledge, accepting the fact that she must learn to adapt to this one aspect (i.e., classroom discussion) of college life; she would eventually reshape her cultural habitus and beliefs about debate and competition. Alternatively, she may choose to drop the introduction to sociology and enroll in a primarily lecture-style course to avoid experiencing further cognitive dissonance arising from participating in classroom discussions and debates.

This hypothetical situation provides one illustration of how incongruence between an individual's internal cultural systems and that person's experiences within a newly encountered cultural terrain can shape their experiences, reactions, and behaviors. To describe what happens in such a situation, I use the term *cultural dissonance*—conflict or tension perceived and experienced by an individual as a result of inconsistencies between that individual's cultural habitus and newly encountered culturally-specific information and experiences. Such cultural dissonance can contribute to increased levels of cognitive dissonance experienced by college students. In the context of higher education, if the predominantly White cultures of a campus perpetuate values, beliefs, perspectives, and assumptions that are drastically incongruent with the precollege cultures of racial/ethnic minority students, the result can be a noticeably high level of cognitive dissonance among those minority students.

Such experienced cultural dissonance may ultimately hinder their desire or willingness to engage in particular environments and situations on that campus.

UNDERSTANDING THE ROLE OF CULTURAL PROPERTIES IN CREATING CULTURAL DISSONANCE AND SHAPING CROSS-CULTURAL ENGAGEMENT

Cultural events are prevalent on college campuses, but they often fail to attract diverse crowds. Even if an event does attract a diverse group of students, institutional leaders who wish to realize the benefits of cross-cultural engagement face the task of fostering such engagement in sustained and meaningful ways. How can institutional leaders use the concept of cultural dissonance to enhance their understanding of ways to promote meaningful and sustained cross-cultural engagement? One logical starting point might be to examine the cultural charac-teristics of a campus, paying particular attention to which elements increase or decrease levels of cultural dissonance among students. Because minority students are more likely to experience cultural dissonance when engaging in mainstream campus cultural activities and events, a particular point of interest should be attempting to understand how to foster more inclusive campus cultures that minimize cultural dissonance among minority students. In the next section, I provide examples of how cultural values, assumptions, perspectives, and physical artifacts can constitute major sources of cultural dissonance.

TWO FACETS OF INSTITUTIONAL DIVERSITY VALUES: ESPOUSAL AND ENACTMENT

In March 2005, the University of Minnesota announced its strategic plan to become one of the top three public research universities in the world. One corollary of that strategic plan was the closure of the uni-versity's General College, which had historically served as a gateway for under-prepared high school graduates aspiring to attend the university. While the administration simultaneously underscored the importance of diversity, many people interpreted the General College's closing as a symbolic gesture that contradicted the university's espousal of the value of diversity. As a result, faculty, staff, and students created organizations focused on saving the college and protests ensued.

The difference between espoused and enacted diversity values is critical. Whereas *espoused* values refer to shared beliefs about what is important, *enacted* values are beliefs upon which actions are taken by members of the group (Whitt, 1996). There is some indication that whether diversity is an espoused *and* enacted value of an institution may be an important factor in how racial/ethnic minority students, in particular, experience their campus environment (Museus, in press). The situation at the University of Minnesota illustrates how incongruence, or perhaps perceived incongruence, between espoused and enacted values can create cultural dissonance within a particular institutional culture.

Evidence consistently indicates that minority students at predominantly White institutions (PWIs) can experience feelings of alienation, devaluation, exclusion, and isolation (Allen, 1992; Cabrera, Nora, Pascarella, Terenzini, & Hagedorn, 1999; Feagin, Vera, & Imani, 1996; Harper & Hurtado, 2007; Lewis et al., 2000). These manifestations of cultural dissonance can be generated by specific experiences with prejudice and discrimination, but it is also possible, if not probable, that minority students' negative perceptions of their institutional environments are likely to be exacerbated by perceptions of institutional leaders' devaluing of diversity. The arousal of such negative feelings can diminish a student's sense of belonging to, desire to contribute to, and likelihood of engaging in the mainstream campus community. Regardless of the extent to which they espouse the value of diversity, institutions should be aware of whether diversity is perceived as an espoused *and* enacted value of the institution and consider how this might influence student engagement.

CULTURAL ASSUMPTIONS ABOUT GENDER AND RACE: CULTURAL STEREOTYPES

A predominantly White fraternity decided to hold a "Netcong Delta" party, during which the fraternity brothers dressed up as American soldiers and the female students at the party dressed up as Vietnamese prostitutes. Asian students on the campus were extremely offended and concerned about how the fraternity had objectified Asian women.

The incident fueled some minority students' resentment of the climate on their campus.

This incident was revealed during a culture assessment of a rural northeastern public research university. The choice of the theme of the fraternity party was, in part, based on knowledge of and belief in a cultural stereotype. Stereotypes of specific genders and races are ubiquitous in American society. By turning on the television, one can instantly and frequently be exposed and re-exposed to stereotypes of the Asian American nerd, the Black gangster, or the Latina housekeeper. While these stereotypes are often the butt of offensive jokes and popular in race-themed parties organized by predominantly White fraternities and sororities, the preceding example is evidence that stereotypes are potent and anything but benign. The manifestation of the submissive Asian female stereotype reinforced the sexual objectification of Asian women and had a negative impact on race relations on the campus. Such culturally derived assumptions about the behaviors and thoughts of gender and racial groups permeate the media and society; they play a fundamental role in shaping our way of thinking about cultures, communities, and people who differ from ourselves.

Scholars have recently illuminated the hidden dangers intertwined with the existence, perpetuation, and internalization of gender and racial stereotypes. Steele (1999) has exposed stereotypes for their ability to induce anxiety among persons who belong to stereotyped groups—anxiety that, his research indicates, can result in lower academic performance. Moreover, there is some indication that stereotypes can also influence students' predispositions to engage in and out of the classroom (Museus, in press). Administrators hoping to understand the dynamics underlying students' willingness or desire to engage across cultures would benefit from an exploration of how stereotypes generate cultural dissonance and influence students' behavior on their campuses.

CULTURAL PERSPECTIVES: UNWRITTEN RULES AND SOCIAL NORMS

In the movie *Remember the Titans*, a White high school football player, Louie Lastik, sat down at a lunch table to eat with a group of his Black peers. In reaction, one of the Black players at the table asked him what he was doing and why he wasn't sitting with "his people."

The setting of the movie was a recently racially integrated high school in the mid-twentieth century, a period of peak racial tensions in American society. When Lastik sat down at the Black student table, he violated a social norm—an unwritten rule—that governed human behavior in his highly segregated and racially tense community. Though policies banning racial segregation were implemented over 40 years ago, similar factors continue to drive the behavior of college students. This scene highlights the cultural phenomenon at the core of students' decisions about whether to engage in cross-cultural activities. Their decisions are, in part, a function of what they see as normal or socially acceptable behavior in the cultures and subcultures in which they are immersed.

Formal student organizations and affinity groups can be critical sources of academic and social support (Guiffrida, 2003; Kuh & Love, 2000), constituting a venue for the expression of students' cultural heritages and contributions to their minority communities (Guiffrida, 2003; Harper & Quaye, 2007). Such subcultures can also provide spaces where students can experience less cultural dissonance. A gay male student, for example, can often find comfort in joining a student organization or a resource center that provides support for lesbian, gay, bisexual, and transgender (LGBT) students. Because those students have experienced similar struggles, they may have developed some congruent core values, assumptions about sexuality in society, and perspectives that many heterosexual students might not understand; they eventually gravitate toward each other to form a socially cohesive support system. Such cohesive groups are critical to the success of minority students in college (Kuh & Love, 2000; Tierney, 1999; Tinto, 1993). Administrators face the task of respecting the importance of these groups, while simultaneously crafting methods to help students see past their own social norms to recognize the importance of sustained and meaningful cross-cultural engagement.

THE SYMBOLIC MEANING OF SPACE: RACIALLY EXCLUSIVE SPACES

In 2007, shortly after a Black student was noticed sitting under what some students referred to as the "White Tree" at Jena High School, a group of White students hung a noose from the tree. The incident sparked a series of racially charged incidents. After four Black students physically beat a White peer who was involved in the noose hanging at the high school, they faced assault charges and incarceration. As a result of the charges, which many believed to be a manifestation of lingering racial discrimination and differential treatment in the town of Jena, Black communities were joined by individuals of other races across the nation in rallies to have the charges expunged. This course of events was galvanized, in part, by the designation and, in the eyes of some White students, violation of a racially exclusive space.

Physical spaces serve several purposes. They constitute places for people to gather and venues for events to take place. They can carry rich symbolic cultural meaning. In some cases, they play a fundamental role in driving human behavior (Strange & Banning, 2002). The "White Tree" at Jena High School in Jena, Louisiana, served all three of those functions. It served as a physical space for students to gather, it represented a racially exclusive space to some Black *and* White students, and it played prominently in a sequence of politically charged events.

On predominantly White campuses, it is not uncommon for students of color to experience difficulty trying to locate other racial minorities in physical spaces that serve as venues for mainstream campus events. Racial minority students often experience cultural dissonance in situations in which they are the only students of color, or one of few students of color. On some campuses, it can be difficult for students of color to find a space where they feel a real sense of belonging. The reasons for this difficulty are intuitive but may not be obvious. For example, the lawns and courtyards of many campuses are lined with statues of White male alumni, the halls of buildings are covered with paintings of White male presidents, and the rooms are filled with White students. These artifacts can be considered celebrations of a history rich with contributions of White historical figures and their accomplishments, but they can also be interpreted as a reminder that voices of women and people of color have historically been marginalized or excluded on that campus. Institutional leaders should be mindful of how physical environments are structured and the cultural meanings that students attach to those spaces and structures.

CONDUCTING CAMPUS CULTURE ASSESSMENTS FOCUSED ON UNDERSTANDING CROSS-CULTURAL ENGAGEMENT

Both qualitative and quantitative research and evaluation methods can be useful for understanding the impact of cultural factors on the experiences and behaviors of college students (Whitt, 1996). Surveys can provide valuable insight into the extent to which a particular cultural phenomenon permeates a campus, but qualitative methods are indispensable for gaining a holistic understanding of the elements of campus cultures and how they interact to drive behavior and thought. Because the concept of cross-cultural engagement is so complex, qualitative techniques should provide the primary tools for data collection and analysis. Specific techniques useful for conducting culture assessments include individual and group interviews, participant observations, and document analyses. Scholars have discussed these methods as well as their strengths and weaknesses in the context of campus culture assessment (Kuh & Whitt, 1988; Museus, in press; Whitt, 1993; Whitt, 1996), so they will not be discussed in detail here. Instead, the remainder of this chapter contains a brief discussion of several methodological considerations in conducting culture assessments to understand cross-cultural engagement on campus.

Each aspect of a campus culture assessment should be a function of the purpose and focus of that assessment (Whitt, 1996). Nevertheless, useful guidelines can help ensure effectiveness in the design and execution of a campus culture assessment (Kuh & Whitt, 1988; Museus, in press; Whitt, 1993, 1996). This section provides an overview of 12 recommendations that should be considered when assessing campus cultures to understand cross-cultural engagement.

1. **Focus on student attitudes, feelings, thoughts, and experiences about cross-cultural engagement.** Students' meanings, thoughts, feelings, and experiences should be the primary sources of data in attempts to understand cross-cultural engagement on campus. Indeed, student perspectives are the best source for gaining a comprehensive understanding of how various interactive elements of a campus culture shape student decisions about whether to engage in particular activities or interactions with members of other cultures.

2. **To the extent possible, diversify data sources.** Do not assume there is a single truth because there are likely to be multiple truths (Whitt, 1993). The viewpoints of students are most likely a function of a plethora of factors, such as their gender, sexual orientation, race/ethnicity, religion, precollege communities, and political orientations (Whitt, 1996). Moreover, students' perspectives of the campus culture and cross-cultural engagement will probably be a function of the subcultures in which they are most often immersed. A student who spends a majority of the time engaged in Black student union activities might have a very different perspective of campus cultures than a student of the same gender, race, ethnicity, and sexual orientation, who is involved in a wide variety of mainstream cultural activities.

3. **Be prepared to hear things that challenge existing institutional cultures.** Student cultures should not be studied if institutions are unwilling to consider students' perspectives (Whitt, 1996). Institutions of higher education have adopted and, for so long, maintained a magical way of thinking about cross-cultural interaction. Discovering students' perspectives about elements of campus culture that may impede cross-cultural engagement and contribute to segregation and hostile climates on campus may challenge long-standing institutional policies, programs, and practices.

4. **Be aware of your own biases, assumptions, values, perceptions and attitudes throughout the assessment.** Anyone conducting a campus culture assessment to understand cross-cultural engagement has interacted with people of different genders, races, ethnicities, sexual orientations, or religions. Based on those experiences, they are likely to have their own notions about how people feel and what they think when interacting across cultures. While researchers' experiential knowledge and beliefs can be informative and useful, those conducting campus culture assessments should be aware of how those preconceived notions may influence their interpretation of assessment data. If the purpose of assessment is discovery, prejudgments about what is appropriate or *right* should be suspended (Whitt, 1996).

5. **Pay attention to cultural contexts.** Culture exists on many levels. Everyone on college campuses, for example, functions within the broader culture of society, the institutionwide culture of their college or university, and the organizational subculture of their department or office. Organizational subcultures should be studied in the context of institutional cultures, and institutional cultures should be studied in the context of external cultures (Whitt, 1996). With regard to cross-cultural interaction, the importance of this consideration is particularly salient. Case in point: After the terrorist attacks on September 11, 2001, many students on college campuses across the country perceived or experienced an upsurge of cultural, racial, and religious tension. Many Muslim students were concerned about backlash and may have avoided environments with low levels of monitoring and security to evade racial and religious discrimination. This is just one example of how consideration of cultural contexts is critical to understanding the cross-cultural relations of students on campus—and the importance of involving someone in the culture assessment who is knowledgeable about those various levels of culture.

6. **Be prepared to invest resources to study culture.** Developing an understanding of an institution's culture requires extensive immersion in that culture and can be costly, in terms of both time and money (Whitt & Kuh, 1991). Several considerations factor into the cost of a culture assessment: the number of investigators involved, training for researchers, and the scope of the study (Whitt, 1996). Especially on large campuses, the amount of resources needed to capture a holistic understanding of the impact campus cultures have on students' behaviors and experiences across subcultures can be a daunting task. Moreover, because of the focus on cross-cultural engagement, culture assessments will require the inclusion of several people across multiple subcultures to gain a comprehensive understanding of cultural influences on such engagement.

7. **Expect and embrace ambiguity.** Campus cultures are messy, because many elements of culture are multifaceted, contradictory, intertwined, hidden, and unarticulated (Kuh & Whitt, 1988; Whitt, 1996). If a culture assessment is focused on understanding cross-cultural engagement, it is likely to become even more complicated and confusing. Understanding

a student's attitudes toward a particular institutional value, for instance, can be a complicated task, but is probably easier than trying to discover how a particular institutional value might facilitate or hinder that student's willingness or desire to engage in situations conducive to interacting across cultures. Researchers should, therefore, be ready to engage in extensive and mentally rigorous immersion in those cultures.

8. **Understand that more time spent studying a culture leads to a better understanding of that culture.** Researchers conducting campus culture assessments should allow sufficient time for cultures to reveal themselves in all their complexity (Whitt, 1993, 1996). Unfortunately, administrators and institutional researchers are often limited in how much time and energy they can invest in assessing their own campus cultures. Because an understanding of a campus's culture is likely to evolve over time, those who wish to understand how cultural factors influence cross-cultural engagement must be prepared to continue a culture assessment over extended periods if they are to develop a more holistic and complex comprehension of the forces at work in that culture.

9. **Use external researchers and evaluators.** External researchers and evaluators can provide a more objective perspective of the cultural dynamics at work on a particular campus. Unless they are newcomers to the campus culture, administrators and institutional researchers usually have fairly well-developed perceptions of, attitudes about, and beliefs regarding the students and environments on their campus. While their perspectives may be a valuable contribution to the culture assessment, their biases can get in the way of objective interpretation of other people's perspectives and attitudes. When resources permit, the use of external evaluators or researchers is desirable.

10. **Consider the benefits of triangulation and integration.** Triangulation—the use of multiple data sources and data collection methods—is a common technique among qualitative researchers that helps enhance the quality and trustworthiness of the findings of a particular study (Lincoln & Guba, 1986). When conducting campus culture assessments, researchers should also consider the importance of integrating the various data sources and methods. Consider the scenario earlier

in this chapter in which a Hispanic student attended an alumni event and left shortly after her arrival. The cultural dissonance that surfaced for this student drove her behavior and, therefore, is likely to be fresh in her mind. Researchers observing this incident could solicit the student's participation in an interview and gain rich data about the relationship between the cultural tensions she experienced and her decision to leave the event. Thus, while data collection methods might be separated into different phases, flexibility should be maintained so that such opportune moments can be used to inform the assessment.

11. **Consider the overlap of institutional subcultures.** College students often belong to several institutional subcultures. Indeed, one student can simultaneously be engaged in an academic department, student government, an ethnic student organization, and multiple affinity groups—all of which might have their own unique dominant cultural properties. As a result of the influences from multiple subcultures, several students within one subculture might have disparate perspectives, attitudes, and beliefs than others engaged in the same subculture. Thus, researchers should be careful not to generalize the viewpoints of a few individuals to an entire subculture on campus, for one student's views may partially represent many subcultures but holistically represent none. This overlap of institutional subcultures blurs the lines between what is and is not thematic or common across subcultures, and complicates understandings of how one can make sense of an institutional culture. Martin (1992) has provided a typology of cultural perspectives that can be useful in studying campus cultures. Her *integration* perspective focuses on common and shared elements of culture; the *differentiation* perspective is centered on understanding what is inconsistent across subcultures; and the *fragmentation* perspective focuses on the ambiguities of culture. Employing all three perspectives contributes to a more complete and intricate understanding of cultures and subcultures.

12. **Be aware of the difficulty in understanding cross-cultural engagement.** Researchers should not expect to gain an understanding of how cultures influence cross-cultural engagement by simply asking questions, listening to responses, and reporting what was found. It is

possible that some college students have never thought deeply or meaningfully about their interactions and engagement across cultures. Asking them questions about why they do not attend cultural awareness events may produce more moments of silence and uncomfortable attempts to respond to a question for which they do not have an answer. It is critical, therefore, for researchers to understand how they can engage assessment participants in deep and meaningful discussion about the various factors that contribute to cultural dissonance. By focusing on the concept of dissonance, researchers can overcome the ambiguity of the influence of culture and focus the discussion on which institutional artifacts, values, perspectives, and assumptions create internal conflict and tension for students.

Conclusion

In his discussion of the limitations of organizational theorists' study of organizational culture, Schein (1996) explained:

> We did not grasp that norms held tacitly across large social units were much more likely to change leaders than to be changed by them. We failed to note that 'culture,' viewed as such taken-for-granted, shared, tacit ways of perceiving, thinking, and reacting, was one of the most powerful and stable forces operating in organizations. (p. 231)

The purpose of this chapter is twofold. First, it is designed to offer a new perspective for viewing institutional realities and efforts to facilitate cross-cultural engagement by bringing to administrators' attention the power of culture as a tool for acquiring rich insights into the intersection between institutional environments and individual behavior. Second, while transforming institutional cultures is beyond the scope of this chapter, the current discussion highlights the potential power of culture as a vehicle for fostering environments conducive to sustained and meaningful cross-cultural engagement. Despite the messiness and difficulty encountered when using cultural perspectives, higher education administrators and institutional researchers stand to benefit a great deal from employing such cultural perspectives.

References

Allen, W. R. (1992). The color of success: African-American college student outcomes at predominantly white and historically black public colleges and universities. *Harvard Educational Review, 62*(1), 26–44.

Allport, G. (1954). *The nature of prejudice.* Cambridge, MA: Addison-Wesley.

antonio, a. l. (2001a). Diversity and the influence of friendship groups in college. *Review of Higher Education, 25*(1), 63–89.

antonio, a. l. (2001b). The role of interracial interaction in the development of leadership skills and cultural knowledge and understanding. *Research in Higher Education, 42*(5), 593–617.

Astin, A. W. (1993). *What matters in college: Four critical years revisited.* San Francisco: Jossey-Bass.

Becher, T. (1984). The cultural view. In B. Clark (Ed.), *Perspectives in higher education.* Berkley: University of California Press.

Bolton, C. D., & Kammeyer, K. C. W. (1972). Campus cultures, roles orientations, and social type. In K. Feldman (Ed.), *College and student: Selected readings in the social psychology of higher education.* New York: Pergamon Press.

Bourdieu, P., & Passeron, J. C. (1977). *Reproduction in education, society, and culture,* London: Sage Publications.

Bowen, W. G., & Bok, D. (1998). *The shape of the river: Long-term consequences of considering race in college and university admissions.* Princeton, NJ: Princeton University Press.

Cabrera, A., Nora, A., Pascarella, E. T., Terenzini, P. T., & Hagedorn, L. (1999). Campus racial climate and the adjustment of students to college: A comparison between white students and African-American students. *Journal of Higher Education, 70,* 134–160.

Chang, M. J. (1999). Does racial diversity matter?: The educational impact of a racially diverse undergraduate population. *Journal of College Student Development, 40*, 377–395.

Chang, M. J. (2002). Racial dynamics on campus: What student organizations can tell us. *About Campus, 7*(1), 2–8.

Chang, M. J., Astin, A. W., & Kim, D. (2004). Cross-racial interaction among undergraduates: Some consequences, causes, and patterns. *Research in Higher Education, 45*(5), 529–553.

Chang, M. J., Chang, J. C., & Ledesma, M. C. (2005). Beyond magical thinking: Doing the real work of diversifying our institutions. *About Campus, 10*(2), 9–16.

Chang, M. J., Denson, N., Sáenz, V., & Misa, K. (2006). The educational benefits of sustaining cross-racial interaction among undergraduates. *Journal of Higher Education, 77*(3), 430–455.

Chang, M. J., Witt, D., Jones, J., & Hakuta, K. (Eds.). (2003). *Compelling interest: Examining the evidence on racial dynamics in colleges and universities.* Stanford, CA: Stanford University Press.

Cross, K. (1971). *Beyond the open door: New students to higher education.* San Francisco: Jossey-Bass.

Feagin, J. R. (1992). The continuing significance of racism: Discrimination against black students in white colleges. *Journal of Black Studies, 22*(4), 546-78.

Feagin, J. R., Vera, H., & Imani, N. (1996). *The agony of education: Black students at white colleges and universities.* New York: Routledge.

Festinger, L. (1957). *A theory of cognitive dissonance.* Stanford, CA: Stanford University Press.

Fries-Britt, S., & Turner, B. (2001). Facing stereotypes: A case study of black students on a white campus. *Journal of College Student Development, 42*, 420–429.

Gonzalez, K. P. (2003). Campus culture and the experiences of chicano students in a predominantly white university. *Urban Education, 37*(2), 193–218.

Gratz v. Bollinger, et al., 123 S.Ct. 2411.2003.

Grutter v. Bollinger, et al., 123 S.Ct. 2325. 2003.

Guiffrida, D. A. (2003). African American student organizations as agents of social integration. *Journal of College Student Development, 44*(3), 304–319.

Gurin, P., Dey, E., Hurtado, S., & Gurin, G. (2002). Diversity in higher education: Theory and impact on educational outcomes. *Harvard Educational Review, 72,* 330–366.

Harper, S. R., & Hurtado, S. (2007). Nine themes in campus racial climates. In S. R. Harper & L. D. Patton (Eds.), *Responding to the realities of race on campus: New Directions for Student Services, No. 120.* San Francisco: Jossey-Bass.

Harper, S. R., & Quaye, S. J. (2007). Student organizations as venues for black identity expression and development among African American male student leaders. *Journal of College Student Development, 48*(2).

Hurtado, S. (2001). Linking diversity and educational purpose: How diversity affects the classroom environment and student development. In G. Orfield & M. Kurleander (Eds.), *Diversity challenged: Evidence on the impact of affirmative action* (pp. 187–203). Cambridge, MA: Harvard Education Publishing Group.

Hurtado, S., Dey, E. L., Gurin, P. P., & Gurin, G. (2003). College environments, Diversity, and student learning. In J. C. Smart (Ed.), *Higher Education: Handbook of Theory and Research.* Vol. 18. Amsterdam: Kluwer.

Hurtado, S., Milem, J. F., Clayton-Pedersen, A. R., & Allen, W. R. (1998). Enhancing campus climates for racial/ethnic diversity: Educational policy and practice. *Review of Higher Education, 21*(3), pp. 279–302.

Kohlberg, L. (1971). Stages of moral development. In C. Beck, B. Crittenden, & E. Sullivan (Eds.), *Moral education.* Toronto: University of Toronto Press.

Kuh, G. D. (2001/2002). Organizational culture and student persistence: Prospects and puzzles. *Journal of College Student Retention: Research, theory, & Practice, 3*(1), 23-39.

Kuh, G. D., & Hall, J. E. (1993). Using cultural perspectives in student affairs. In G. D. Kuh (Ed.), *Cultural perspectives in student affairs work.* Lanham, MD: American College Personnel Association.

Kuh, G. D., & Love, P. G. (2000). A cultural perspective on student departure. In J. M. Braxton (Ed.), *Reworking the student departure puzzle* (pp. 196–212). Nashville: Vanderbilt University Press.

Kuh, G. D., & Whitt, E. J. (1988). *The invisible tapestry: Culture in American colleges and universities.* ASHE-ERIC Higher Education Report Series. Washington, DC: Association for the Study of Higher Education.

Lewis, A. E., Chesler, M., & Forman, T. A. (2000). The impact of "colorblind" ideologies on students of color: Intergroup relations at a predominantly white university. *The Journal of Negro Education, 69*(1/2), 74–91.

Lincoln, Y. S., & Guba, E. G. (1986) But is it rigorous? Trustworthiness and authenticity in naturalistic evaluation. *New Directions for Program Evaluation, 30,* 73–84.

Love, P. G., & Others (1993). Student culture. In G. D. Kuh (Ed.), *Cultural perspectives in student affairs work.* Lanham, MD: American College Personnel Association.

Manning, K. (1993). Properties of institutional culture. In G. D. Kuh (Ed.), *Cultural perspectives in student affairs work.* Lanham, MD: American College Personnel Association.

Milem, J. F. (1994). College, students, and racial understanding. *Thought and Action, 9*(2), 51–92.

Milom, J. F., & Hakuta, K. (2000). The benefits of racial and ethnic diversity in higher education, featured report. In D. Wilds (Ed.), *Minorities in higher education: Seventeenth annual status report* (pp. 39-67). Washington, DC: American Council on Education.

Museus, S. D. (In Press). Using qualitative methods to assess diverse campus cultures. In S. R. Harper & S. D. Museus (Eds.), *Using qualitative methods in institutional assessment: New Directions for Institutional Research*. San Francisco: Jossey-Bass.

Nora, A., & Cabrera, A. (1996). The role of perceptions of prejudice and discrimination on the adjustment of minority students to college. *Journal of Higher Education, 67*, 119-148.

Pascarella, E. T., Edison, M., Nora, A., Hagedorn, L. S., & Terenzini, P. T. (1996). Influences on students' openness to diversity and challenge in the first year of college. *The Journal of Higher Education, 67*(2), 174-195.

Perry, R. (1970). *Forms of intellectual and ethical development in the college years: A scheme*. New York: Holt, Rinehart & Winston.

Regents of the University of California v. Bakke, 438 U.S. 265. [http://laws.findlaw.com/us/438/265.html]. 1978. Retrieved November 4, 2004.

Sax, L., & Astin, A. W. (1997). The development of civic virtue among college students. In J. N. Gardner & G. Van der Veer (Eds.), *The senior year experience: Facilitating integration, reflection, closure, and transition*. San Francisco: Jossey-Bass.

Schein, E. H. (1992). *Organizational culture and leadership* (2nd ed.). San Francisco: Jossey-Bass.

Schein, E. H. (1996). Culture: The missing concept in organization studies. *Administrative Science Quarterly, 41*(2), 229-240.

Smith, D. G., Gerbick, G. L., Figueroa, M. A., Watkins, G. H., Levitan, T., Moore, L. C. et al. (1997). *Diversity works: The emerging picture of how students benefit*. Washington, DC: Association of American Colleges and Universities.

Steele, C. (1999). A threat in the air: How stereotypes shape intellectual identity and performance. *American Psychologist, 52*(6), 613–629.

Suzuki, B. H. (2002). *Revisiting the model minority stereotype: Implications for student affairs practice and higher education: New Directions for Student Services, No.* 97 (pp. 21–32). San Francisco: Jossey-Bass.

Tierney, W. G. (1999). Models of minority college-going and retention: Cultural integrity versus cultural suicide. *The Journal of Negro Education, 68*(1), 80-91.

Tinto, V. (1993). *Leaving college: Rethinking the causes and cures of student attrition* (2 ed.). Chicago: University of Chicago Press.

Whitt, E. J. (1993). Making the familiar strange. In G. D. Kuh (Ed.), *Cultural perspectives in student affairs work.* Lanham, MD: University Press of American and American College Personnel Association.

Whitt, E. J. (1996). Assessing student cultures. In M. L. Upcraft and J. H. Schuh (Eds.), *Assessment in student affairs: A guide for practitioners.* San Francisco: Jossey-Bass.

Whitt, E. J., & Kuh, G. D. (1991). The use of qualitative methods in a team approach to multiple institution studies. *Review of Higher Education, 14*(3), 317–337.

Chapter Twelve

○○○○○

Enacting Multicultural and Democratic Ideals on Campus: Challenges and Possibilities

Dominique C. Hill and Peter M. Magolda

○○○○○

Multiculturalism and *democracy* are popular buzzwords in higher education. Despite the ease with which colleges and universities espouse these ideals, enacting them remains a challenge. This chapter introduces and critiques multiple discourses centering on multiculturalism and democracy by examining two narratives based on our experience in higher education. The analysis and recommendations that follow illuminate the complexities, paradoxes, and struggles associated with creating and maintaining multicultural democratic communities in the diverse, politically charged, and ever-changing world of higher education.

Lonely, Not Alone: The Value of Collegiate Subcultures

College was my road toward self-discovery and self-redefinition. In 2001, soon after I (Dominique) arrived at a small predominantly White university in upstate New York, I immediately searched for peers with whom I could identify and relate. I expected and feared that I would be the only Black student in most of my classes, and I was correct. I had been down this road before, but this time I was in uncharted territory without my family. I was determined to "make it" no matter what.

Colgate University, a private institution atop a hill in the middle of remote upstate New York, made me an offer I couldn't refuse. The academic grant the university awarded me covered most of my $35,000 annual tuition. I earned the right to attend college as a result of hard work, rigorous academic preparation, and family support, which was a significant accomplishment since the majority of my neighborhood peers considered it a monumental achievement to graduate from high school. An educational opportunity not available to everyone awaited me. And I correctly suspected that this college education came with a price. Once again I had to prove to my professors and peers that *I deserved to be here*. Like I did in high school, I embraced the challenge.

During orientation, the three days before the start of my first semester, I attended several programs and workshops. Topics included student success, academic integrity, decision-making, and, of course, the importance of campus diversity. Exposing new students to the *realities* of college was a primary goal. Colgate prides itself on celebrating diversity; annually it dedicates an entire day of orientation to diversity, where students participate in various workshops and discussions. For 12 continuous hours, new students, faculty, and staff discuss and debate multicultural-related topics. The university's commitment to diversity actually surprised me during this epic transition.

I usually relish dialogue about differences—racial, gender, sexual orientation, or otherwise. Yet, during this diversity marathon my enthusiasm waned. Too often, workshop facilitators and peers singled me out and asked questions such as, "What's YOUR experience like?" or "How do Black people feel . . . ?" I had no idea how other Black people felt; nor did I possess the arrogance to speak for them as if I did "know." I contemplated—if I remained silent, my peers would miss out on hearing a Black student's perspective; if I candidly and passionately spoke, I might shut down the conversation, offend some attendees, or even worse, become *the* voice of Colgate Black students. Despite these apprehensions, I shared my views. I concluded that I would rather have my peers misinterpret *my* views as those of *all* Black students than allow the workshop dynamics to silence me. As the daylong session concluded, my peers and I experienced diversity fatigue and overload, while concurrently realizing that we merely scratched the surface.

In 2001, of the 2,800 Colgate undergraduates, only about 13% were students of color. During my first week on campus, while crossing the academic quad, I passed numerous clusters of almost identically dressed White peers. They did not resemble me. My wardrobe did not include bright polo shirts with popped collars, For-All-Mankind jeans, Gucci and Coach purses, and J. Crew jackets. Popular chatter, usually centering on working out or hooking up, seldom interested me. Amid hundreds of people, I felt alone, like an outsider. Eventually I encountered a student of color; we engaged in the "knowing nod" ritual, acknowledging each other's presence. I cherished the nod since this transient peer was one of the few persons of color I would likely encounter all day. During my early weeks on campus, faculty, students, and student affairs administrators reached out and tried to support me. Still, uneasy feelings of loneliness and marginalization ensued.

Two weeks later, the university sponsored a student involvement fair. Organizers encouraged first-year students to attend to gather information about student organizations and clubs that might interest them. Hundreds of students clogged the narrow aisles surrounding closely aligned tables; I struggled to navigate this event. Occasionally, organizational members offered me informational brochures about their group. No doubt, recruitment was the implicit aim of this gathering, while making connections was my goal. As I struggled to maneuver the crowded aisles, I avoided eye contact with representatives whose organizations did not interest me. Quickly, I became proficient at smiling, while looking downward. Some representatives looked past me as I stood at their table and perused their brochures.

I wondered if anyone else noticed that all of the racial/ethnic organizations occupied a single row? The segregated tables intrigued me. Representatives from these organizations—African American Student Alliance, Caribbean Student Association, and Sisters of the Round Table—bombarded me with welcoming rhetoric, brochures, and candy. I exchanged contact information with too many organizations, mostly because I felt obligated to support them. Secretly, I hoped most of these organization representatives would not contact me. Still, I wanted to find at least one group where I might belong.

Exhausted, I began to conclude my whirlwind participation in the fair. En route to the exit, I encountered the Rainbow Alliance, a group of nonheterosexual identified students and supporters. They offered me a handout and a condom. I knew little about the goals of a lesbian, gay, bisexual, transgender, or queer student organization. Should I exchange contact information with the Rainbow Alliance? I quickly concluded that I should, so I did.

I returned to my residence hall and sorted through my fair artifacts. I pondered with which groups, if any, I should affiliate. Ultimately, I joined the African American Student Alliance (AASA) because the members took the time to talk to me and they seemed genuinely interested in my experience. Because several of my new acquaintances also intended to join AASA, my decision made sense. Initially, I resisted my urge to attend a meeting of the Sisters of the Round Table (SORT), a women's organization, fearing what others might think if I actually joined a *women's* group. As I deliberated, I mentally rehearsed my rationale—I need more racial affirmation and I could get my gender identity affirmed at the same time as I celebrated my racial self. I eventually joined.

Throughout my first semester I regularly attended AASA meetings and involved myself with SORT. I grew close to members of both organizations. We regularly attended campus lectures that featured speakers of color. I eagerly anticipated these campuswide programs and spent considerable time afterward sitting with SORT and AASA members, informally processing the experiences. I appreciated Colgate's decision to fund programs that brought these distinguished speakers to campus. Yet a sense of discomfort persisted. Speakers and other racial/ethnic programming such as cultural banquets and "appreciation of difference" symposia simultaneously felt both grand and shallow. These programs spawned dialogues centering on diversity that appeared to make my White peers comfortable. Oddly, safe within the confines of AASA and SORT, I remained uncomfortable.

During my second semester, I accepted a job at the Center for Women's Studies to fulfill my work-study obligation. It was one of the few places hiring on campus. I had no idea that accepting this part-time job would significantly contribute to my development as a Black woman. As a staff member, I began to understand my struggles related to gender. I became more aware of sexism and the ways it complicates the lives of Black students, particularly Black women. Intellectually stimulating formal and informal discussions regularly occurred at the center. During these gatherings, attendees voiced their opinions about complex and contentious issues. At first, I realized that my views and opinions were raw. I felt unprepared and ill-informed. But the longer I participated in these discussions, the more comfortable and educated I became. I learned to freely share my informed views. For the first time, I perceived myself as a Black woman rather than a Black person.

My work-study job and cocurricular experiences shaped my identity. SORT, a group that once seemed too political and radical, genuinely appealed to and influenced me. SORT functioned both as a support network for women of color as well as a vehicle to bring about awareness of issues affecting women of color to local and global audiences. Many SORT women were extremely vocal, strong-willed, and supportive (descriptors others eventually conferred on me). Initially, these women's views intimidated me. I feared their power, rooted in knowledge and conviction. Over time, my fright subsided and *my* voice emerged. I became more comfortable with myself.

From the outset of my undergraduate experience at Colgate, I searched for communities that welcomed me, wanted to *know* me, challenged me, supported me, and ultimately respected me. At first, I perceived the university's demographics and organizational structures as barriers to attaining this goal. I eventually discovered ways and some places to fit in; I was no longer lonely and definitely not alone.

COLLEGIATE SUBCULTURE ASSETS: AN ANALYSIS

We begin this chapter with a story about Dominique's first semester of college for two reasons. First, the story reminds readers that new students' transitions to college are both challenging and stressful. Adjusting to new surroundings, managing academic demands, meeting new peers, and finding comfortable niches are not easy tasks. The proliferation of scholarly writings centering on the importance of the first year of college (e.g., Erickson, Peters, Strommer, & Erickson, 2006; Reason, Terenzini, & Domingo, 2007; Rendón, Garcia, & Person, 2004; Barefoot, Gardner, Cutright, Morris, Schroeder, Schwartz, Siegel, & Swing, 2005; Ward-Roof & Hatch, 2003) and the ever-increasing number of student affairs educators dedicated exclusively to support new students suggest that higher education recognizes the importance of this complex rite of passage for new students. Without sufficient human resources, a supportive institutional ethos and infrastructure, mentors, and a theoretically sophisticated understanding of this transition, new students at best will not likely optimize their collegiate experiences; at worst, they will drop out of college (Seidman, 2005; Tinto, 1987).

The story also reminds readers that this transition is more complex and challenging for students if they are underrepresented at their higher education institution (Allen, 1992; Jackson, 1998; Martinez-Aleman, 2000; Williamson, 1999). Being a Black woman attending a predominantly White and male-dominated university adds layers of complexity (e.g., racial insensitivity, cultural assimilation) onto an already challenging transitional experience (Constantine & Watt, 2002; Cureton, 2003; Howard-Hamilton, 2003).

Some implicit institutional expectations—e.g., to be successful in college, students of color need to leave behind their cultural heritage; students of color should educate the larger campus community about "the students of color experience"—challenged Dominique. Nine years earlier, Stage and Manning (1992) in *Enhancing the Multicultural Campus Environment: A Cultural Brokering Approach* documented similar institutional expectations for students of color. In 2007, these unreasonable expectations and burdens persist. New students of color often struggle to celebrate their racial/ethnic identities and find it challenging to locate racial/ethnic enclaves and secure spaces that are both supportive and free of insensitivity (Weis, 1985). These issues lead us to key questions: How do students of color achieve similar rights and responsibilities as White students, while not abandoning their own identities? How can higher education be more responsive to these dynamics?

As Dominique navigated the campus, she was keenly aware that her peers neither looked like her nor dressed like her. She also encountered similar dynamics at her all-female predominantly White Catholic high school, which had no faculty of color. Comparable past experiences are helpful but never fully prepare students for this unique collegiate transition. Students of color may fantasize about higher education being an island of equity and justice in a societal sea of racial insensitivity, but soon after they arrive on campus, they recognize that higher education mirrors society. Feelings of estrangement are typically commonplace.

Admittedly, the assertions that students' transition to college is complicated and that those from underrepresented groups often experience unique transition challenges are hardly groundbreaking revelations. Yet there is a third theme embedded in Dominique's story, which centers on the importance of student subcultures in helping new students, especially students of color, adjust to college. Oddly, despite the presence and proliferation of collegiate student subcultures, higher education scholars and practitioners seldom scrutinize this concept by posing and answering these two important questions: "Why do subcultures form?" and "What functions do these communities of interest serve?"

The formation of university subcultures in general and collegiate student subcultures in particular is often linked to an idyllic dream of community in the academy. A Duke University department chair's ruminations included in a faculty newsletter capture this quest for community in academia: "I crave a sense of belonging, the feeling that I am a part of an enterprise larger than myself, part of a group that shares some common purposes . . ." (Willimon & Naylor, 1995, p. 144). A Carnegie Foundation (1990) survey of college presidents found that 98% stated it was either "very important" or "somewhat important" to devote "greater effort to build a stronger overall sense of community" (p. A-4). Seventeen years after the Carnegie Foundation published these survey findings, this desire for community—linked to belonging and common purpose—remains a priority; for most, the quest continues.

Few faculty, staff, or students would disagree with the assertion that building and maintaining community is important, as it is a near-universal ideal. The more interesting and contentious issue centers on a question seldom posed: "What kind of community should higher education aspire to be?" Answering this question illuminates some of the liabilities and dangers associated with academia's community quest and the rise of subcultures.

Carlson's (1994) critique of community synthesizes many of the concerns implicit in that question. He asserts that the dominant idea of community in America (including the field of higher education) is a normalizing community. Such a community is built upon common ideas; its goal is homogeneity. By virtue of answering the question, "What kind of community should higher education aspire to be," institutional/organizational values emerge, which become the foundation for what is normal. Within normalizing communities, those in power define a "natural" cultural center that renders dominant group behaviors and values acceptable, while relegating others to the margins.

Normalizing communities privilege certain individuals, activities, roles, and relationships. Marginalized groups that speak out and challenge their marginalized status often form new (or join existing) subcultures that provide much-needed support and safe space, a foundation for identity development. These oppositional subcultures encourage members to forge a group identity and deconstruct their individual and collective campus experiences to reveal the social and power inequities that contribute to their ostracized feelings.

Most colleges and universities value community. Like the aforementioned department chair at Duke University, colleges and universities want students to feel a sense of belonging, of being part of an educational enterprise larger than themselves. Dominique's orientation program exemplified one way Colgate encouraged students to connect with the institution and each other. Glimpses of this particular school's conceptualization of community (and core values) emerged. It purposefully oriented and socialized new students by sponsoring a three-day orientation program. It valued diversity, symbolically conveyed by its decision to allocate one third of its orientation program to this topic. The university also affirmed its commitment to diversity in the cocurriculum by sponsoring a fair showcasing an eclectic array of student organizations aimed at supporting students and facilitating their sense of belonging.

Every collegiate community espouses core values of the institution (which could otherwise be characterized as *the natural cultural center*); these values, if enacted, become the foundation for what becomes normal. Individuals who embrace these values are deemed normal, and thus privileged. Colgate students' bright polo shirts with popped collars, For-All-Mankind jeans, Gucci and Coach purses, and J. Crew jackets exemplified what was normal for Colgate students in 2001. This informal dress code privileges certain individuals and relegates others to outsider status. As Rhoads (1994) noted, "We develop languages and social practices that exclude, order, disperse, and limit any behaviors or characteristics outside the mainstream" (p. 101).

This normalizing process is seldom manifested via coercion or blatant socialization efforts. Instead, it occurs by making the acts seem legitimate and natural. Stuart Hall (as cited in Hebdige, 1979) notes that dominant cultures exert "'total social control' over subordinate groups, not by coercion or by the direct imposition of ruling ideas, 'but by winning and shaping consent so that the power of the dominant classes appears both legitimate and natural'" (pp. 15–16). Colgate students were not required to adhere to a dress code. Instead, those in power shaped student consent so that wearing a J. Crew jacket and For-All-Mankind jeans became perceivably normal and natural.

Declaring what is *normal* inevitably creates insiders and outsiders. Carlson (1994) argued that communities of interest and subcultures emerge as the idea of a single "unified in thought and action" community eludes the larger social entity, such as a college campus. These norms are prescribed codes to which insiders must adhere. Outsiders or those who do not hold fast to these dominant norms (e.g., Dominique's resistance to subscribe to the dominant dress code or join mainstream student organizations) are relegated to the margins. Outsiders are keenly aware of these social controls that govern their daily lives and how power is aligned with allegiance to dominant ideologies. Their reluctance to embrace them often contributes to feelings of estrangement or marginalization.

Culture shapes social life. Subcultures form in reaction or opposition to the hegemony of dominant groups and the voids within the existing dominant culture (Hebdige, 1979). Subcultures provide voice and identity to their members. For example, most Black students on predominantly White campuses are visually different. An implicit norm is for the Black students to "act White," which will ensure that the institution maintains the status quo. The assumption is that Black students can gain insider status by accepting these dominant norms and expectations.

An alternative path is to forge alliances with others through subcultures that also reject these norms. Peers who asked Dominique to speak on behalf of all Black students revealed their lack of understanding about the complexities of race and, more specifically, Black people. These normalizing expectations accelerated her desire to locate more ideologically compatible communities with shared interests including race, culture, and style of dress. She met and befriended other Black students and women who sustained her on campus, gave her voice, and shaped her identity. Students of color must stand together or face oppression alone (Thompson & Fretz, 1991).

Collegiate Subculture Assets: Some Caveats

Implicit in this particular conceptualization of subculture are three caveats. First, subcultures come in all shapes and sizes including formal and easily delineated enclaves (e.g., College Republicans) as well as informal and less-bounded communities of interest (e.g., politically conservative students). Subcultures are not synonymous with formal organizations and need not be sanctioned in order to exist. Individuals also involve themselves with multiple subcultures concurrently. For Dominique, her involvement in SORT exemplifies a formal and delineated subculture, while her affiliation with women hanging out in the Center for Women's Studies represents a more informal and less-bounded subculture. Participating in both kinds of subcultures helped Dominique greatly with her adjustment to college and supported her curricular and cocurricular pursuits.

Second, the labels of culture and subculture are fluid, not absolute, categories. Subcultures are dependent on and qualified by the dominant culture. Thus, the larger dominant culture defines the subculture. One could designate all student organizations as the larger and more dominant *culture* while designating racial/ethnic student organizations as the *subculture*. Likewise, one could characterize racial/ethnic organizations as the *culture*, while defining the Caribbean Student Association as a *subculture*. Subcultures regularly nest within subcultures. For example, racial/ethnic student organizations could be a subculture of all student organizations; the Caribbean Student Association could be a subculture of the racial/ethnic student organization category; women members could be a subculture of the Caribbean Student Association; and Jamaican women could be a subculture of the women members of the Caribbean Student Association. Understanding the interrelationship between culture and subculture is more important and productive than defining what counts as a culture or subculture. Nested within subcultures such as SORT and the Center for Women's Studies (which in Dominique's context were subcultures of the larger university) were other subcultures (e.g., activist SORT members and passive SORT members). These subcultures within subcultures also provided Dominique the much-needed challenge and support she desired to forge her identity and fit in.

Third, subcultures, like the larger dominant culture, have normalizing expectations for their members. Though these expectations may or may not be explicitly stated, they are part of the subculture's identity. These socially constructed assumptions and values illuminate the interdependence between one's self and the subculture, and reveal how power affects group relationships and individual identity. The subcultures and subcultures within subcultures of Dominique's affiliation expected her to function not merely as a participant, but also to advance the group's agenda of making peers aware of the issues women of color encounter locally and globally (i.e., this subculture's normalizing expectation).

Students' past cultural experiences and social histories contribute to their identities. Many students of color, in particular, resist the idea of casting aside their "irrelevant" cultural pasts in order to fit in and earn a college degree (Rendón,

1994). As a result, collegiate subcultures arise out of voids in a particular context and provide safe spaces for members to build on their past cultural experiences and celebrate their histories. Affiliations with subcultures, especially for underrepresented students, allow them to gain a deeper understanding of the self as well as the other. Subcultures reveal normalizing expectations, inequities, and injustices. Prior to her involvement in the Center for Women's Studies, Dominique viewed her life solely through a racial lens. As she interacted with this enclave of women, she expanded her understanding of the importance of both race and gender in her identity development. These revelations prompted her to think differently about power, inequalities, and injustice.

College student subcultures are valuable and worth forming, maintaining, and celebrating. Without the presence of these subcultures, new student transitions would be more difficult and turbulent. This is especially true on a predominantly White campus, where support for racial and ethnic diversity is more complicated. That said, student subcultures on college campuses are necessary but insufficient. In the narrative that follows, we reveal subculture liabilities—most notably, the reluctance of subcultures to cross borders and engage in multicultural democratic discourses with other subcultures.

CAN'T WE ALL GET ALONG? SUBCULTURES AND THE CHALLENGE OF INITIATING PUBLIC DISCOURSE

Since 1992, the year I (Peter) joined the Miami University College Student Personnel (CSP) program faculty, we have engaged in an annual ritual of identifying prospective graduate students for our academic community. In the short term, we hope many of these prospective students will enroll in our program. In the long term, we hope these individuals will join the student affairs profession and passionately educate college students, both inside and outside the classroom.

CSP faculty have been down the recruitment road many times. Will we be able to recruit enough men, non-traditional-age students, and students of color? Enrolling a diverse graduate student cohort—reflecting the gender, ethnic, age, sexual orientation, and socioeconomic demographics of the universities where these students will eventually work and the societies in which they will live—is a faculty priority. Although we desire a diverse student cohort, we also desire an academic community that values solidarity. Achieving these two aims is easier said than done.

Encouraging diverse applicants to enroll at a mid-size predominantly White public university in the remote southwest corner of Ohio is a formidable undertaking. We try to make prospective students an offer they can't refuse—tuition, a modest stipend, and a challenging and supportive curriculum that integrates seamlessly with assistantship or fellowship opportunities. The financial package helps students get by. The seamless integration of classroom and out-of-class learning coupled with supportive peers offset applicants' realization that they will not accumulate financial wealth anytime soon. Faculty and continuing students promote the distinctive CSP culture as well as tout the numerous CSP subcultures that provide safe spaces for students to teach, learn, and succeed. Faculty recognize that having a diverse cohort of continuing students encourages diverse students to apply to the program.

When candidates visit campus, they participate in a two-day interview program. Throughout the two days, they interview with faculty for admission into the academic program, ascertain compatibility with assistantship providers, tour the campus, participate in a simulated graduate seminar, and attend several panel discussions. Current students play a major role in candidate recruitment (e.g., answering e-mail inquiries and conducting informational interviews) during their campus visits. Often these students subconsciously engage in a form of reproduction theory; current students recruit candidates who are like them and share their values. If the current student cohort is diverse, this reproduction strategy increases the likelihood that the new cohort of students also will be diverse. If the current student cohort is homogeneous, this reproduction strategy increases the likelihood that the program's goal of diversity will remain elusive.

CSP faculty encourage current students to share their honest perceptions of the program with candidates. Revealing "the good, the bad, and the ugly" (with the hope that the good will eclipse the bad and the ugly) will assist all parties in their deliberations. Yet, during these dialogues, current students usually overemphasize commonalities, consensus, and harmony, while frequently downplaying differences, disagreements, and conflict. When current students acknowledge differences, similarities still remain at the forefront.

Current students frequently acknowledge the existence of numerous CSP enclaves, such as full-time students and part-time students. When talking about these different enclaves, though, the topic of within-enclave consensus overshadows discussions about between-enclave differences. These dynamics worry me. Do they symbolically convey a sense of artificial coherence and solidarity, which comforts the CSP community and candidates during the recruitment process but will be problematic over time? Is the idea of a community based on differences too challenging a concept to infuse into a recruitment process?

Annually, a cohort of about 25 new graduate students accepts our invitation to join our learning community. This cohort merges with about 25 continuing graduate students. In total, the roughly 50 students experience a two-year journey toward self-discovery and self-redefinition. These students are academically capable, interpersonally adept, and committed to the student affairs profession. Their numerous accomplishments and accolades are ample evidence to support this claim. Yet many of these students arrive on campus with two temporary phobias: a fear of failing (both in the classroom and in their work settings) and a fear of not fitting in. For our graduate students from underrepresented groups, these phobias influence their transitions inside and outside the classroom.

Once new students receive their first wave of feedback from faculty and assistantship supervisors evaluating their performance (usually around the third week of the semester), one of two outcomes results. Students conclude that they can "make it" and the first phobia disappears, or students realize they need to make performance adjustments. In the latter instance, the students plot corrective courses of action with their faculty advisor or supervisor. Regardless of the scenario, by mid-semester, the collective phobia centering on failing gradually dissipates for most students.

Remedying the fitting-in phobia is more difficult. Soon after arriving on campus, students express feelings of loneliness and disconnectedness. No doubt the diverse personalities and ideologies of the 50 students exacerbate these temporary feelings of estrangement. One way the CSP faculty address these struggles is to sponsor a retreat during the first week of the academic year that focuses on students' adjustment to graduate school. Retreat topics include student success, academic integrity, community standards, and, of course, the importance of self-reflection. CSP faculty hope the retreat will illuminate the realities of graduate school, but more importantly, identify strategies to relieve new students' fitting-in phobia.

During the retreat, to combat feeling of loneliness, students usually situate themselves in informal enclaves, usually based on common attitudes, habits, and beliefs. Students holding Office of Residential Life assistantships often sit together; so, too, do the part-time, non-traditional-age students. Also obvious are student enclaves based on gender, sexual orientation, and race. CSP subcultures come in all shapes and sizes, though some—especially those based on race and gender—are more obvious and easier to classify (and therefore more scrutinized) than subcultures of part-time students, queer students, and residence life staff.

Soon after retreat discussions begin, students acknowledge the existence of these enclaves and frequently speak of them in terms of binaries: new versus continuing students; married versus single students; serious versus not-so-serious students; White students versus students of color. An "us–them" binary transcends these discussions. The power of these enclaves is unmistakable; the us versus them dichotomies, especially with the hyper-need of students to fit in, are more perplexing.

Graduate students accept the existence of some enclaves; others they contest. The Residential Life assistantship students, who live in the same quad and dine in the same campus eateries, exemplify an *accepted* enclave. It seems natural for these students who spend so much time together to cluster together during the retreat. Yet, students grapple with the appropriateness of, for example, racial enclaves. "Why did all the Black CSP students sit together during the retreat?" This question, seldom verbalized, weighs heavy on White students' minds. Why does segregation seem natural in some contexts and unnatural in others?

Retreat participants tread lightly when discussing individual, religious, socioeconomic, and sexual orientation differences. They appear especially apprehensive and cautious though when discussing race or ethnicity. Based on my informal observations over 12 years, I have noted three unwritten norms that guide students' retreat dialogues about race and ethnicity. First, as the percentage of students of color in the cohort increases, the risk-taking on the part of White students decreases. Talking about race with a homogeneous group is much more comfortable for retreat participants than a similar discussion with a diverse group of participants. Second, when the discussion topic centers on race, White students yield to students of color—inviting and sometimes expecting them to speak first. And students of color do not always accept these invitations; often they bask in the silence, gaining power from the awkward dynamics. Oddly, when discussing race, disproportionate numbers of extroverted CSP students, who usually initiate and dominate conversations, remain mostly silent. Some students' discomfort with silence usually breaks the impasse. They offer innocuous comments to jump-start the conversation, a strategy that rarely works. Finally, when a member of one's enclave eventually speaks, other members offer silent nods—a powerful gesture of approval and solidarity.

Processing these unusual dynamics with White students, I learn that they remain mostly silent because they worry that their underdeveloped and unfiltered comments might possibly shut down the conversation, offend peers, or worse yet, lead others to conclude they are racists. Intellectually, all CSP students appear to recognize the importance of discussing diversity, especially racial and ethnic differences, yet their goal of fitting in seems to trump their goal of openly and honestly discussing these topics.

The CSP faculty's response to reluctance to engage in a public conversation about sensitive topics, such as race, is to encourage students to form smaller discussion groups of their choosing. This strategy responds to students' resistance to public discourse. Yet, when the larger group reconvenes to share insights gained during the smaller group discussions, silence or safe comments prevail. The hesitancy to engage in substantive public conversations in a large, multiethnic context is unmistakable and frustrating, yet understandable. Do these awkward, painful, and sincere retreat discussions about difference help or hinder these new students as they embark on this complex rite of passage into the CSP learning community? How do students of color interpret these awkward dynamics?

Graduate student engagement in the profession, both locally and nationally, is another retreat topic. New students learn about national professional organizations such as the National Association of Student Personnel Administrators, the American College Personnel Association, and the National Orientation Directors Association. Faculty encourage students to join professional groups that will augment the formal curriculum and better prepare them to work in higher education. Faculty also showcase campus organizations that might help students as well. For example, students learn about Miami's Graduate Student Association as well as the Graduate Students of Color Association. Students of color struggle as they decide which organization, if any, to join. White students lament that they have less options than their student of color peers. Does White students' lack of access to certain organizations (or subcultures) add to the mystique of those groups and lead to greater scrutiny?

New members of the CSP community want to fit in and succeed. They join subcultures while attempting to remain connected simultaneously to the larger CSP community. New CSP students appear more comfortable with consensus than difference and more comfortable with harmony than conflict. CSP subcultures aid with their transition, help them fit in, combat loneliness, and shape their identity. Yet some subcultures make some CSP students nervous. The idea of supporting segregated enclaves seems unnatural and antithetical to conventional wisdom about community, but publicly raising this concern could traumatize the community. These uneasy feelings about subcultures are even more disconcerting when the issue of race entangles itself with subcultures. Are there ways to maintain these much-needed subcultures and diminish these uneasy feelings about segregation and assumed exclusivity? Are there other ways to support new students of color without promoting subcultures?

COLLEGIATE SUBCULTURE LIABILITIES: AN ANALYSIS

Higher education plays an important and fundamental role in shaping students' personal and professional development. The transition to graduate school, like undergraduate students' transition to college, is complicated and full of twists and turns. Subcultures, aimed at supporting students in their graduate school transition, are alive and well. Segregated graduate subcultures connect students to like-minded peers, who help them navigate the perils of academia and assist them with the challenging rite of passage. This is particularly true for CSP students of color.

The CSP narrative also reveals an inherent limitation of subculture—the reluctance of subcultures to venture out of their comfort zones, cross borders, and interact with outsiders. bell hooks (1994), in *Teaching to Transgress*, affirms these idiosyncratic findings. She argued that enclaves that cross subculture boundaries and interact with others are the exception rather than the rule (especially in higher education):

> It is fashionable these days, when 'difference' is a hot topic in progressive circles, to talk about . . . 'border crossing,' but we often have no concrete examples of individuals who actually occupy different locations within

structures, sharing ideas with one another, mapping out terrains of commonality, connection, and shared concern . . . (p. 130)

Collegiate student subcultures occupy distinct locations, and share ideas, commonalities, and concerns with other subculture members. Only infrequently do they engage in these activities with outsiders. When these discrete subcultures do cross paths, the interactions are more often superficial than substantive. Collegiate subcultures peacefully coexist (e.g., Colgate student organizational subcultures jointly participating in a student activities fair or CSP subcultures jointly participating in a graduate student retreat). Without outsider interventions, such as the CSP faculty facilitating the discussion, subcultures rarely engage in substantive dialogue with others. When subcultures engage in dialogue, harmony and consensus is in the foreground, while differences remain in the background.

During the Colgate student organization fair, members of the political clubs rarely interacted with the performing arts organizations. The racial/ethnic organizations seldom talked to members of the queer student groups. Even after a speaker of color addressed the entire campus community, Dominique informally processed the speaker's comments with her like-minded peers; she did not participate in any public conversation. The absence of a public discourse reflects the existence of these entrenched communities.

In the Miami CSP context, during the campus interview process, the panel discussions (involving students representing multiple subcultures) overemphasized similarities and underemphasized differences. During the CSP retreat, initiating a public conversation about difference was a tough task, yet within-subculture discussions were robust. When CSP subcultures interacted, safe and innocuous comments were the rule. The idea of forging a new academic community based on difference appeared too risky for retreat participants. Yet, the absence of a genuine public discourse sustains the status quo, which is equally disconcerting. For students who recognize their difference and celebrate it, these dynamics are troubling.

Encouraging subcultures to cross borders is admittedly risky. When one subculture considers challenging the legitimacy of subcultures, the goal of border crossing seems a remote possibility. For example, in the CSP example, some White students privately expressed ambivalence about supporting the existence of some racial/ethnic subcultures (e.g., the Graduate Students of Color organization). These contested subcultures appear exclusive, unnatural, and a fragmentation threat to the larger community. Implicit is a level of distrust of the others' ideologies and points of view, complicating the goal of border crossing. It is easier to dismiss, suppress, ignore, or deny these differences.

Encouraging subcultures to cross borders requires a thoughtful "conscientization"—a combination of self-awareness, self-reflection and action (Freire, 1970). The process of making a subculture's values and experiences (often repressed or hidden) conscious and visible to outsiders is demanding. Carefully, gently, and thoroughly processing with White students why the existence of some subcultures (e.g., residence life staff) is permissible but the existence of others (e.g., Graduate Students of Color Organization) is not, will likely lead to temporary discomfort and conflict. Conscientization is a prerequisite to subcultures crossing borders and entering into borderland discussions.

COLLEGIATE SUBCULTURE LIABILITIES: CAUTIONS INVOLVING COMMUNITIES OF INTEREST

There is some merit in the subculture or communities of interest perspective, but these discourses are fundamentally limiting because the discrete, autonomous groupings make it difficult to engage in dialogue about the public interest (Carlson, 1994). Substantive dialogue about the pubic good was absent from the Colgate fair as well as the Miami CSP retreat.

A second limitation associated with communities of interest is that while they appear responsive to nonmainstream interests, creating space for marginalized enclaves does not disturb the existing power structure (Carlson, 1994). Although Sisters of the Round Table and the African American Student Alliance were two student organizations that responded to nonmainstream interests, these organizations seldom disturbed the existing student organization hierarchy or initiated systemic change at the institutional level. During the CSP retreat, the lack of public discourse ensures that the program maintains the status quo; the power of subcultures to influence the entire academic program is less probable.

Carlson (1994) advocated for a discourse that focuses on difference and diversity; he situates this discourse in multicultural democratic ideals. This multicultural democratic discourse provides space for communities of interest to form and prosper, while a common, public culture is constantly and consciously being constructed and reconstructed through dialogues across and about difference.

INITIATING MULTICULTURAL DEMOCRATIC DISCOURSES

There are many strategies and pathways to initiate multicultural democratic discourses. Most of these strategies focus on understanding and appreciating the interrelationships of power, race, socioeconomic status, social mobility, gender, and sexual orientation. Multicultural democratic discourses recognize and appreciate the commonalities and differences of both dominant and underrepresented groups. Through these dialogues, the goal is to coconstruct ways these similarities and differences might result in the formation of alliances for change (Bensimon & Tierney, 1992/1993).

We highlight four strategies (Carlson, 1994) aimed at initiating multicultural democratic discourses. First, before initiating multicultural democratic discourses, the subcultures must *rupture the borders that separate these enclaves into separate camps or neat categories*. In the two case studies, members of student organizations or members of the various CSP subcultures would assume responsibility for blurring subcultural boundaries. As the two case studies reveal, this is unlikely without outside interventions. More likely, someone like the director of Colgate's Center for Leadership and Student Involvement or the CSP faculty would need to initiate and model this boundary-blurring process. Regardless of the impetus for the ruptures, they must occur.

Second, multicultural democratic discourses must *maximize public participation, providing room for divergent perspectives, and become sensitive to the concerns of all*. In the Colgate and Miami narratives, organizations and students must talk to each other, listen to divergent viewpoints, and openly discuss points of agreement as well as differences. This multicultural democratic discourse is a form of political expression; within this political arena, conflict is inevitable. Accepting rather than repressing conflict and negotiating difference are important considerations for those who aspire to form multicultural democratic discourses by maximizing public participation. Gamson (1993) advocates embracing conflict and difference in higher education:

> [Higher education communities] must develop ways for members to disagree with one another without losing the respect of other members. People in colleges and universities are notoriously uncomfortable with conflict. We run away from it or stomp it into the ground. We deny it or over-dramatize it . . . Dealing with conflict . . . requires respect and

civility. It does not ask that parties love or even like each other, just that they continue interacting. (p. 6)

Multicultural democratic discourses mandate a public space for conflict and difference to flourish, and require encouragement and mediation on the part of all participants. This discourse also encourages members of all subcultures to negotiate realms of meaning, social relations, knowledge, and values. This dialogue should celebrate difference and accept conflict as a way of life, while realizing that dealing with difference is hard work, time consuming, and discomforting (Tierney, 1993).

Third, *multicultural democratic discourses stand for something in the way of moral or ethical vision for the reconstructing of the larger culture.* This discourse is not simply a technical or mechanical exercise to bring diverse people together to exchange ideas; it must include a moral or ethical component. Multicultural democratic discourses grapple with the question, "What is good?" In the Colgate case, what is good for SORT is supporting Black women collegians. What is good for the CSP retreat is bringing differences to the surface and encouraging participants to respect them. In both cases, the subcultures grappled with the questions centering on goodness and what is right, recognizing that answering this question will restructure the larger culture.

Finally, this multicultural democratic discourse must be directed toward subcultures, building alliances and recognizing the interconnectedness between identity formation and cultural struggle. Success in collegiate organizations and graduate school necessitates that students participate in subcultures, and these subcultures must build alliances with other subcultures. Forging these alliances will reveal cultural struggles and provide participants greater clarity about individual and subculture identity development. In the next section, we describe the struggles and benefits associated with building these multicultural democratic alliances; if enacted, they will enhance the quality of life for members of subcultures and benefit the larger culture in which such subcultures exist.

Putting Multicultural Democratic Ideals into Action: Easier Said than Done

Embracing and enacting multicultural democratic ideals leads to multicultural democratic campuses. This is a complex, constant, and immense struggle. It necessitates educating and challenging the dominant culture, while empowering those on the margins. Enacting these ideals is not something an individual or a collective decides to do, does, and then checks it off a task list. Championing difference, democracy, and multiculturalism is a perpetual process, continually contested.

How do we encourage individuals to commit to multicultural and democratic ideals in higher education? How do we structure higher education to value multiculturalism and democracy? How do we move from "monolithic centers of power to democratic constellations in which organizational structures reflect diverse cultures and perspectives?" (Rhoads & Valadez, 1996, p. 9). We recognize there are numerous paths that cultures or subcultures can take to answer these three questions and enact multicultural democratic aims; we offer seven modest recommendations that we intend to serve as guides, not prescriptions for action.

1. **Recognize the value of assembling individuals committed to multicultural democratic ideals.** Multiple cultural identities exist in the United States, and higher education should reflect this diversity. Having a diverse group of individuals committed to multicultural democratic ideals will facilitate the enactment of these ideals on college campuses. The particular collegiate context will dictate what counts as diverse, but it is essential to assemble a cross-section of individuals and subcultures. Disenfranchised or underrepresented individuals need to be at the proverbial table and participate in this transformative process. This inclusiveness agenda connects democracy with education. Assembling a diverse cadre of individuals will give voice to historically silenced or absent stakeholders, lessen power differentials, challenge the status quo, infuse multiple agendas to achieve collective aims, and aid in recruiting the next generation of agents for democracy to champion equity, justice, and freedom.

2. **Recognize the value of subcultures and support their existence on college campuses.** Culture shapes identity and people engaged in interaction shape culture. Subcultures help new students, especially students of color on predominantly White campuses, with their transition to college. Subcultures help students fit in and make it. Subcultures provide voice to their members, outlets for identity development and expression, and a safe haven for members to escape the normalizing expectations of the larger culture. Subcultures form in opposition to the hegemonic culture as well as fill voids within the existing dominant culture (Hebdige, 1979). In uncertain times, when the many fragmented subcultures appear to eclipse the whole of the community, some individuals perceive subcultures as a threat to community and want to eliminate them (or at least diminish their influence). Often, these individuals want to return to "the good old days," to a romanticized notion of a monoculture (Rhoads, 1994) that probably never existed. It is essential to resist romanticized notions that devalue subcultures and lead to efforts to dismantle them. Advocates of multicultural democracy must support the existence of subcultures on college campuses. Understanding why subcultures form and the positive functions these communities of interest serve is essential.

3. **Recognize that not all subcultures are created equal and give voice to the less powerful.** Power differentials exist within and between collegiate cultures and subcultures. An African American fraternity at a predominantly White institution possesses different degrees of power and influence than the same organization at a historically Black college. Context dictates the power differential between this subculture and others. It is important to call attention to, monitor, and (if necessary) challenge these power differentials to diminish hierarchies, lend support to the less powerful subcultures, and ensure justice for the underrepresented.

4. **Recognize, monitor, and challenge what counts as normal.** Colleges and universities are normalizing communities. Each institution subscribes to sociopolitical values that become the foundation for what counts as normal. Declaring what is normal inevitably creates insiders and outsiders. Those who embrace these values are deemed normal and thus are privileged; others are relegated to the margins. Every culture

and subculture has normalizing expectations, and the establishment of insiders and outsiders is both inevitable and unavoidable. What is possible, however, is the constant monitoring of what counts as normal, bringing to the forefront of the group's consciousness these values, evaluating the assets and liabilities, and advocating for change. Asking and answering two questions is essential: "What counts as normal?" and "Whose interests are being served by these norms?"

5. **Encourage subcultures to cross borders, build alliances, and engage in multicultural democratic dialogues.** Too often, members of subcultures are reluctant to venture out of their comfort zones, cross borders, and interact with outsiders. When these discrete subcultures do cross paths with others, interactions tend to be more superficial than substantive. To enact multicultural democratic ideals, subcultures must cross borders and begin to negotiate realms of meaning, social relations, knowledge, and values through substantive dialogue with other subcultures. Dialogue should validate the unique border knowledge of participants. These diverse groups should be empowered to (a) assemble and collectively struggle with important campus and societal issues centering on equity, diversity, and participatory democracy; (b) provide space for communities of interest to form and prosper, while constructing and reconstructing a common, public culture; and (c) criticize the cultural, historical, social, economic, and political forces that lead to injustice and thwart democracy on campus. Ideally, these dialogues will forge trusting relationships that provide room for divergent perspectives respected by all.

6. **Recognize that multicultural democratic ideals and discourses must involve a moral and ethical vision for reconstructing the subculture and the larger culture.** Enacting multicultural democratic ideals is not simply a technical or mechanical exercise that assembles diverse people together to exchange ideas. Instead, this discourse must be built upon a moral and ethical foundation. With this political agenda, subcultures must continually generate multiple and competing responses to the questions: "What is good?" and "Why is it good?" Subcultures also must reach a consensus about the responses to these questions.

7. **Recognize the value of conflict and celebrate differences**. Conflict is an integral and necessary aspect of predominant cultures and subcultures in higher education. Broad public participation in dialogue centering on "what is good" will no doubt yield differences in perspectives, leading to conflicts and probably resistance. Subscribing to multicultural democratic ideals invites participants to celebrate rather than repress differences and negotiate conflict rather than limit it. Exploring differences and accepting conflict necessitates mediation on the part of all, and the benefits outweigh the liabilities despite the inevitable tensions. As Rhoads (1994) argued, ". . . dialogue about difference can serve as a connective fabric among diverse people. In this light difference is not something to be erased but it is instead something that can bring people together" (p. 36). Conflict is inevitable and healthy if multiple voices are to be heard and increased understanding of "the other" is a goal.

CONCLUSION

Transforming higher education to make it more democratic and multicultural should be an ongoing quest. Assembling individuals committed to these ideals; supporting and advocating for seldom-heard voices from subcultures; monitoring and challenging normalizing expectations; facilitating border crossings; creating environments and attitudes that embrace cultural differences; and mediating conflict are challenges that higher education faculty, students, and staff encounter daily. If we are to embrace and enact these multicultural and democratic ideals on campus, we must accept these challenges and perpetually contemplate possibilities.

REFERENCES

Allen, W. R. (1992). The color of success: African American college student outcomes at predominantly white and historically black public colleges and universities. *Harvard Educational Review, 62*, 26–44.

Barefoot, B. O., Gardner, J. N., Cutright, M. Morris, L. V., Schroeder, C. C., Schwartz, S. W., Siegel, M. J., & Swing, R. L. (2005). *Achieving and sustaining institutional excellence for the first year of college.* San Francisco: Jossey-Bass.

Bensimon, E., & Tierney, W. (1992/93). Shaping the multicultural campus: Strategies for administrators. *The College Board, 166*, 4–7, 30.

Carlson, D. (1994). Gayness, multicultural education, and community. *Educational Foundations, 8*(4), 5–25.

Carnegie Foundation for the Advancement of Teaching. (1990). *Campus life: In search of community.* Princeton, NJ: Carnegie Foundation for the Advancement of Teaching.

Constantine, M. G., & Watt, S. K. (2002). Cultural congruity, womanist identity attitudes, and life satisfaction among African American college women attending historically black and predominantly white institutions. *Journal of College Student Development, 43*(2), 184–194.

Cureton, S. R. (2003). Race-specific college student experiences on a predominantly white campus. *Journal of Black Studies, 33*, 295–311.

Erickson, B. L., Peters, C. B., Strommer, D. W., & Erickson, B. L. (2006). *Teaching first-year college students.* San Francisco, CA: Jossey-Bass.

Freire, P. (1970). *Pedagogy of the oppressed.* New York: Continuum.

Gamson, Z. (1993). The destruction and re-creation of academic community: A personal view. *ASHE Open Forum, 6*, 4–7.

Hebdige, D. (1979). *Subculture: The meaning of style.* London: Routledge.

hooks, b. (1994). *Teaching to transgress: Education as the practice of freedom.* New York: Routledge.

Howard-Hamilton, M. F. (Ed.). (2003). *Meeting the needs of African American women: New Directions for Student Services, No. 104.* San Francisco: Jossey-Bass.

Jackson, L. R. (1998). The influence of both race and gender on the experiences of African American college women. *The Review of Higher Education, 21,* 359–375.

Martinez-Aleman, A. M. (2000). Race talks: Undergraduate women of color and female friendships. *The Review of Higher Education, 23,* 133–152.

Reason, R. D., Terenzini, P. T., & Domingo, R. J. (2007). Developing social and personal competence in the first year of college. *Review of Higher Education, 30*(3), 271–299.

Rendón, L. I. (1994). Validating culturally diverse students: Toward a new model of learning and student development. *Innovative Higher Education, 19*(1), 33–51.

Rendón, L. I., Garcia, M., & Person, D. (Eds.). (2004). *Transforming the first year of college for students of color.* Columbia, SC: Center for the First-Year Experience and Students in Transition.

Rhoads, R. (1994). *Coming out in college: The struggle for a queer identity.* Westport, CT: Bergin & Garvey.

Rhoads, R. A., & Valadez, J. R. (1996). *Democracy, multiculturalism, and the community college: A critical perspective.* New York: Garland.

Seidman, A. (2005). *College student retention: Formula for student success.* Westport, CT: Praeger.

Stage, F. K., & Manning, K. (1992). *Enhancing the multicultural campus environment: A cultural brokering approach.* San Francisco: Jossey-Bass.

Thompson, C. E., & Fretz, B. R. (1991). Predicting the adjustment of black students at predominantly white institutions. *Journal of Higher Education, 62,* 437–450.

Tierney, W. G. (1993). *Building communities of difference: Higher education in the twenty-first century*. Westport, CT: Bergin & Garvey.

Tinto, V. (1987). *Leaving college: Rethinking the causes and cures of student attrition*. Chicago: University of Chicago Press.

Ward-Roof, J. A., Hatch, C., National Orientation Directors Association, & National Resource Center for the First-Year Experience & Students in Transition. *Designing successful transitions: A guide for orienting students to college*. Columbia, SC: National Orientation Directors Association and the National Resource Center for the First-Year Experience & Students in Transition, University of South Carolina.

Weis, L. (1985). *Between two worlds: Black students in an urban community college*. Boston: Routledge & Kegan Paul.

Williamson, J. A. (1999). In defense of themselves: The black student struggle for success and recognition at predominantly white colleges and universities. *Journal of Negro Education, 68*, 92–104.

Willimon, W. H., & Naylor, T. H. (1995). *The abandoned generation: Rethinking higher education*. Grand Rapids, MI: Wm. B. Eerdmans.

ABOUT THE EDITOR

SHAUN R. HARPER is an assistant professor of higher education management at the University of Pennsylvania, and director of research on the NASPA Board of Directors. He maintains an active research agenda that examines race and gender in higher education; Black male college achievement; the effects of college environments on student behaviors and outcomes; student affairs at historically Black colleges and universities; and gains associated with educationally purposeful student engagement. In September 2007, Harper was featured on the cover of *Diverse Issues in Higher Education* for his National Black Male College Achievement Study, the largest-ever empirical research project on Black male undergraduates. He has presented more than 100 research papers, workshops, and symposia at national higher education and student affairs professional conferences since 2000. He also is the author of more than 40 peer-reviewed journal articles, book chapters, and other academic publications. His four books and monographs include *Responding to the Realities of Race on Campus* and *Using Qualitative Methods in Institutional Assessment* (both published by Jossey-Bass in 2007).

In 2004, Harper received the NASPA Melvene D. Hardee Dissertation of the Year Award. In addition, the American College Personnel Association (ACPA) presented him the 2005 Emerging Scholar Award and the 2006 *Annuit Coeptis* Award for early career achievement. He has prior professional experience in student activities, sorority and fraternity affairs, graduate admissions, and academic program administration. He has also served as a trustee for the Association of College Unions International, a member of the advisory committee for the National Conference on Race and Ethnicity in American Higher Education, and on the editorial boards of the *NASPA Journal*, the *Journal of College Student Development*, and the *American Journal of Education*. He earned his bachelor's degree in education from Albany State, a historically Black university in Georgia. His master's degree in college student affairs administration and Ph.D. in higher education administration are from Indiana University.

ABOUT THE AUTHORS

anthony lising antonio is an associate professor of education and assistant director of the Stanford Institute for Higher Education Research at Stanford University. antonio's research interests focus on stratification and postsecondary access, racial diversity and its impact on students and institutions, student friendship networks, and student development. His current work also includes an international study of engineering education. antonio has served on the editorial boards of a number of scholarly journals, including *Educational Evaluation and Policy Analysis*, the *American Educational Research Journal*, the *Review of Higher Education*, the *Journal of College Student Development*, and *Change Magazine*. He received the Promising Scholar/Early Career Award from the Association for the Study of Higher Education in 2004. His Ph.D. is in higher education and organizational change from the University of California, Los Angeles.

BRIGHID DWYER is a doctoral candidate in the Center for the Study of Higher and Postsecondary Education at the University of Michigan. Her research and scholarly interests are in the areas of access to college for students of color, minority-serving institutions, and the relationships of urban universities to their surrounding communities. Currently she works as a research assistant for the Transition to College and Early College Experiences of Minority Students Project at the University of Michigan. Prior to this appointment, Dwyer worked as an evaluator for the Kellogg Minority Serving Institutions Leadership Fellows Program, which was cosponsored by The National Forum on Higher Education for the Public Good and the Institute for Higher Education Policy. She has presented several scholarly papers at both the American Educational Research Association and the Association for the Study of Higher Education. As a graduate student, Dwyer has been active in community service projects and graduate student leadership. Her prior professional experiences have been in multicultural student affairs and athletics.

KIMBERLY A. GRIFFIN is a doctoral candidate in the Higher Education and Organizational Change program at the University of California, Los Angeles. She received her master's degree in education policy and leadership from the University of Maryland, College Park, and worked previously as an administrator in both undergraduate and graduate admissions at Stanford University. Her research interests focus primarily on understanding the experiences and outcomes of African

Americans and other underserved populations in higher education, and include projects on high-achieving students of color; outcomes of Black faculty and students; exploring relationships within the higher education context, specifically interactions between faculty and students; and maximizing the benefits of campus diversity. She also studies how relationships between individuals and their families, peers, students, and faculty at critical time-points influence outcomes along the educational spectrum. Griffin's research has been published in the *Journal of College Student Development* and the *Journal of Negro Education.*

MICHAEL D. HANNON is a counselor for the Princeton University Preparatory Program (PUPP), a college preparation initiative for high-achieving, low-income students. His work as an educator and counselor is highlighted by his desire to prepare students to gain access to and succeed in higher education. Hannon's professional experience includes student affairs administration at historically Black and predominantly White institutions. He has also worked as a high school counselor in the Trenton, New Jersey, public school district. Before assuming his current post, he was employed as a consultant in college admissions counseling for PUPP. Hannon has presented at conferences and been published in journals, discussing topics including the functions of Black culture centers, creating successful peer-mentoring programs, and perceived student oppression within college and university settings. His most treasured work, however, is the initiative on which he has embarked with his wife: the development of the nonprofit organization *Greater Expectations Teaching & Advocacy Center (GETAC) for Childhood Disabilities, Inc.* Through GETAC, they are working to open a developmental preschool for children with disabilities.

DOMINIQUE C. HILL is a graduate student in the College Student Personnel Program at Miami University. She earned a B.A. in education and women's studies from Colgate University in 2005. As an honors student in education, she wrote a thesis titled, "What Does It Mean to Be Racialized as Black: Comparing How African American and West Indian Women Negotiate Being Racialized as Black on a Small Predominantly White Campus." In 2005–2006, Hill served as a program coordinator of the Cultural Center at Colgate University, where she created and managed VISION, a council comprising 13 cultural/ethnic organizations, and mentored female students of color. In 2008, she hopes to enroll in a doctoral program that will allow her to pursue her research interests, which include resiliency in Black women, the intersection of race and gender as it relates to educational experiences, and self-agency and student activism in Black and Brown students. She remains committed to enhancing the educational experiences of women of color, particularly those of the Black diaspora.

SYLVIA HURTADO is a professor and director of the Higher Education Research Institute at the University of California, Los Angeles. Formerly, she served as director of the Center for the Study of Higher and Postsecondary Education at the University of Michigan. Hurtado has published numerous articles, chapters, and books related to her primary interests in student educational outcomes, campus climates, college impact on student development, and diversity in higher education. She has coordinated several national research projects, including a U.S. Department of Education-sponsored study of how colleges are preparing students to achieve the cognitive, social, and democratic skills to participate in a diverse democracy. In addition, she has examined assessment, reform, and innovation in undergraduate education for a project through the National Center for Postsecondary Improvement. *Black Issues in Higher Education* (now *Diverse Issues in Higher Education*) named her among the Top 15 Influential Faculty whose work has had an impact on the field. Hurtado serves on numerous editorial boards for journals in education and is past president of the Association for the Study of Higher Education. She earned her Ph.D. in higher education and organizational change from UCLA, an Ed.M. from Harvard Graduate School of Education, and an A.B. in sociology from Princeton University.

TOBY S. JENKINS is the director of the Paul Robeson Cultural Center at The Pennsylvania State University. She has also worked at the Nyumburu Cultural Center, Office of Campus Programs, and the Institute for Urban & Minority Education at the University of Maryland, College Park. Her educational outreach programs have received honors from the president of the United States and the governor of the state of Maryland. Jenkins' past professional experiences, research interests, and studies have taken her to the United Kingdom, Greece, Spain, Norway, Italy, Morocco, Egypt, Russia, Belgium, Turkey, South Africa, and various parts of the West Indies. She has worked with students from more than 40 countries at the Johns Hopkins University Office of Summer Programs. She received her master's degree in college student personnel from the University of Maryland, College Park, and her Ph.D. in educational theory & policy/social foundations of education from Penn State University. Her professional interests focus on various cultural issues, including how young adults of color define culture in a contemporary society, culture as a social foundation in communities of color, culture's impact on leadership proxy, and the social responsibility of cultural arts.

SUSAN R. JONES is an associate professor and director of the College Student Personnel Program at the University of Maryland, College Park. She has published in educational journals including the *Journal of College Student Development* and the *Journal of Higher Education* on such topics as multiple dimensions of identity development, the role of meaning-making capacity in the construction of multiple identities, enduring influences of service–learning on college student's identity development, shifts and continuities in community service participation from high school to college, developing student understanding of HIV/AIDS through community service–learning, understanding diversity through community service–learning, disability as social construction, and dynamics of lesbian college students' multiple dimensions of identity. With Vasti Torres and Jan Arminio, she coauthored the book *Negotiating the Complexities of Qualitative Research in Higher Education: Fundamental Elements and Issues* (Routledge, 2006). Jones is the recipient of several prestigious awards including The Ohio State University Alumni Award for Distinguished Teaching, ACPA's Emerging Scholar Award, and ACPA's Diamond Honoree for significant contributions to higher education and student affairs. She served ACPA as director of the Core Council for the Generation and Dissemination of Knowledge and on the planning committee for the 2007 ACPA/NASPA Joint Meeting.

JILLIAN KINZIE is associate director of the NSSE Institute for Effective Educational Practice and the Indiana University Center for Postsecondary Research. Kinzie coordinates research and project activities to facilitate the use of student engagement data and promote educational effectiveness. She earned her Ph.D. in higher education with a minor in women's studies at Indiana University. Prior to this, she held a visiting faculty appointment in the Higher Education and Student Affairs Department at Indiana University and worked as an administrator in academic and student affairs for many years at several institutions. In 2001, she was awarded a Student Choice Award for Outstanding Faculty at Indiana University. Kinzie has coauthored a monograph on theories of teaching and learning, and the Lumina Foundation monograph *Continuity and Change in College Choice: National Policy, Institutional Practices and Student Decision Making*. She has also conducted research on women in undergraduate science, retention of underrepresented students, and educational effectiveness and institutional change. She is coauthor of *Student Success in College: Creating Conditions that Matter* (Jossey-Bass, 2005), *One Size Does Not Fit All: Traditional and Innovative Models of Student Affairs Practice* (Routledge, 2006), and *Piecing Together the Student Success Puzzle: Research, Propositions, and Recommendations* (Jossey-Bass, 2007).

PETER M. MAGOLDA is a professor in the Miami University College Student Personnel Program. He received a B.A. from LaSalle College, an M.A. from The Ohio State University, and a Ph.D. in Higher Education Administration from Indiana University. He teaches educational anthropology and research seminars. Magolda's scholarship focuses on ethnographic studies of college students, critical issues in qualitative research, and program evaluation. His recent research centers on evangelical student subcultures and the political actions of college students. Magolda has authored numerous articles, book chapters, policy briefs, and invited essays. He also coedited a book about new professionals in student affairs positions. He serves on the editorial boards of *Research in Higher Education* and the *Journal of Educational Research*. Magolda is a 2007 ACPA Senior Scholar inductee. In 2004, he received the Miami University's Richard T. Delp Outstanding Faculty Member award and the Maude Stewart Alumni Award from The Ohio State University. In 2007 the Higher Education and Student Affairs Program at Indiana University awarded him the Robert H. Shaffer Distinguished Alumni Award. Prior to joining the Miami University faculty in 1994, Magolda worked in the division of student affairs at Miami University, The Ohio State University, and the University of Vermont.

WILLIAM MAXWELL is a sociologist who studies international comparisons of student access, persistence, and degree attainment, particularly in 2-year and community colleges. He currently serves as an associate professor and research associate in the Center for Higher Education Policy Analysis at the University of Southern California, Rossier School of Education. Maxwell's community college research has focused on race and ethnic relations, African American male retention, and learning communities. In addition, he has compared educational policies in several societies of the Pacific Rim. His Ph.D. is from the University of California, Los Angeles.

JEFFREY F. MILEM is a professor in the Center for the Study of Higher Education at the University of Arizona and president-elect of the Association for the Study of Higher Education, the major professional research organization for scholars of higher education. His work focuses on education policy, racial dynamics in higher education, the educational outcomes of diversity, the impact of college on students, and the condition and status of the professorate—including the ways in which faculty effectively use diversity in their classroom teaching. As a widely recognized expert in the area of racial dynamics in higher education, Milem has been commissioned to do research by the Institute of Medicine of the National Academies, the Harvard Civil Rights Project, the American Council on Education, and the American Educational Research Association's Panel on Racial Dynamics in Higher Education. He received his B.A. in political science from Michigan State University, his M.Ed. from the University of Vermont, and his Ph.D. from the University of California, Los Angeles. In addition to his employment in higher education, Milem has worked as a photographer, a janitor and maintenance worker, a house painter, a landscaper, a bartender, a cook, and a hospital orderly.

SHAILA MULHOLLAND is a doctoral candidate in higher education administration at New York University (NYU). Her research interests are in education policy, with a focus on policy development and implementation; governance as a way of improving access and equity for underrepresented students; and international perspectives on education. Mulholland has worked in student affairs in the areas of diversity education, multicultural affairs, and student services, and as a biology teacher with precollege summer programs, including Upward Bound and the Jim Holland Biology Program for underrepresented students in the sciences at Indiana University (IU). Mulholland was also a research assistant with the Alliance for International Higher Education Policy Studies at NYU and a project associate with the National Survey of Student Engagement Institute at IU. Her dissertation, *Fifty Years of Higher Education Access and Equity Strategies in Indiana,* explores the causes and consequences of how Indiana developed its community college system. Mulholland holds a bachelor's degree in biology and a master's degree in higher education and student affairs, both from IU.

SAMUEL D. MUSEUS is an assistant professor of higher education and an affiliate faculty member in the Asian American Studies Program at the University of Massachusetts, Boston. He earned his Ph.D. in higher education at The

Pennsylvania State University. Museus maintains a research agenda focused on examining the impact of public policy and institutional environments on the access, experiences, and success of low-income and racial/ethnic minority college students. Specifically, his current research is aimed at understanding the role of institutional environments on the experiences and outcomes of students of color in higher education. He has given more than a dozen presentations at national conferences on campus environments and minority college student success and is currently the principal investigator of multiple qualitative and quantitative inquiries aimed at analyzing the impact of campus climates and cultures on minority student engagement and persistence. With Shaun R. Harper, Museus recently coedited *Using Qualitative Methods in Institutional Assessment* (Jossey-Bass, 2007).

ANDREW H. NICHOLS, a Bunton-Waller Graduate Fellow and Edward & Susan Wilson Graduate Scholarship recipient, is a doctoral candidate and research assistant in the Center for the Study of Higher Education at The Pennsylvania State University. Formerly, he worked in residence life and the Topping Student Center at the University of Southern California (USC). Nichols' research agenda examines the influence of race and ethnicity on student outcomes, experiences, and behaviors; diversity and equity in higher education; and race relations on predominantly White campuses. He received a master's degree in postsecondary administration and student affairs from the USC Rossier School of Education and a bachelor's degree in psychology from Vanderbilt University.

LORI D. PATTON is an assistant professor of higher education in the Department of Educational Leadership and Policy Studies at Iowa State University. She has administrative experiences in a wide range of student affairs functional areas including student activities, Greek life, admissions, and residence life. Patton's research has examined the effects of Hurricane Katrina, LGBT populations at HBCUs, and spiritual dimensions of student development. Most notably, her research has highlighted the relevance of Black culture centers in higher education. With Shaun R. Harper, she is coeditor of *Responding to the Realities of Race on Campus* (Jossey-Bass, 2007). Patton serves on the ACPA Governing Board as the director of Equity & Inclusion. In 2004 she was recognized as an ACPA Emerging Scholar and was an ACPA *Annuit Coeptis* Award recipient. She has published, edited, and contributed to numerous books, articles, and book chapters. Patton regularly presents educational sessions at ACPA, NASPA, ASHE, and AERA annual conferences. Her bachelor's degree is in speech communication from Southern Illinois University at Edwardsville, and her master's degree is in college student personnel from Bowling Green State University. She earned her Ph.D. in higher education administration from Indiana University.

DAVID PÉREZ II is a doctoral candidate in the higher education program at The Pennsylvania State University. His research focuses on high-achieving Hispanic/Latino college students; the purposeful engagement of racial/ethnic minority students; diversity and social justice education in postsecondary institutions; educational outcomes associated with diversity; and inclusive pedagogical practices. He has prior professional experience in residence life, student activities, and multicultural affairs at Syracuse University and New York University. In 1993, Pérez was selected as a Posse Scholar and earned his B.S. and M.Ed. from Vanderbilt University. He participates actively in NASPA and ACPA.

STEPHEN JOHN QUAYE is an assistant professor in the College Student Personnel Program at the University of Maryland and a department editor for *About Campus*. His research focuses on the influence of race relations on college and university campuses, specifically the gains and outcomes associated with inclusive racial climates, cross-racial interactions, and color-conscious pedagogical approaches. Over the past 3 years, Quaye has given 18 presentations at national higher education and student affairs conferences. With Shaun R. Harper, Quaye is coeditor of the forthcoming book *Student Engagement in Higher Education: Theoretical Perspectives and Practical Approaches for Diverse Populations* (Routledge, 2008) and author of nearly a dozen peer-reviewed journal articles, book chapters, and other scholarly publications. He is an editorial board member for the *Journal of the Professoriate* and the *NASAP Journal*. His previous experience in student affairs includes residence life, multicultural affairs, and learning assistance. Quaye received his Ph.D. in higher education from The Pennsylvania State University.

DIANE SHAMMAS is a doctoral candidate at the University of Southern California, Rossier School of Education. Her dissertation research focuses on social relations, campus racial climates, and sense of belonging among Arab and Muslim community college students. She has combined survey methods and focus groups to collect data from students at 18 community colleges in California and Michigan. Her broader research interests focus on the effects of global and U.S. national politics on the marginalization and racialization of Arab American and Muslim American college students, and the absence of Arab and Muslim perspectives in the curricula of American postsecondary institutions. Shammas has presented at the annual conference of the Council for the Study of Community Colleges. She also serves on the National Advisory Board of the Levantine Cultural Center, a nonprofit organization in Los Angeles dedicated to promoting peace among all peoples of the Middle East and effecting social change through the presentation of literary, performing, and visual arts.

K. DEX TUTTLE is a graduate of North Dakota State University (NDSU) with a B.A. in computer science. His ties to the programming board at NDSU helped him find a career in student affairs, where he worked advising student groups and planning campus activities. After 4 years in the field full-time, Tuttle pursued his master's degree in College Student Affairs at The Pennsylvania State University. During his studies, he found an interest in how spaces on campus affect student behaviors. After graduating in May 2007, he found a job as assistant director of campus life at Southeast Missouri State University. He is currently serving as the staff advisor to the Gay/Straight Alliance and working to develop major campus programming initiatives. Tuttle has also had professional responsibilities with leadership development programs, student organization administration, and facility and vendor operations. He also strives to combine his computer science background with his student affairs work, identifying technical solutions to improve work processes and data management.

PAUL D. UMBACH is an assistant professor of higher education in the Department of Educational Policy and Leadership Studies at the University of Iowa. His research explores the effects of the organizational contexts of colleges and universities on college students and faculty. Central to much of this work are issues of equity and diversity. He also studies survey research methods, particularly as they apply in college settings. He has published more than 30 peer-reviewed articles, book chapters, and other scholarly publications. His work has appeared in the *Journal of College Student Development*, the *Journal of Higher Education*, *Research in Higher Education*, and the *Review of Higher Education*. He currently serves on the editorial boards of the *Journal of College Student Development*, *Research in Higher Education*, and the *Review of Higher Education*. In 2007, the Association for the Study of Higher Education awarded him the Promising Scholar/Early

Career Achievement Award. He earned his Ph.D. in higher education from the University of Maryland.

CLAYTON L. WALTON serves as associate dean of student life and director of the Paul Robeson Campus Center at Rutgers University–Newark. He came to Rutgers from the John Jay College of Criminal Justice (City University of New York), where he served as the assistant director of student activities. Prior to John Jay, Walton worked at the University of Maryland, where he received his master's of education in counseling and personnel services and served as the assistant director of student Involvement and leadership. A graduate of St. John's University (Queens Campus) with a bachelor's degree in sociology and minors in secondary education and social work, Walton started working in higher education as a student program coordinator in the St. John's Office of Student Activities. He has spent the last 10 years working in numerous positions where he has constructed program initiatives and student development models geared toward challenging students to intentionally engage their college experience.